Navigating the Maze of Social Security

Previous books by Stephen J. Stellhorn

Brokers, Financial Advisors & Insurance Agents

*An Investigative Process – the Book that **Some** May Not Want Their Clients to Read*

Available in digital format only on Kindle, Apple and Nook platforms

Navigating the Maze of Medicare

A Comprehensive Look at your Coverage Options
2013 and 2014 Editions

Available in softcover at Amazon and Barnes & Noble, 2014 Edition available in digital format on Kindle, Apple and Nook platforms

Navigating the Maze of Health Insurance Choices

A Comprehensive Look at Individual & Small Business Options

Available in softcover at Amazon and Barnes & Noble, digital format on Kindle, Apple and Nook platforms

Navigating the Maze of Social Security

Claiming Strategies for Fifty Shades of Grey

STEPHEN J. STELLHORN, RMA^{SM}

CALMSEASMEDIA
Tampa, Florida

Published by **CALMSEAS**MEDIA, Tampa, Florida

Cover design: Don Saunders
Photos: iStockphoto® and Photography by Robin
Quotations: Courtesy *BrainyQuote®* unless otherwise noted.

Library of Congress Cataloging-in-Publication Data

Stellhorn, Stephen, 1954
    Navigating the maze of social security: claiming strategies for fifty shades of grey / Stephen Stellhorn.

        p. cm.
    Includes index.
    ISBN: 978-0-9894265-5-8
    CIP data applied for.

First Edition

Printed in the United States of America

Table of Contents

Request for Feedback

I am very respectful of your time and privacy. I will not share information you provide without your expressed consent to do so. I also want to thank you in advance for your consideration.

I invite readers to share their feedback with me on this subject matter. What topics did I cover too much and what should I have covered more? Did I not cover a topic that should have been covered? Should I have completely deleted a topic?

Your comments are very valuable in helping to make future updates better. I've established an email address for receiving your feedback: readercommunity@msmcapital.net. Please insert the name of the book, "Navigating the Maze of Social Security" in the subject line of your email.

Acknowledgement

I'd like to acknowledge Mary Beth Franklin. Mary Beth is a Contributing Editor at InvestmentNews, writing a column for the print edition and a blog for their website. Though I have never met her, reading her columns over the last few years inspired me to learn more about the inter-workings of Social Security and ultimately write a book for individuals wanting to expand their own knowledge of the Social Security system also.

"Live your life and forget your age!"

Norman Vincent Peale
Minister and Author

Setting the Context

Welcome to the tantalizing and seductive world of Social Security. Many say seduction starts with the mind. Whether you're single, married, divorced, widowed or even remarried and divorce a second time, you will discover something intriguing and thought provoking when you pull back the sheets of this book. Shockingly, you will find situational examples of over fifty shades of grey when devising your Social Security claiming strategy. And you didn't think Social Security could be so sexy, did you.

During the depths of the Great Depression, the FDR administration had both the leadership and the visionary insight to create a program which would touch so many lives and have such a positive impact on individual's financial situations in the years that would come. Ida May Fuller retired in November 1939. On January 31, 1940, she became the first individual to receive retirement benefits under the new Social Security system. Her monthly benefit check was $22.54 (approximately $375 in today's dollars).

Why should you buy this book? For one, you may find Social Security bewildering and perplexing. Google, Social Security, and you get about 460,000,000 results to choose from. Next, Google Social Security Claiming Strategies, and you get about 3,100,000 results. You may not even realize there are various claiming strategies which can be implemented. According to Dr. Laurence Kotlikoff, Ph.D., there are over 817 possibilities from 57 basic variations. No wonder people get confused. Can you the answer some of the following basic questions about Social Security?

- How many earnings credits do I need to be eligible for Social Security?
- If my earnings record is wrong how can I fix it?
- What are earnings cap restrictions?
- Can my benefits be reduced?
- What are delayed retirement credits?
- When can I claim spousal benefits?
- How can I ensure my spouse gets the biggest benefit she is entitled to?
- Are my benefits subject to federal income taxes?
- I'm 59 and getting remarried. Should I wait?
- I'm divorced. Can I claim benefits on my cheating ex-husband who is an executive?
- How does the repeal of DOMA, by the Supreme Court, affect same-sex marriages?
- Could buying an immediate fixed annuity be the wrong use of your investable assets today?
- What does Medicare cover and is it free?

If these basic questions appear challenging, this book is for you. To be fair and honest with the reader, all the information contained in this book is available through Social Security free of charge. However, you will need to wade through 123 different online publications the Social Security Administration (SSA) has available as PDFs from their website. This doesn't include the SSA's 20 chapter Social Security Handbook, which has 2,728 rules covering Social Security and is available only online and very difficult to navigate. What this book offers the reader is to consolidate much of this information into one easy to read and concise format. It is designed to provide you with a solid educational foundation and increase your knowledge on how Social Security works. In turn, it will make you a more informed consumer by eliminating much of the confusion you might have about Social Security. This translates to better decision making as to what's most appropriate for your particular situation. In addition, the book offers a basic primer on Medicare, which may be the next major decision you have to make as you transition into retirement.

When it comes to divesting assets during retirement, to create an income stream, individuals and couples basically have four fundamental options to fund their retirement.

- Preserve the principal and live off the interest.
- Invest in a portfolio of stocks and bonds and draw out a portion as income.
- Buy an annuity to generate monthly income.
- Win the lottery.

In a recent survey, conducted by Market Strategies International (MSI), affluent Americans expect to delay retirement to age 68. MSI surveyed 900 investors for the Cogent Reports, who were 55 or older with at least $100,000 in investable assets. The average participant in the study had $623,000 in investable assets. There were several variables driving this trend. There were only 22% of pre-retirees who are relying on a pension as their primary source of retirement income compared with 39% of current retirees who are relying on a pension. Just 28% of pre-retirees, those older than 55 who had not yet retired, were very confident about their ability to generate enough income during retirement to meet their needs. There are serious concerns about either outliving their money or not being able to financially handle unexpected costs. Only 23% of pre-retirees expressed confidence they would not outlive their assets. As will be seen in subsequent studies and surveys, these are legitimate fears which are pushing even affluent individuals and couples to remain in the workforce longer than they had anticipated.

Savvy individuals and couples should think of Social Security as another "asset class", though not in the traditional sense, within their investment portfolio which needs to be planned for. Yet most don't realize what a critical decision this is and simply look at Social Security as a bucket of money to spend once they reach age 62; not realizing they may be leaving thousands of dollars on the table along with the constrained consequences they may be placing on their spouse long after they're gone. However, if you're really struggling each month to pay your essential living expenses, claiming early benefits when you turn 62 is what you should probably do then. It will provide an immediate benefit to you right now.

In March 2014, Financial Engines, founded by Nobel Laureate Dr. William Sharpe, Ph.D., released the results of an online survey which asked more than 1,000 near and current retirees 8 questions about claiming Social Security benefits. Of those respondents who had not claimed Social Security yet, 74% scored a grade C or lower while only 5% were able to answer all 8 questions correctly. You can take the quiz at http://corp.financialengines.com/social-security/test-your-knowledge-quiz.html. In addition, for a married couple, based on their own earnings record or as a spouse when all the options to claim retirement benefits between age 62 and age 70 were examined, the research uncovered more than 8,000 possible Social Security claiming strategies. Their conclusion was individuals are over-confident when it comes to Social Security. They believe they know what they're doing but they really don't.

If you really don't need the money, for a typical individual, claiming early benefits could result in an opportunity cost to you in excess of $100,000 in lifetime benefits. For a married couple, claiming early could mean they are leaving $250,000 in lifetime benefits on the table. As an example, someone who is single and eligible to collect $1,500 per month at their full retirement age of 66 and lives to age 85, this bucket of money could become either $310,000, $342,000 or $356,400 depending on if they collect at ages 62, 66 or 70, respectively. This does not include any intervening cost-of-living adjustments the individual would be entitled to receive over those years. If a couple is eligible to cumulatively collect $2,500 per month, at their full retirement ages of 66, the bucket of money becomes

$517,500, $570,000 or $594,000 depending on whether they begin to collect at ages 62, 66 or 70, respectively. Again, this doesn't include any intervening cost-of-living adjustments the couple would be entitled to receive over those years. Suddenly, when looked at in this manner, this bucket gets to be pretty large.

Should you claim benefits at 62? It depends on a number of factors which will be different for each individual and couple. Decisions as to when to begin claiming your benefits usually involve the following macro-factors:

- Beliefs and emotions.
- Genetics
- Health status.
- Life expectancy.
- Cashflow needs.

While these may seem like simple concepts, the decision analysis can be extremely complex. Looking at these you may believe Social Security is going to go broke so I better get it now or they'll have to cut benefits. You may have adequate cashflow but it might be nice to have the additional money each month from Social Security. You may also be in the best shape of your life with no health issues or you may have heart disease, are obese with diabetes and taking ten different medications a day and you don't know how long you may live. You could be in the situation where you have really been struggling since the Great Financial Recession of 2008-2009 and this money will be a godsend to help meet your essential expenses each month. You may be in the inviable position where you really don't need the money from Social Security and are just going to wait.

These are all valid concerns which need to be evaluated against the backdrop of when is the optimal time to claim Social Security benefits. Researcher L. Stephen Coles, M.D., Ph.D. has done extensive work in gerontology. In collaboration with colleagues at Stanford University, he expects to soon publish findings regarding the genetic basis of extreme potential longevity, which they now know to be inherited and little influenced by one's lifestyle.

The last of the baby boom generation will be turning 50 this year. There have been numerous surveys done, asking those already in retirement what their greatest regrets were since retiring. The survey results are all fairly consistent in their responses. The majority regretted:

- The failure to plan.
- Excessive borrowing.
- Retiring too early.
- Psychological impact of retiring – what to do now?
- Not having planned for long-term care.

Health care is not a topic most individual want to discuss. It makes individuals contemplate their own mortality; a scary subject for most people. Nobody wants to think about the possibility of their own incapacitation due to an unforeseen accident or medical event and all the expenses that go with it. The fear is more health care coverage means more expenses they will have to deal with; possibly for something they may or may not ever need.

Medical achievements in disease treatment and anti-aging, which many take for granted today, just recently as a decade ago were little more than theoretical science. Advances in biomedical science, an integrated process of employing the principles of biology, biochemistry, physiology and other basic sciences to solve problems in clinical medicine have clearly helped in extending our life spans. Through biomedical engineering, advances in the design and functionality of artificial limbs have greatly improved quality of life issues for those in need of limb replacement. Advances are now starting to extend to organ replacement through research in regenerative biology.

Americans will likely continue to have the capacity to live longer than their forbearers. Today in fact, healthy 65-year-olds have at least a 40% chance of living into their 90s.

That's great news. The bad news is many will likely live their lives with some sort of chronic illness such as diabesity, cardiovascular disease, some form of neurological degenerative process, skeletal issues involving orthopedics or Type-2 diabetes, which will require ongoing medical care. Longevity plus chronic illness may place many at risk of outliving their savings, the biggest peril of old age.

Controlling the escalating costs of funding government entitlement programs and the premiums worker's pay for health insurance are paramount. Otherwise, this country may well face a health care crisis before the end of the second decade of the 21st century. Decreasing health is not the issue. The real issue for many will be decreasing health which results in a major "health event" occurring. Health care costs have the potential to torpedo many future retirement plans if individuals and couples don't engage in comprehensive planning, ahead of time, to ensure they are adequately protected against the rising risks to their health as they age. You can have all the wealth in the world but if you don't have your health, your quality of life can be an agonizing ordeal to live with each day, every day.

When I began my business career, just over 30 years ago, my own belief was Social Security wouldn't be around by the time I would be eligible to collect it. It was going to be broke by then and, my God, that's 40 years into the future. Well - time has passed and age 62 is not that far away for me now. Social Security is still here with even better benefits than in 1981. Who would have thought? Yet, the same concerns exist among younger individuals today.

Cheers! Here's to a healthy and full-filled life!

Stephen

Stephen J. Stellhorn
July 2014
Tampa, Florida

"Financial literacy is an issue that should command out attention because many Americans are not adequately organizing finances for their education, healthcare and retirement."

Ronald E. "Ron" Lewis
Former Member U.S. House of Representatives –
Kentucky's 2nd Congressional District

CHAPTER ONE

PRELUDE TO RETIREMENT

"... Circumstance has forced my hand
To be a cut price person in a low budget land
Times are hard but we'll all survive
I just got to learn to economize

I'm on a low budget
I'm on a low budget
I'm not cheap, you understand
I'm just a cut price person in a low budget land

... I'm dropping my standards so that I can buy more
Low budget sure keeps me on my toes
I count every penny and I watch where it goes"

Written by: Ray Davies. Published by: Davray Music Ltd.

The Kinks were an English rock band formed in Muswell Hill, North London, by brothers Ray and Dave Davies in 1964. The Kinks, who rose to fame during the mid-1960s were part of the British Invasion and are recognized as one of the most important and influential rock groups of the era. The hard rock sound of *Low Budget,* released in July 1979, helped make it the Kinks' second gold album and the group's highest charting original album in America, where it peaked at number 11. In a review by Stephen Thomas Erlewine; he writes, *"Ray Davies cleverly designed the album as a sly satire of the recession and oil crisis that gripped America in the late '70s, thereby satisfying his need to be a wry social commentator while giving American audiences a hook to identify with. It was a clever move that worked."* At the time the song was released, the U.S. economy was dealing with double digit inflation rates. Interest rates were on the rise and approaching double digits and America would soon be coping with the Iranian hostage crisis. I thought the lyrics to this Kink's song were an appropriate introduction to this chapter.

Are the song's lyrics and message appropriate for today? Let's compare a few statistics. In 2013, a record 20% of American households, one in five, were on food stamps according to data from the U.S. Department of Agriculture (USDA). In a 2011 study by the Congressional Budget Office (CBO) titled, *"Trends in the Distribution of Household Income Between 1979 and 2007",* it found the top earning 1% of households increased their income by about 275% after federal taxes and income transfers over a period between 1979 and 2007. That compares to a gain just under 40% for the 60 % in the middle of America's income distribution. In a 2012 analysis of Internal Revenue Service (IRS) figures, dating back to 1913, by economists at the University of California at Berkeley, the Paris School of Economics and Oxford University titled, *"Top Incomes and the Great Recession: Recent Evolutions and Policy Implications",* they found the gap between the richest 1% and the remaining 99% was the widest it's been since the 1920s. Incomes of the wealthiest 1% rose nearly 20%, whereas incomes of the remaining 99% rose a meager 1% in comparison. These statistics and the ones that follow are

2

pretty sobering as to what is happening for a majority of individuals in the United States today. You be the judge.

Spectrum of Population Cohorts

A number of surveys are going to be discussed concerning the level of savings, investments and attitudinal beliefs across population groups. These are the commonly used terms when discussing population groups.

- Silent Generation (before 1946): Currently age 69 and older.
- Baby Boom Generation (1946 – 1964): Currently between ages 50 and 68.
- Generation X (1965 – 1985): Currently between the ages of 29 and 49.
- Millennial Generation (1986 – 2002): Currently between the ages of 12 and 28. A.k.a. Generation Y.

Figure 1.1 displays the population by generation size. Depending on the book or study you read you may find differences in the age bands by 2-3 years.

Figure 1.1 Population Cohorts by Size

Generational Size

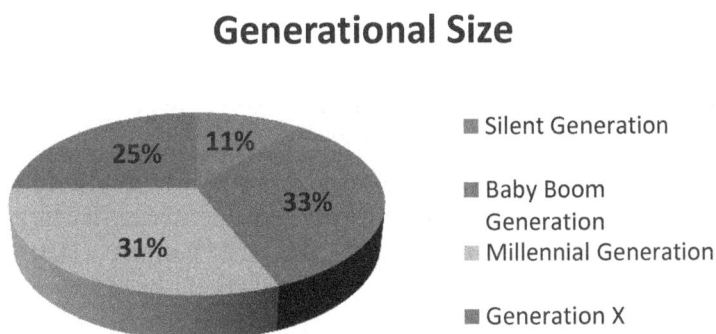

Source: FINRA, 2012 National Financial Capability Study

Prelude to Retirement Thinking

This book is not about financial/retirement planning. Ninety percent of it concerns Social Security. However, there are a few topically themes worth introducing because optimizing your Social Security retirement benefits involves planning. Unfortunately, few do this and just claim at age 62 for a mired of reasons. Planning for Social Security integrates income, spending, tax and longevity metrics along with potential health care needs and a healthy dose of emotional attributes. As the research is beginning to show, thinking about when you retire and when you claim your Social Security benefits can be two entirely different questions which need to be planned for accordingly.

Linear Life Plan – the Old Normal

Retirement planning in the "old days" would probably be considered very simple by today's standards. You may or may not have gone to college but you typically worked for one company, maybe two, your entire life.

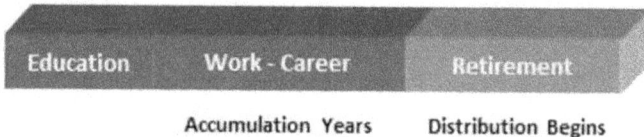

Education | Work - Career | Retirement

Accumulation Years | Distribution Begins

The transition, from school to career to retirement was predictable, formal and few. At age 65, the company gave you a retirement party where you received your gold watch and the paperwork to file so you could begin collecting your pension from the company's defined benefit (DB) plan. Within the week you then probably filed the paperwork to begin collecting your Social Security retirement benefits. Ah, the quaint ritual of a bygone era. You were now officially retired and trying to figure out what to do with all that free time now. Retirement planning was commonly

4

referred to as the three-legged stool approach. The three legs of the stool comprised Social Security, pensions and personal savings. Typically, one's income during retirement came from about 1/3 Social Security, 1/3 from a pension and 1/3 from personal savings. Thus, two-thirds of your income stream was guaranteed for the rest of their life. A key attribute of retirees then was by the time they got to retirement, they typically had their house paid for and they entered retirement with very little debt.

The New Normal

Just after the new millennium came the Great Dot-Com Bust of 2001-2002, followed by the Great Financial Recession of 2008-2009, which have ushered in a new normal for most individuals. However, this new normal has been anything but normal. It has been defined by not only how individuals save for retirement but also by how they transition through their employment career. It's not a clear smooth transition as it was in the "old days".

Figure 1.1 New Retirement Paradigm

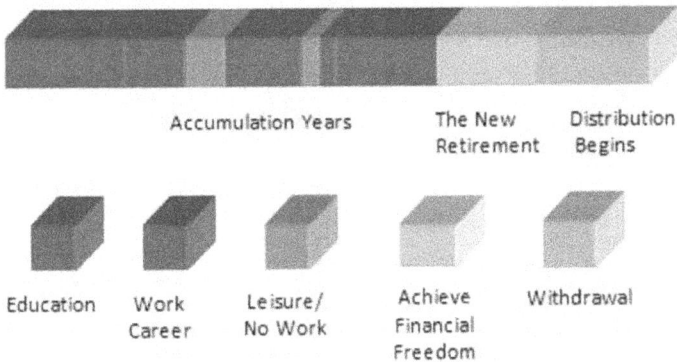

| Accumulation Years | The New Retirement | Distribution Begins |

| Education | Work Career | Leisure/ No Work | Achieve Financial Freedom | Withdrawal |

Courtesy: The 2013 RMA℠ Curriculum, Fifth Edition
Source: The 2005 Merrill Lynch New Retirement Study: A
Perspective From the Baby Boomer Generation

Serial employment, coupled with flexible or reversible retirement dates is now the new normal. Many individual's careers are now punctuated by extended breaks (voluntary or otherwise) for education, re-training or some other kind of mental refresher. Retirement is not an "event" as it was under the linear life plan but now more of a process which you transition through continually as you age.

Figure 1.2 below displays the distribution of retirement plan coverage among those who have a retirement plan. In 1979, 62% of workers with a retirement plan had only a defined benefit (DB) plan while 16% participated only in a defined contribution (DC) plan. As can be seen in the chart, by the late 1980s and early 1990s the shift in trend was clearly underway.

Figure 1.2 Private Sector Participates in a Retirement Plan

Private-Sector *Participants* in an Employment-
Based Retirement Plan, by Plan Type, 1979–2008

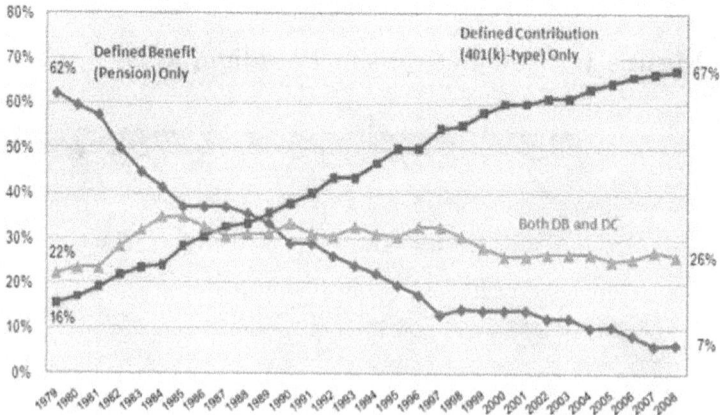

Source: U.S. Department of Labor Form 5500 Summaries for 1979-1998; PBGC, Current Population Survey data for 1999-2008; Employee Benefit Research Institute estimates for 1999-2008

Source: U.S. Department of Labor; Employee Pension Institute

By 2008, those with a defined benefit plan had decreased to 7%, while those in a 401(k) type defined contribution plan increased to 67%. In the new normal fewer will have a company pension to draw on while transitioning through retirement.

During those recessions, companies which adopted defined contribution plans such as the 401(k) found they could make adjustments to those plans. Contributions aren't mandatory as in DB plans. Contributions are measured as a percentage of their payroll so any savings from benefit cuts are realized immediately. In the wake of the Great Financial Recession the benefit consulting firm, Towers Watson, surveyed 334 companies and found that about 18% had either suspended or reduced 401(k) company matches to conserve cash. Yet when economic conditions improved, about 23% of those companies which reinstated their company match now offered less generous matching contributions than before the recession occurred.

Health care costs have been rising faster than the inflation rate with companies now beginning to make employees shoulder a larger portion of the cost while also cutting benefits. With the passage of the *Affordable Care Act,* many companies are saying they have to reduce, eliminate or change the funding process for the company match in 401(k) plans to offset their higher health costs. Bloomberg has analyzed hundreds of government filings which corporation are required to file when changes are made to their benefit programs. A difference of just three percentage points on a match can add up to hundreds of thousands of dollars lost for employees over the course of their careers. In a continuing effort to cut expenses and boost profits, employers are squeezing workers' retirement savings, holding back on both the amount and the timing for matching funds and dragging out vesting schedules.

The Good, the Bad and the Ugly

Below are a few examples of what is occurring. Kroger Company matches 100% of the first 3% of employee salary deferrals, plus 50% of the next 2% of workers compensation.

7

The company also pays another 1% to 2% based on tenure. Amgen Inc. contributes 5% of workers' salaries whether they contribute or not. Whole Foods provides an annual match of 15.2% on the first $1,000 which workers contribute. Prior to the recession, Caesars Entertainment match was 50% of the employees' contribution up to 6% of pay. In 2009 the company suspended its match and when it was reinstated in 2012, the maximum contribution was $450 for that year and $600 for all of 2013. During the recession, Hewlett-Packard lowered its match from 6% to 4% where it has remained. Facebook has not offered a match but has indicated it will later in 2014. IBM shifted to a lump-sum payment at year-end in 2013. As a result of what the CEO termed "distressed babies" and higher health costs, in February 2014, AOL, Inc. indicated it would make the matching payments in a lump-sum at the end of each year, forcing employees who leave before then to forfeit the benefit but will continue with its 3% contribution. After an employee uproar and negative media press, the CEO reversed its decision. UPS indicated it was discontinuing health coverage to white-collar employees' spouses who can get health coverage through another company.

Your ability to build your "nest egg" is slowly becoming totally dependent on YOU. Today, the term retirement means many different things to many people. Some view it when they stop work altogether. For others, when they begin collecting Social Security or when they start their "second act" in their life.

Retirement in the 21st Century

Retirement in the 21st century is feeling much different for many than it did for those who retired during the 20th century. It is anything but linear. Since the start of this century we have had the dot.com bust, the war on terrorism begin and still continuing, two devastating bear markets, a housing boom and bust, millions simply leaving the workforce, an extended period of historically low interest rates and a sluggish economic cycle despite massive stimulus efforts on the part of the Federal Reserve Bank. And just think, we're only 14 years into this century.

The process of transitioning from accumulation to decumulation is becoming much more challenging in ensuring retirement success. Accumulation is simply the process of saving and investing while you work. Decumulation is the process of living off what you have saved and invested. It is a time when the "standard" paycheck stops coming in every two weeks. Managing risk during this period becomes critically important as you approach retirement. Without understanding how these risks affect your retirement, you could be stepping into the twilight zone. These risks include:

- Inflation
- Sequence of returns
- Health
- Longevity

The retirement model in the 21st century will be driven by developing a blueprint for understanding and efficiently utilizing your personal capital. It is the totality of this personal capital which will drive a sustainable income stream. When optimized, these capital sources; human, social and financial work synergistically to create a floor of income to offset "essential" expenses no matter what market conditions exist, yet still provides an opportunity for upside potential in retirement balance growth. Retirement income planning is not static and shouldn't be thought of as a one-and-done process. As you navigate this process you may need to make many course adjustments along the way. You need to be prepared to be flexible in your thinking. Corporate benefits are being reduced which is adding to employees' financial anxieties at a time when income levels for a vast majority of workers have been stagnant. This holistic approach to longevity planning is vastly different from traditional investment planning.

The State of Retirement Readiness

Research reports and surveys provide insight into attitudes, beliefs and circumstances of the public at specific points in time. The real value lies in those studies and surveys which have been done consistently over a period of time, allowing one to see changes taking place on what is being assessed. The research reports and surveys which follow are not focused on just Social Security but also on saving for retirement in general.

Household Incomes Drive Everything

For many this has been an economic recovery which has simply left many Americans behind, especially when evaluating income growth. The graph in figure 1.3 below illustrates median household income in the U.S.

Figure 1.3 Median Household Income in the U.S.

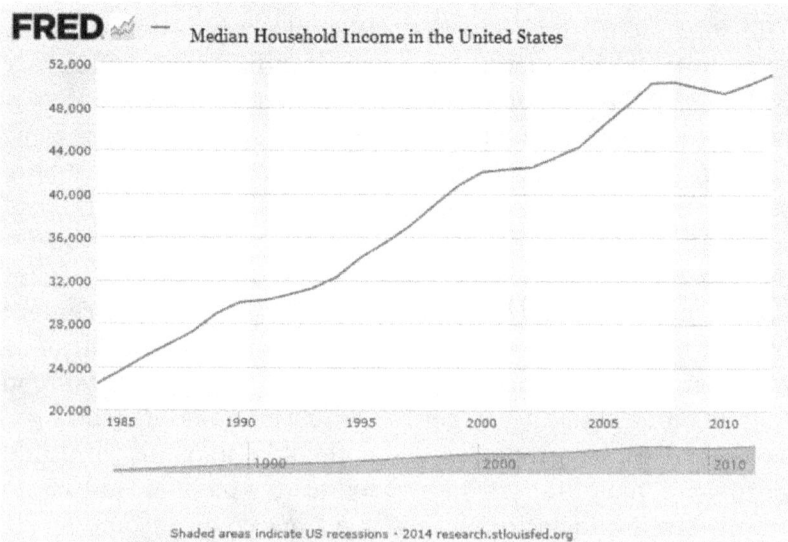

Source: Federal Reserve Bank of St. Louis

At first look, the graph is upward sloping indicating growth in median incomes. However, since reaching its peak at the beginning of 2008, right at the onset of the Great Financial Recession, median household incomes have flatten out. In 2008, median household income peaked at $50,303. Four years later median household income is only at $51,017, a *cumulative* increase of only 1.4%. In *nominal terms* we've had virtually no income growth over a four year period.

What happens if we adjust the data to take into account the effects of inflation over the intervening period? Figure 1.4 below displays the same graph for the level of real median household income in the U.S., adjusted for the effects of inflation. A totally different picture emerges.

Figure 1.4 Real Median Household Income in the U.S.

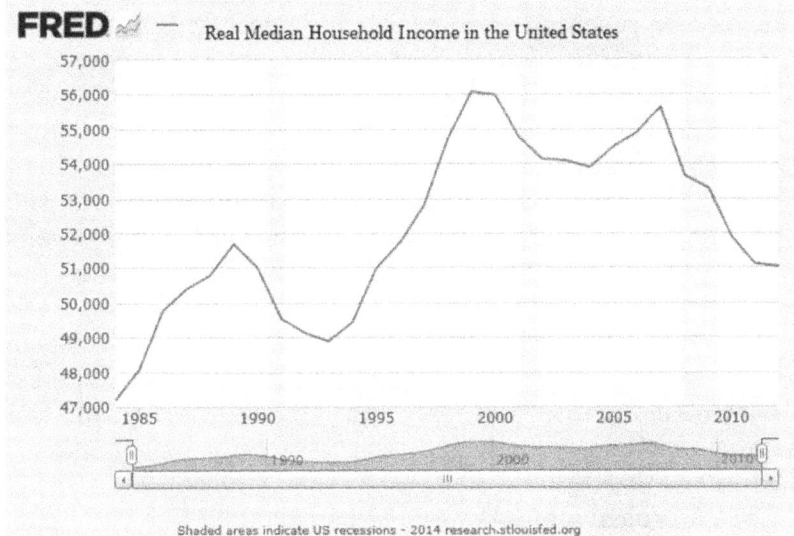

Source: Federal Reserve Bank of St. Louis

After peaking at $56,080, at the beginning of 1999, real household incomes have fallen to just $51,017 as of the beginning of 2012, a *cumulative decline* of nearly 10% over the 13 year period. Real median household incomes are now back to levels last seen in 1995. Real incomes for many are just not keeping up with inflation, which further constrains already limited household budgets. As a result, many people are being pushed into poverty levels where they have little choice but to turn to public assistance programs to help meet life's essential needs such as food and health care.

Research Reports and Surveys on Non-Retired Outlooks

The National Institute on Retirement Security (NIRS), located in Washington, D.C., is a non-profit research and education organization established to contribute to informed policymaking by fostering a deep understanding of the value of retirement security to employees, employers, and the economy as a whole. In December 2013 they released a research report titled, *"Race and Retirement Insecurity in the United States."* The study's research is based on an analysis of data from the U.S. Bureau of Labor Statistics' Current Population Survey Annual Social and Economic Supplement and the Federal Reserve's 2010 Survey of Consumer Finance. The study calculates the retirement security racial divide in the U.S. which every racial group faces. The findings of the study reveal the typical working-age American household is far off track toward accumulating sufficient savings to meet their basic needs in retirement. The situation is particularly dire for African-Americans, Latinos and Asians. Some of the findings include:

- A typical white household has $30,000 in retirement accounts and $112,000 in retirement savings.
- A typical African-American household has nothing set aside in a 401(k) or IRA and $20,000 in retirement savings.
- A typical Latino household also has nothing set aside in a 401(k) or IRA and only $18,000 in retirement savings.

This study served as a companion report which the NIRS released in July 2013 titled, *"The Retirement Savings Crisis: Is It Worse Than We Think?"* The study uses the Federal Reserve's Survey of Consumer Finances to analyze retirement plan participation, savings and overall assets of all U.S. households, between the ages of 25 to 64, not just those with retirement account assets. This is important because some 45% or 38 million working-age households do not have any retirement account assets. The study's conclusions found today's American workers are less prepared for retirement than at any point since 1979, some 25 years ago.

The U.S. Senate Finance Committee recently held a special hearing on needed reforms for Social Security, defined benefits and private retirement accounts. The December 2013 hearing was called by the Subcommittee on Social Security, Pensions and Family Policy. A series of statistics were presented to the subcommittee which paints a bleak picture of the ability of today's retiree to face a comfortable and secure retirement.

- One-third of Americans aged 45 to 65 have no retirement savings at all.
- Of those that do, 75% of Americans nearing retirement age have less than $30,000 in their retirement accounts.
- Among minority workers the situation is especially dire with 89% of Latino workers having less than $10,000 in retirement savings.

When you consider the racial disparities in wealth, the picture gets even worse. The median wealth of white households is 20 times that of African-American households and 18 times that of Hispanic households. These numbers represent the largest ratios, since the federal government began publishing this data, some 25 years ago. The percentage of workers covered by traditional defined benefit plans has steadily declined for 35 years. In the mid-1980s, there were roughly 112,000 DB plans. That number is now down to roughly 30,000. The number of those actually covered by a BD plan has dropped from 62% to 7% during the same period.

In February 2014, the Consumer Federation of America (CFA) released its *7th Annual Savings Survey*. Its findings reveal that despite the economic recovery of the last four years, most Americans continue to face significant personal savings challenges. While many individuals struggle to save, most are able to meet their day-to-day financial obligations. One-third of the households in the survey are barely saving. Two factors may account for this. First, Americans with annual household incomes between $25,000 and $50,000 were much less likely to report good savings habits than those in higher income groups. Second, there are fewer individuals in 2014 that have savings plans with specific goals or spending plans that include savings goals than the previous year's survey.

In March 2014, a study was released by the FINRA Investor Education Foundation titled, *"The Financial Capability of Young Adults – A Generational View"*. The study was based on an examination of data from the FINRA Foundation's National Financial Capability Study (State-by-State Survey) and was conducted online with 25,509 American adults from July to October 1012. The study found that millennials are struggling financially. In particular they exhibit a number of problematic financial behaviors, display low levels of financial literacy and express concerns about their debt. When asked about their financial satisfaction the survey found the following levels.

- Millennials: 23%
- Gen Xers: 17%
- Baby Boomers: 25%
- Silent Generation: 42%

There are concerns across the generations about having too much debt in general, not including student loans.

14

- Millennials: 46%
- Gen Xers: 50%
- Baby Boomers: 38%
- Silent Generation: 23%

Also in March 2014, Capital One ShareBuilder, Inc., a subsidiary of Capital One Financial Corporation, released its *Financial Freedom Survey*. The survey completed by ORC International's Online CARAVAN® interviewed 1,008 non-retired landline and cell phone users ages 18 and older. While the results corroborate the findings from those surveys mentioned previously, for those who are not retired, the survey found that financial stress is keeping three out of four non-retired individuals (75%) up at night. The leading cause of sleepless nights for most non-retirees (34%) is supporting children and saving for college, while retirement is a top concern for only 13%. Women (61%) are significantly more concerned than men (52%) that they may never save enough for retirement.

In a study by the LIMRA Secure Retirement Institute, it found that 27% of U.S. workers, ages 55 to 64, say they do not know how they will use their defined contribution plan savings after they retire. Women are twice as likely to not have a plan for using these retirement assets as men do.

Research Reports and Surveys on Retired Outlooks

In a survey which was conducted by Fidelity Investments, it found those who are 55 or older and have been with their current employer for at least ten years have an average retirement account balance of $255,000.

The Employee Benefits Research Institute (EBRI), located in Washington, D.C., produces credible, reliable, and objective research, data, and analysis. The EBRI does not take advocacy positions on policy proposals, lobby for or against proposals, or recommend specific approaches/prescriptions and is funded by membership

15

dues, grants, and contributions. We're going to take a look at two different studies which they conducted.

In February 2013, the EBRI released a paper titled, *"Debt of the Elderly and Near Elderly, 1992–2010"*, which found housing debt is increasing for older Americans. Debt levels among those with housing debt have obvious and serious implications for the future retirement security of these Americans, perhaps most significantly that these families are potentially at risk of losing what is typically their most important asset—their home. Housing debt, both home mortgages and home equity loans, was the major component of debt for families with a head of household, age 55 or older. During the study period the proportion of families with heads age 55 or older, housing debt increased steadily from 24% in 1992 to 42% in 2010. Nearly 75% of debt payments are for housing for this group. For families with heads of households ages 65–74, this debt increased from 18% in 1992 to 41% by 2010, and for families with heads of households age 75 or older, from 10% to 24%. According to the EBRI, these debt results are troubling as far as retirement preparedness is concerned. They indicate American families just reaching retirement or who are newly retired, are more likely than past generations to have debt—and significantly higher levels of debt.

The EBRI also conducts the *Retirement Confidence Survey (RCS)*, the longest running annual retirement survey of its kind in the U.S., now in its 24th year. For 2014, a random, nationally representative telephone survey of 1,501 individuals (1,000 workers and 501 retirees), age 25 and over was conducted by Greenwald & Associates during January 2014. The percentage of workers confident about having enough money for a comfortable retirement, at record lows between 2009 and 2013, increased in 2014. Eighteen percent are now very confident, up from 13% in 2013, while 37% are somewhat confident. Twenty-four percent are not at all confident (statistically unchanged from 28% in 2013). What's interesting is this increased confidence level is observed almost exclusively among those with higher household incomes ($75,000 and up). The survey also found confidence was strongly correlated with household participation in a retirement plan, including an individual retirement account (IRA). Nearly 50% of workers without a retirement plan were not at all confident about their financial security in retirement, compared with only 1 in 10 with a plan.

Retiree confidence in having a financially secure retirement, which historically tends to exceed worker confidence levels has also increased, with 28% very confident, up from 18% in 2013 and 17% not at all confident (statistically unchanged from 14% in 2013).

Findings from the current survey indicate a sizable percentage of workers have virtually no money in savings and investments. Nearly 60% of workers have less than $25,000 in savings, excluding ownership in their primary home and defined benefit plans. Equally distributing is that 36% surveyed say they have saved less than $1,000. Those with between $25,000 and less than $100,000 in savings and investments total 18%. These numbers are slightly worse than the previous year and are skewed by millennials and Gen-Xers who have little in savings but it does provide some perspective regarding the trends in saving for the future.

For retirees, 58% have less than $25,000 in savings, excluding ownership in their primary home and defined benefit plans. Again, equally distributing is that 29% surveyed say they have saved less than $1,000. Those with between $25,000 and less than $100,000 in savings and investments total 15%. These numbers are mixed from the previous year.

Existing debt levels is also an issue prohibiting workers from saving for retirement. Fifty-eight percent of workers and 44% of retirees report having a problem with their level of debt. Furthermore, 24% of workers and 17% of retirees indicate that their current level of debt is higher than it was five years ago.

17

As a result, more Americans are becoming reliant on their Social Security benefits to be the foundation of their retirement plan, not just a supplemental source of additional income which is what it was originally designed to be. What we've known as the traditional retirement model is imploding and rapidly vanishing. Without retirement savings, aging parents become dependent on their working-age adult children, preventing them from saving for their own retirement. Even with retirement savings, boomeranging adult children are coming back home, forcing their parents to deplete their own savings in helping them to get back on their feet.

Again in March 2014, Franklin Templeton released their *Retirement Income Strategies and Expectations (RISE) Survey.* The survey was conducted online among a sample of 2,011 adults comprising 1,008 men and 1,003 women, 18 years of age or older. The survey was conducted by ORC International's Online CARAVAN® between January 2 and 16, 2014. The survey uncovered many contradictions relating to retirement income planning. The biggest: while a majority of people have a positive view of retirement, most aren't taking steps to reach the retirement they aspire to. Of those surveyed, 72% were looking forward to retirement. What is interesting is that not only are just 25% confident that their retirement will be better than their parents, 41% actually think it will be worse. In addition, 92% expect retirement expenses to be similar or less than their pre-retirement expenses and nearly 50% were worried about outliving their assets. Of the respondents surveyed, 57% of those who developed a written retirement income plan know with a high degree of confidence how much of their current income will be replace by Social Security.

Expanding Understanding of Social Security

In *Setting the Context*, at the beginning of the book, the results of a survey released by Financial Engines were briefly discussed. Greenwald & Associates conducted the research on behalf of Financial Engines. Information for this study was gathered through a 15-minute online survey with 1,008 near-retirees and retirees between the ages of 55 and 70, who have an annual household income of at least $50,000. The survey included 374 people who have already claimed their Social Security retirement benefits (median age of 65) and 634 people who have not (median age of 59). In determining the survey findings, responses were weighted by the respondent's age, gender and education to reflect the composition of the U.S. population, ages 55-70.

In addition to identifying some costly knowledge gaps, the study found high interest in getting help with selecting the right household Social Security claiming strategy. Near retirees and retirees are receptive to their employers providing access to that assistance. Seven in 10 near-retirees (69%) who have not yet claimed Social Security said they would be at least somewhat interested in a service provided by their employer to help them develop a household claiming strategy. Of these, 39% said that they would be extremely or very interested in this type of Social Security claiming help.

In May 2011, a working paper by Jeffrey R. Brown, Ph.D., Arie Kapteyn and Olivia S. Mitchell, Ph.D. was published in the National Bureau of Economic Research (EBER) titled, *"Framing Effects and Expected Social Security Claiming Behavior"*. In their paper the authors show that individual intentions, with regard to Social Security claiming ages, are sensitive to how the early versus late claiming decision is framed to them. They found that, using an experimental design, the use of a break-even analysis has the very strong effect of encouraging individuals to claim retirement benefits early. On the other hand, if later claiming is framed as a gain, individuals are more likely to report they will delay claiming. Moreover, females, individuals with credit card debt and workers with lower expected benefits are more strongly influenced by framing. The authors conclude some individuals may not make fully rational optimizing decisions when it comes to choosing a claiming date.

Income Replacement and Social Security

In a research study completed by the Employee Benefit Research Institute (EBRI), in January 2014 and authored by EBRI research director, Jack VanDerhei, Ph.D., most workers were found to be able to replace 60% of their pre-retirement income with Social Security and 401(k) savings. This projection holds true if Social Security retirement benefits are not reduced and if the worker has 30 years in a 401(k) savings plan. With these conditions, the EBRI estimates 83% to 86% of workers would be able to replace 60% of their wages earned at age 64 on an inflation-adjusted basis. If the workers amount of income to be replaced is increased to 70%, the percentage of workers who could manage this drops 10 percentage points to 73% to 76%. Even at an 80% replacement threshold, 67% of workers would still be able to manage this. The analysis was done using EBRI's proprietary retirement adequacy computer model.

The EBRI also ran a simulated model where workers would have a proportional 24% reduction in Social Security benefits. The percentage of the lowest quartile with an 80% replacement threshold drops 17 percentage points, from 67% to 50%. For the highest income quartile which receives less proportionate benefits from Social Security, the replacement threshold drops by only 9 percentage points, from 59% to 50%.

The EBRI began to compile data in account balances for 401(k)'s in 1996. Then, account balances for individuals in their 60s averaged $158,000. In 2013, it now averages $224,000. However, to maintain the same buying power, that $158,000 in 1996 would need to be worth $234,000 now, an additional $10,000 to account for the effects of inflation over 17 years.

Understanding Longevity Risk

Longevity risk refers to the risk that actual survival rates and life expectancy will exceed expectations resulting in greater-than-anticipated retirement cash flow needs. In other words, it is the risk of outliving ones' assets which generate the needed cash flow in retirement. The impact of underestimating this risk can include:

- Lower standard of living.
- Reduced care.
- Having to live where you don't want to.
- Need to return to employment at an inopportune age.

There have been a number of studies published on life expectancies. In a 2012 telephone survey of 1,600 adults between the ages of 45 and 80, conducted by the Society of Actuaries (SOA), they found more than 50% of retirees and pre-retirees underestimate how long they may live. Life expectancy for newborn American men over the past fifty years has improved by an average of almost two years each decade, from 66.6 years in 1960 to 75.7 years by 2010. For women, the average increase was about 1.5 years per decade, from 73.1 years in 1960 to 80.8 years by 2010. There is a 40% chance for men and a 50% chance for women of living to age 85, assuming they reach 65 and are in average health.

Let's look at two other sources for life expectancy estimates. According to the U.S. Census Bureau, the U.S. average life expectancy at birth increased 62% from 47.3 years in 1902 to 76.8 years in 2000, with expectations it will reach 79.5 years in 2020. When data, complied by the SSA is examined, their findings indicate a man reaching age 65 today can expect to live, on average, until age 84. For a woman turning age 65 today, she can expect to live, on average, until age 86. These are just averages. According to the SSA, about one out of every four 65-year olds today will live past age 90 and one out of ten will live past age 95.

In a 2012 report, released by the Insured Retirement Institute, they noted that women are far more at risk for outliving their savings due to their unique retirement income challenges. These are longer life expectancies, lower lifetime incomes and higher health care costs in retirement, including long-term care expenses. According to Vanguard's annual report, *How America Saves – 2012*, the average defined contribution balance for a woman was just $59,104 compare with $94,063 for a man.

Dr. L. Stephen Coles, M.D., Ph.D., gave an interview to ThinkAdvisor. Dr. Coles is currently a Lecturer in Gerontology at the UCLA Molecular Biology Institute, Department of Chemistry and Biochemistry. For the past 20 years, he has been the Executive Director of the Los Angeles Gerontology Research Group (GRG). He holds both an M.D. and a Ph.D. in Mathematics. He is a researcher who focuses on super-centenarians, those who have lived to or pass their 110th birth date and on aging in general. As of February 2014, the GRG have validated 71 (66 females and 5 males) living super-centenarians. However, as the GRG indicated, this does not represent every single person age 110 and over. The actual number of worldwide living super-centenarians is more likely to be between 300 and 450 persons. For the U.S., their prediction is between 60-75 persons. While the total number of validated cases is only about 10% of the suspected real-world total, the bulk of true super-centenarians actually fall between 110 and 113 years of age. Few ever surpass 115 years. According to Coles, the most valuable predictors for average life expectancy is not the age of the individual but where they live, their gender and whether they are smokers or not. Interestingly, these are also the main variables insurance companies look at. Coles concluded the interview with a story about a super-centenarian he had met with at UCLA. *"In the middle of our interview she lit up a cigarette. I said, as a doctor I cannot approve of this bad behavior on your part. The woman replied, what are you going to do about it? The last doctor who focused on that is dead."* Go figure. You just never know.

Underestimating life expectancy combined with a short retirement planning horizon can be a recipe for disaster, resulting in inadequate retirement income. When planning for retirement the goal should not be about planning to average life expectancy. It should be about planning beyond life expectancy. The goal should be not to avoid catastrophe, but to optimize the chance of getting the best result.

Longevity Calculators

Longevity calculators may be useful in giving you an idea of how long you may live. I've tried to arrange them in order of complexity, from the simplistic to the more involved. This is just a sampling of what is available.

Estimate Your Life Expectancy: This calculator is located at the Social Security website. You can use the simple Life Expectancy Calculator to get a rough estimate of how long you or your spouse may live. Knowing this information can help you make a more informed choice regarding when to collect Social Security retirement benefits. The calculator is built using Microsoft Excel. You can access it at http://www.ssa.gov/planners/lifeexpectancy.htm.

Life Expectancy Calculator: The Society of Actuaries (SOA) makes available a helpful tool for calculating the life expectancies of an individual and/or couple at different ages. The life expectancies are based on either the SOA Annuity 2000 or Social Security Administration Tables. The calculator allows a user to select either one. The calculator was created by Mary Pat Campbell, FSA and she has graciously donated it to the SOA. It can be accessed at http://www.soa.org/research/software-tools/research-simple-life-calculator.aspx.

How Long Will You Live: This calculator was created by Dean P. Foster, Ph.D., Choong Tze Chua, and Lyle H. Ungar, Ph.D., at the University of Pennsylvania. From their site at http://gosset.wharton.upenn.edu/mortality/ you can calculate predictions as to how long you will live:

- The short form life calculator (less than one minute) is particularly useful for financial planning.
- A longer version of the life calculator (about 5 minutes), is good for exploring more health choices under your control.
- An alternate calculator (not by them) is targeted at the elderly.

Lifespan Calculator: This lifespan calculator available from Northwestern Mutual. It can be accessed at http://media.nmfn.com/tnetwork/lifespan/#0. They also have what they call the Longevity Game you can play at http://www.northwesternmutual.com/learning-center/the-longevity-game.aspx.

Living to 100: The Living to 100 Life Expectancy Calculator uses the most current and carefully researched medical and scientific data in order to estimate how old you will live to be. The calculator asks you 40 quick questions related to your health and family history, and takes about 10 minutes to complete. At the end, you will be asked to create an account store your answers. You can access the calculator at https://www.livingto100.com/calculator.

Retirement Security

In February 2014, Natixis Global Asset Management released their 2014 Global Retirement Index. It is an analysis of 150 countries and the index is based on 20 key trends which are grouped into four thematic areas:

1. Health and health-care quality.

2. Personal income and finance.
3. Quality of life.
4. Socio-economic factors.

The United States ranked 19th in its ability to provide security and overall well-being for retirees. Switzerland, Norway and Austria took the top three spots. Nations in the top rankings share common characteristics which could be useful to U.S. policy makers. Many show a commitment to innovation when comes to improving the savings rate. They emphasize simplicity in retirement plans and they have governments willing to enact bold policy changes when needed.

In March 2014, the National Institute on Retirement Security released their scorecard which ranks states by the economic pressures which are placed on future retirees, using the most recent data from 2012. The reported titled, *"The Financial Security Scorecard: State-by-State Analysis of Economic Pressures Facing Future Retirees"*, finds nearly every state falls short in key areas measuring retirement readiness. The scorecard ranks each of the 50 states plus the District of Columbia in three sources of potential economic pressures for future retirees, as measured through eight specific variables:

- Potential retirement income as measured by private sector workplace retirement plan participation, estimated average 401(k) account balances and effective tax rates on pension income.
- Major retiree costs, focused on housing and health care costs for older households as measured by Medicare out-of-pocket costs, Medicaid generosity and older households' housing cost burden.
- Labor market conditions for older workers as measured by unemployment and median earnings among older workers.

A score of 1 to 10 is assigned to each state in each category of retirement income, retiree costs, and labor markets, with 1 representing the lowest possible score and 10 representing the highest possible score. Then all the rankings are averaged across all variables in order to arrive at an overall state score. The states scoring the highest were Wyoming (9), followed by Alaska, Minnesota and North Dakota (8). The states with the lowest scores were California, Florida and South Carolina (3). Nine states had a score of 4. Two key findings in the study were: (1) across all states there is inadequate private sector retirement savings and (2) seniors now face housing cost burdens in a large majority of states where they pay more than 30% of their income towards housing expenses.

Concluding Thoughts

Retirement is about making choices and compromises. More Americans feel like they are under constant financial duress when it comes to managing life. The replacement of defined benefits plans with defined contribution plans was supposed to help secure and boost the retirement savings for the baby boomers. It would give them more control over retirement planning and better portability of retirement account balances. It hasn't quite worked out the way it was envisioned. According to the Center for Retirement Research at Boston College, the median balance in 401(k) and IRA accounts combined, for households headed by 55 to 64 year olds who had accounts at work, totaled just $120,000 as of 2010. In February 2014, James M. Poterba, Ph.D., published a paper in the National Bureau of Economic Research titled, *"Retirement Security in an Aging Society"*. He notes that a 65 year old who wanted to pay for retirement with annuities, tied to bonds, needed 24% more wealth in 2013 than in 2005.

Today, many living in this country are constrained by limited incomes, forcing them to truly live on a low budget. When it comes to planning for retirement there is much in the way of emotions, guilt and anxiety among many individuals who make these decisions. Many realize they haven't done a good job in saving for retirement. There were just too many competing financial issues for their dollars while they were working. Now many who are in their 50s and 60s feel a tremendous amount of anxiety as to what retirement will bring. In summarizing the previous studies, the following bullet points would probably apply to many.

- The income gap between the wealthiest and the poorest is the widest it's been in 90 years.
- Real household incomes are falling.
- Record numbers for those on food stamps.
- Those with higher incomes have a more confident outlook on retirement.
- The majority of workers have little in the way of current savings and investments.
- Grave concern among many about outliving their financial resources, especially among women.
- There is a knowledge gap in understanding Social Security and benefit levels.

Stock market returns over the past two years, coupled with stabilization and modest improvements in home prices have done much to improve the outlook for many. However, another financial crisis at this juncture would torpedo that optimism very quickly. A pending retirement crisis may well arrive long before the year 2033, a key date we will see for Social Security in the last chapter. What this portends is for the near future, the Social Security system is going to become an even larger component of the retirement foundation for many Americans than what it currently is today, especially for those who are earning minimum wage. Social Security could replace as much as 70% of their income. However, this probably will not improve their socioeconomic situation. This was never the original intent for Social Security when it was created.

"I think that age as a number is not nearly as important as health. You can be in poor health and be pretty miserable at 40 or 50. If you're in good health, you can enjoy things into your 80s."

Bob Barker – Age 90
Former Television Game Show Host
The Price is Right – 1972-2007
Truth or Consequences – 1956-1975

CHAPTER TWO

COST OF HEALTH CARE

One may think this is an odd chapter to include in a book about Social Security claiming strategies. For many individuals, Social Security will represent their main source of income during retirement. Your health, or lack of good health, plays an enormous role in the amount of Social Security benefits you will have left over at the end of the month after you pay for health care expenses. It seems intuitive that as we age our health will naturally decline and a greater portion of our monthly budget will need to be allocated to health care. But does this need to begin in our 60s or 90s? We could have thirty years of good health or thirty years of declining health. The cost of health care is an important topic when discussing Social Security. Good health means more dollars to spend on things other than physician visits, medical procedures and prescription drugs.

According to the Centers for Medicare and Medicaid Services (CMS), in their National Health Expenditures Projections 2011-2021 report, total health care spending in the U.S. is expected to reach $4.8 trillion in 2021. This is up from $2.6 trillion in 2010 and $75 billion in 1970. From the

Bureau of Labor Statistics, medical costs have risen, on average, 5.7% per year for the past twenty years. This is double the rate of inflation as measured by the CPI.

How does health care spending and life expectancy rates, in the United States, compare with those of other developed countries? The facts are not what you might expect. In 2009, health care spending per person was far higher in the United States than any other industrialized country, at nearly $8,000 per person. This probably isn't a surprise to most of you. Switzerland was second at roughly $5,000 per person while New Zealand was the lowest at just under $3,000 per person. Figure 2.1 below illustrates a number of industrialized countries and their health care expenses per person, along with their estimated life expectancy rates for 2009.

Figure 2.1 Health Care Spending Per Person and Life Expectancy

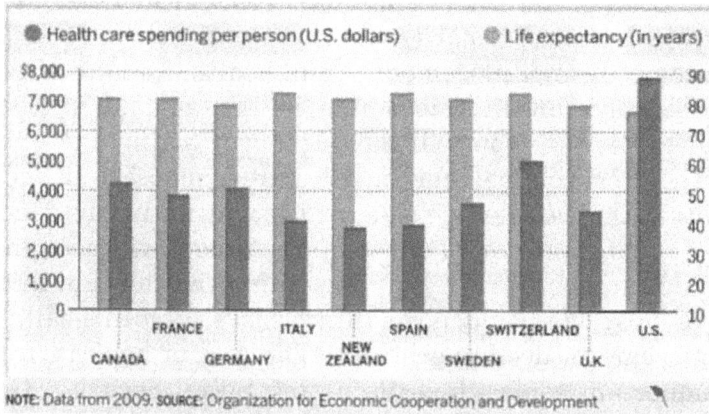

Courtesy: MONEY magazine, October 2011
Source: OECD

What you might not expect from the chart above is Americans aren't necessarily healthier as evidenced by our life expectancy rate which is the lowest.

Measured by GDP, the overall costs for health care have been expanding at a rate of two percentage points faster than the economy. This problem will only get worse in the coming decade as aging baby boomers flood the Medicare system and longer life spans add more years of medical care. In 2012, Americans age 65, have an average life expectancy of 18 additional years.

Under the current law most Americans collect far more from the Medicare system than they pay in. According to calculations by the Urban Institute, a married couple who retired in 2011 can expect to receive $350,000 in lifetime benefits. To receive this benefit they paid in about $150,000 in Medicare taxes. For a couple who are 46 today, they can expect to receive $525,000 in benefits when they retire at 65. Their cost in Medicare taxes; just over $200,000. This example assumes a two-earner couple, one with $69,600 income and the other with $43,500 in income during 2011.

In 1880 there were only 1.7 million individuals 65 and older.

Figure 2.2 Population 65+ by Age: 1900-2050

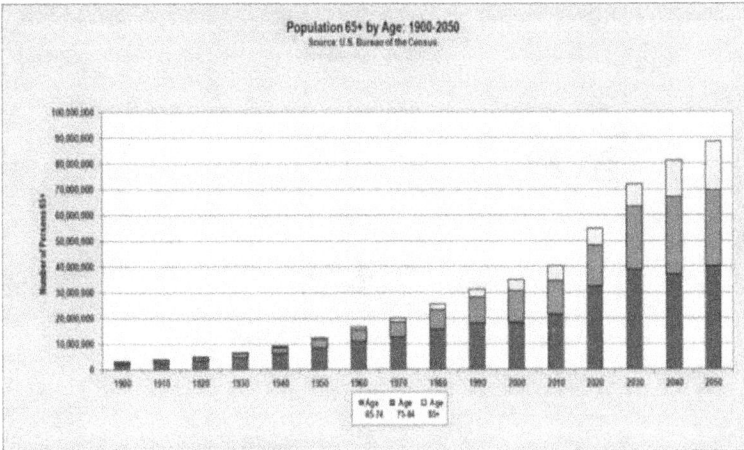

Courtesy: U.S. Administration on Aging
Source: U.S. Census Bureau

Even by 1940, 60 years later, there were still less than 10 million individuals 65 and older. However by 1970, just 30 years later, the figured had double and by 2010 the figure had doubled again to just over 40 million. Between 2000 and 2010, the population, age 65 and over, increased at a faster rate (15.1%) than the total U.S. population (9.7%). According to the U.S. Administration on Aging, by 2050 there will be an estimated 88.5 million individuals 65 and older as illustrated in Figure 2.2 on the previous page.

In Figure 2.3 below the future percentage makeup of GDP is illustrated. The large area at the bottom of the graph, labeled "everything else" includes Social Security.

Figure 2.3 Estimation of Future Percentage Makeup of GDP: 2011-2051

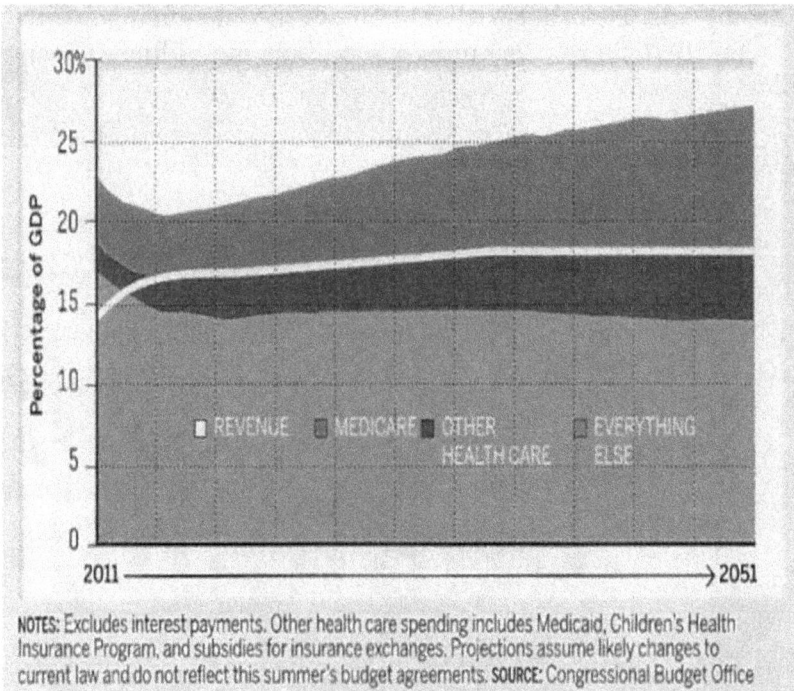

NOTES: Excludes interest payments. Other health care spending includes Medicaid, Children's Health Insurance Program, and subsidies for insurance exchanges. Projections assume likely changes to current law and do not reflect this summer's budget agreements. SOURCE: Congressional Budget Office

Courtesy: MONEY magazine; October 2011
Source: Congressional Budget Office (CBO)

While Social Security is an important issue, it pales in comparison to the rising costs for entitlements for Medicare. By 2030, maintaining benefits at current levels would push government spending to 24% of the economy; with even higher percentages as the years go on. Taxes on the other hand, are expected to generate revenues equal to only 18% of the economy. Clearly this is unsustainable in the long run. While there is a great deal of dissension in Washington on a variety of issues other than health care, both parties agree that controlling Medicare costs is critical to controlling the growing budget gap and future fiscal deficits. Even with reforms, fixing Medicare will be tough. In the end there will need to be some combination of premium/tax increases, increases in copays and coinsurance, higher deductibles, cap limits and possible changes in the eligibility age to receive these benefits. The bottom line; expect and plan for higher costs and less benefits!

Even when health insurance, offered by employer-sponsored plans is examined, the trends are not good. Since 1999, inflation and workers' earnings have risen by cumulative percentages of 40% and 50%, respectively. During the same period, cumulative percentage increases for health insurance premiums and worker' contributions to premiums have seen a three-fold increase since 1999. Figure 2.4, on the next page, plots the *cumulative* increases in health insurance premiums, workers' contributions to premiums, inflation and workers' earnings over a fourteen year period. When average annual health care premiums for single and family coverage are examined over the same time horizon, we see an equally disturbing picture in cost trends. These are the total of both the employee and employer contribution.

Figure 2.4 Cumulative Increases in Health Insurance Premiums

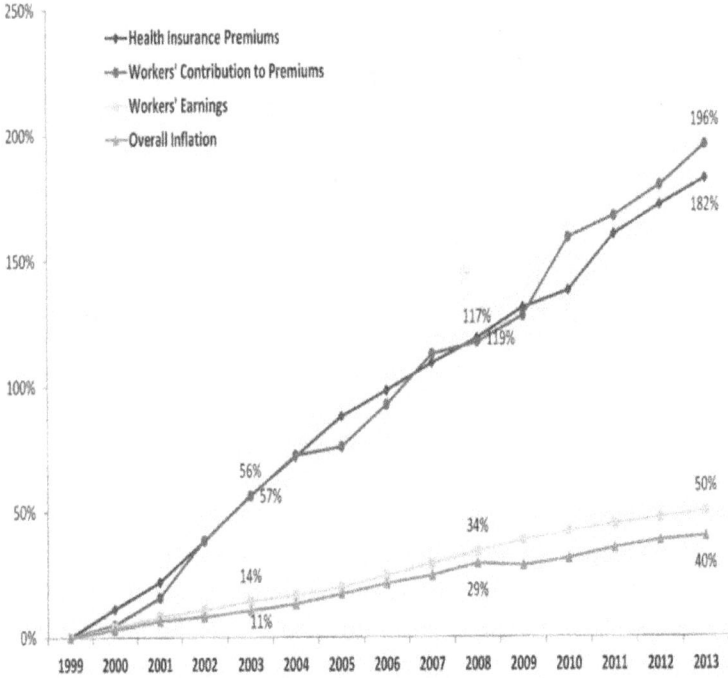

SOURCE: Kaiser/HRET Survey of Employer-Sponsored Health Benefits, 1999-2013. Bureau of Labor Statistics, Consumer Price Index, U.S. City Average of Annual Inflation (April to April), 1999-2013; Bureau of Labor Statistics, Seasonally Adjusted Data from the Current Employment Statistics Survey, 1999-2013 (April to April).

Courtesy: The Kaiser Foundation; 2013 Employer Health Benefit Survey

As illustrated in the graph in Figure 2.5, on the next page, in 1999 the average premium for single and family health insurance coverage was $2,196 and $5,791, respectively.

Figure 2.5 Average Annual Health Insurance
Premiums for Single and Family

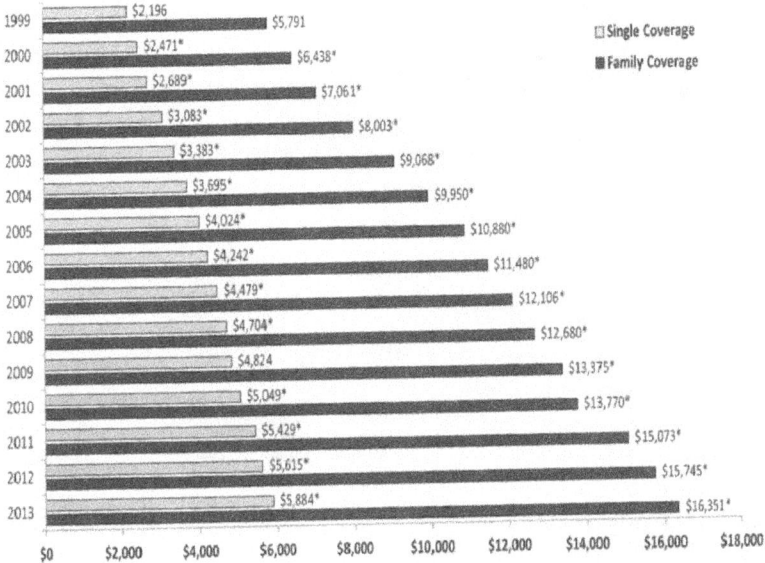

	Single Coverage	Family Coverage
1999	$2,196	$5,791
2000	$2,471*	$6,438*
2001	$2,689*	$7,061*
2002	$3,083*	$8,003*
2003	$3,383*	$9,068*
2004	$3,695*	$9,950*
2005	$4,024*	$10,880*
2006	$4,242*	$11,480*
2007	$4,479*	$12,106*
2008	$4,704*	$12,680*
2009	$4,824	$13,375*
2010	$5,049*	$13,770*
2011	$5,429*	$15,073*
2012	$5,615*	$15,745*
2013	$5,884*	$16,351*

* Estimate is statistically different from estimate for the previous year shown (p<.05).

SOURCE: Kaiser/HRET Survey of Employer-Sponsored Health Benefits, 1999-2013.

*Courtesy: The Kaiser Foundation; 2013 Employer Health B*enefit Survey

Fourteen years later, in 2013, these average annual premiums for single and family coverage had risen to $5,884 and $16,351 per year, respectively.

Where does all the money go? Figure 2.6, on the next page, displays a graph for health care spending for 2010. As can be seen from the pie-chart, the top three spending categories were hospitals at nearly 31%, followed by physicians at 20% and prescription drugs at 10%. These three categories account for 61% of all health care spending in 2010.

Figure 2.6 U.S. Health Care Spending Breakdown, 2010

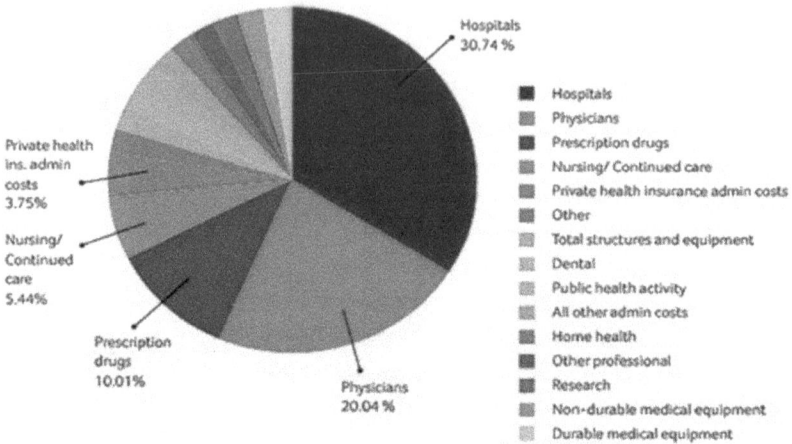

Source: Centers for Medicare and Medicaid Services (CMS)

The *International Federation of Health Plans (iFHP)* was founded in 1968, by a group of health insurance industry leaders. Through its diverse membership, of over one hundred health insurers in twenty-five countries, the iFHP is in a unique position as the leading global network for the industry. The federation is based in London, England. In their *2012 Comparative Price Report,* which is their fourth annual survey, the report contains 28 graphs which display the prices for the cost of specific hospital costs, medical procedures, physician fees and prescription drugs, compiled from data collected by iFHP member plans. The U.S. numbers are based on an aggregate of over 100 million paid claims across multiple payers. What follows is a sampling of eleven graphs reproduced from that report, which can be obtained from the iFHP website at www.ifhp.com.

Figure 2.7 Cost Per Hospital Day

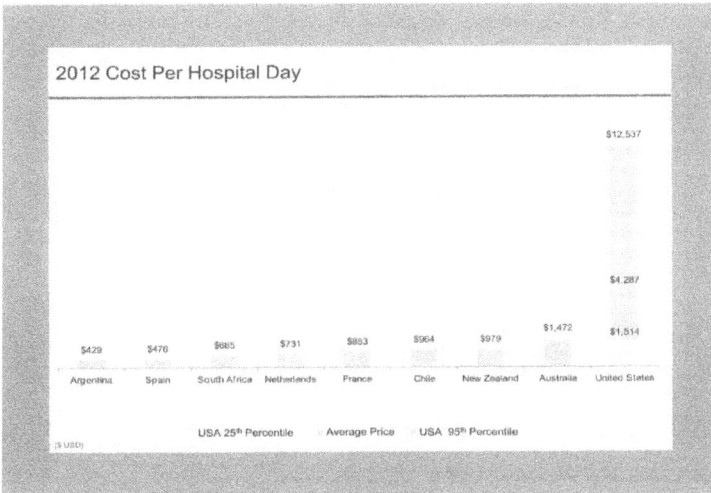

Courtesy: The International Federation of Health Plans;
2012 Comparative Price Report

Figure 2.8 Angiogram Imaging Cost

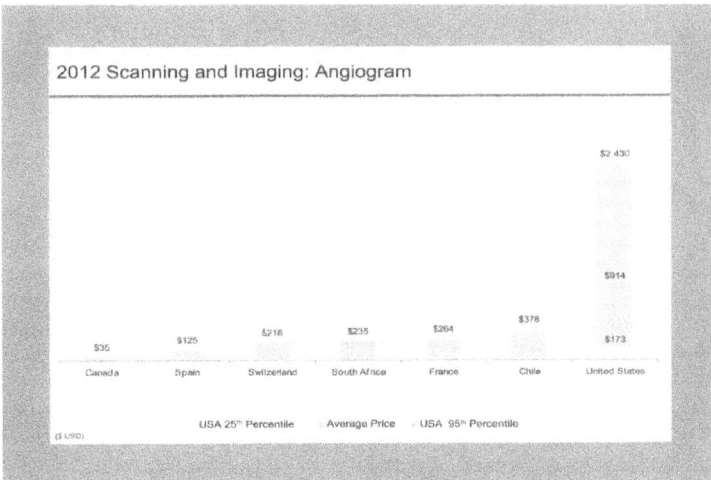

Courtesy: The International Federation of Health Plans;
2012 Comparative Price Report

Figure 2.9 Routine Office Visit Cost

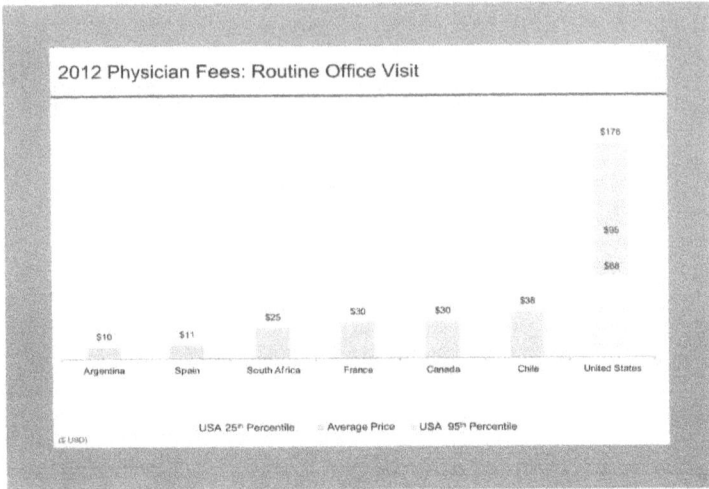

Courtesy: The International Federation of Health Plans;
2012 Comparative Price Report

Figure 2.10 Coronary Artery Bypass Cost

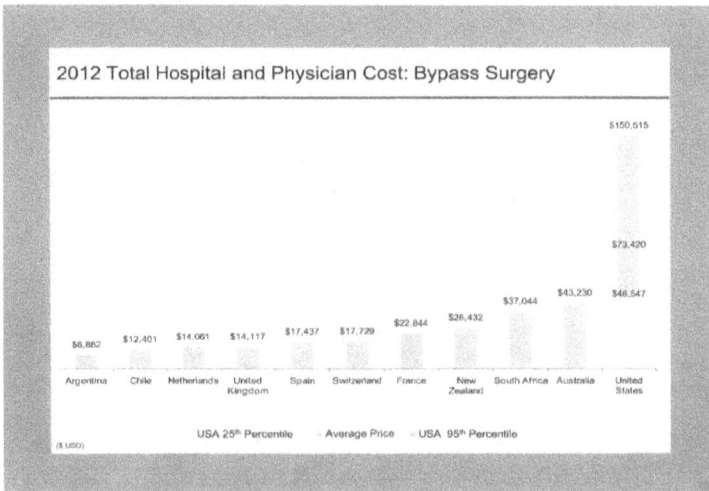

Courtesy: The International Federation of Health Plans;
2012 Comparative Price Report

Figure 2.11 MRI Imaging Cost

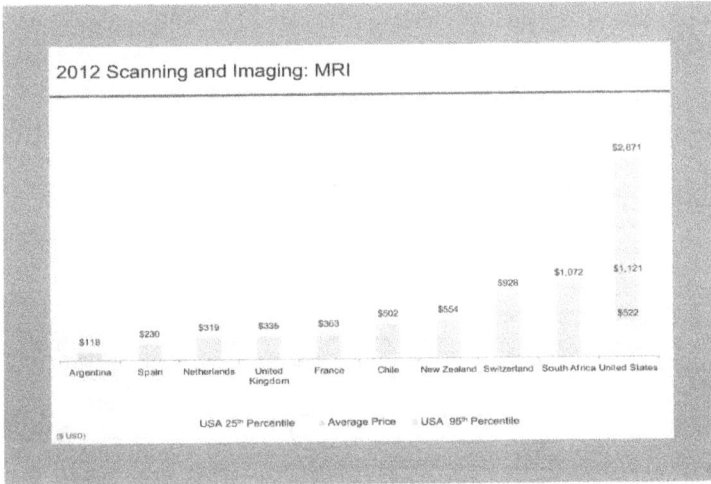

Courtesy: The International Federation of Health Plans;
2012 Comparative Price Report

Figure 2.12 Hip Replacement Cost

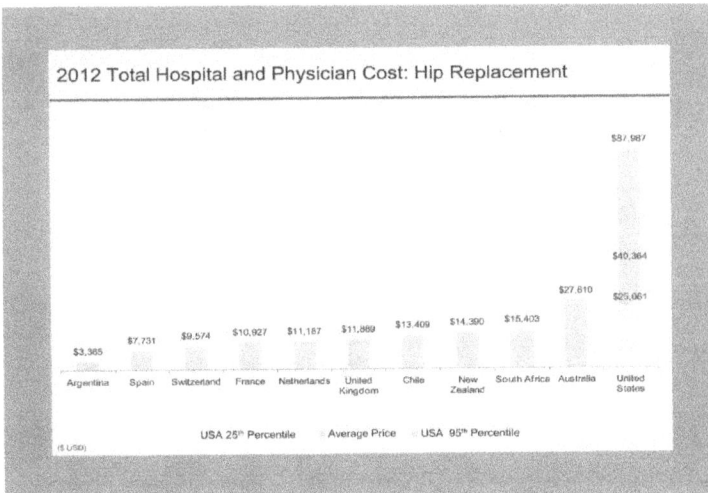

Courtesy: The International Federation of Health Plans;
2012 Comparative Price Report

Figure 2.13 Cataract Surgery Cost

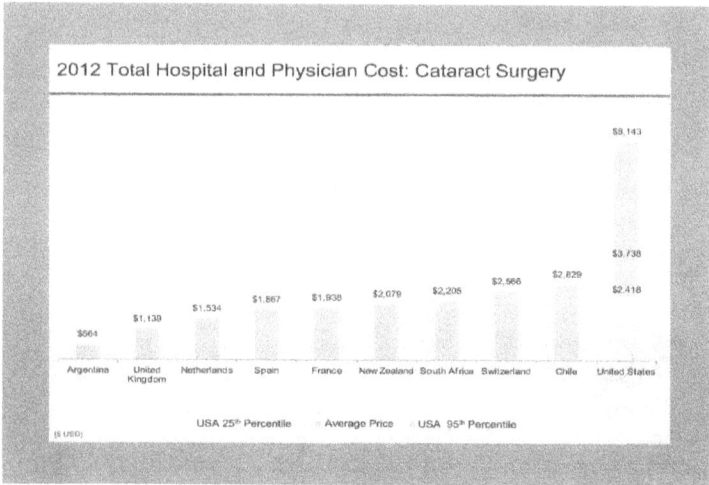

2012 Total Hospital and Physician Cost: Cataract Surgery

$9,143

$3,738

$2,566 $2,829
$2,205 $2,418
$2,079
$1,938
$1,867
$1,534
$1,139
$564

Argentina United Kingdom Netherlands Spain France New Zealand South Africa Switzerland Chile United States

USA 25ᵗʰ Percentile   Average Price   USA 95ᵗʰ Percentile

($ USD)

Courtesy: The International Federation of Health Plans;
2012 Comparative Price Report

Figure 2.14 Colonoscopy Cost

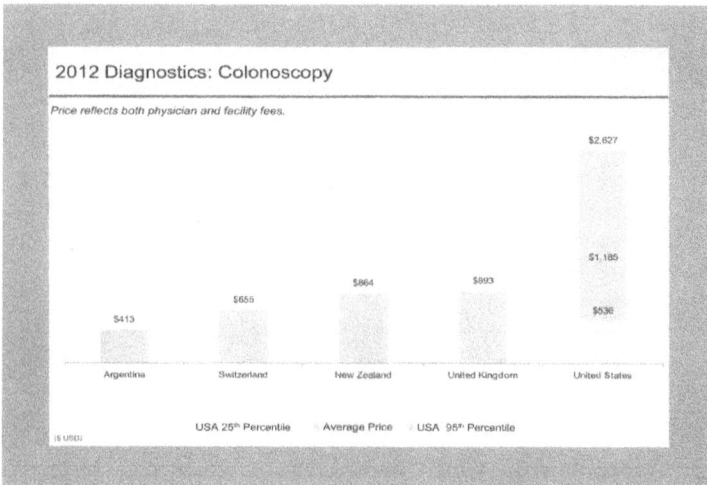

2012 Diagnostics: Colonoscopy

Price reflects both physician and facility fees.

$2,627

$1,185

$993
$864
$655 $536
$413

Argentina Switzerland New Zealand United Kingdom United States

USA 25ᵗʰ Percentile   Average Price   USA 95ᵗʰ Percentile

($ USD)

Courtesy: The International Federation of Health Plans;
2012 Comparative Price Report

Figure 2.15 Nexium Drug Cost

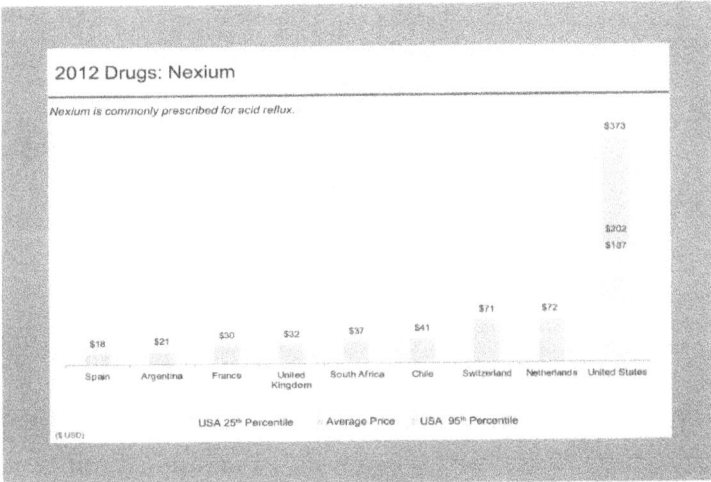

2012 Drugs: Nexium

Nexium is commonly prescribed for acid reflux.

$373

$302
$187

$71 $72

$18 $21 $30 $32 $37 $41

Spain Argentina France United   South Africa Chile Switzerland Netherlands United States
                          Kingdom

USA 25ᵗʰ Percentile   Average Price   USA 95ᵗʰ Percentile

($ USD)

Courtesy: The International Federation of Health Plans;
2012 Comparative Price Report

Figure 2.16 Lipitor Drug Cost

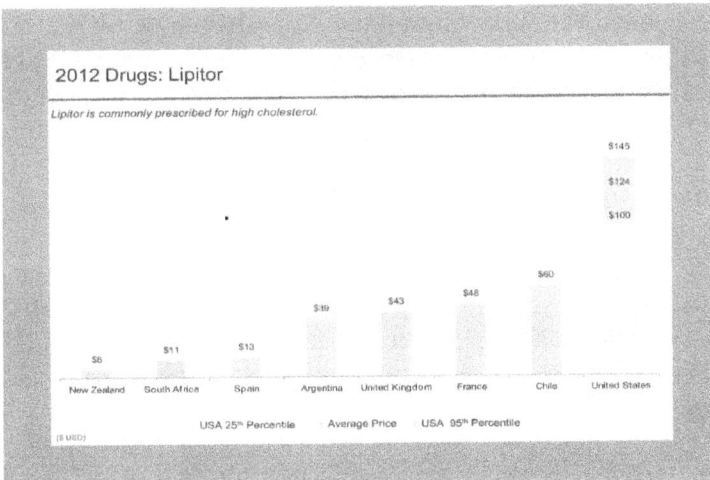

2012 Drugs: Lipitor

Lipitor is commonly prescribed for high cholesterol.

$145
$124
$100

$60

$48
$43
$9

$6 $11 $13

New Zealand South Africa Spain Argentina United Kingdom France Chile United States

USA 25ᵗʰ Percentile   Average Price   USA 95ᵗʰ Percentile

($ USD)

Courtesy: The International Federation of Health Plans;
2012 Comparative Price Report

Figure 2.17 Cymbalta Drug Cost

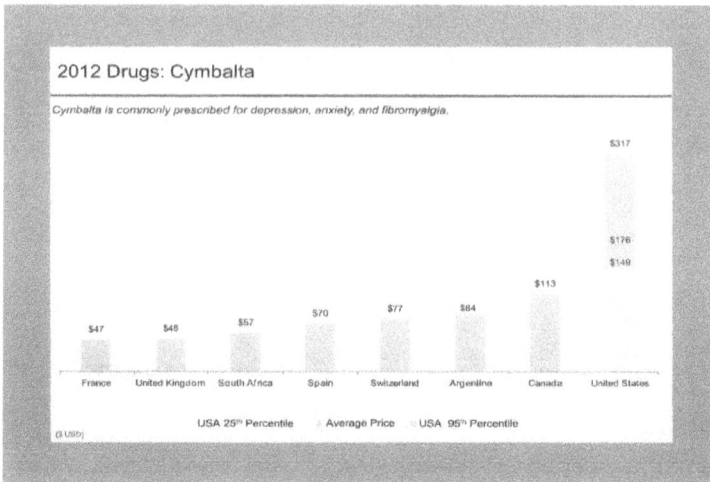

2012 Drugs: Cymbalta

Cymbalta is commonly prescribed for depression, anxiety, and fibromyalgia.

$47	$48	$57	$70	$77	$84	$113	$149 / $176 / $317
France	United Kingdom	South Africa	Spain	Switzerland	Argentina	Canada	United States

USA 25th Percentile   Average Price   USA 95th Percentile

(3 USD)

Courtesy: The International Federation of Health Plans;
2012 Comparative Price Report

FUTURE HEALTH CARE NEEDS

Each year Fidelity Benefits Consulting, a division of Fidelity Investments, calculates an estimate for retiree health care costs. For their 2014 report, they estimate a 65 year old couple, retiring this year will spend $220,000, in out-of-pocket medical expenses while in retirement. This amount remains the same as in 2013 and is down 8% from the 2012 estimate of $240,000. The estimate remains steady, due in part, to lower-than-expected Medicare expenses and continued savings on prescription drugs. Previous declines were in part due to lower-than-expected Medicare spending in recent years, as well as a reduction in projected Medicare spending in the near future. Their analysis is based on a hypothetical couple retiring at age 65, with average life expectancies of 82 and 85 female for the male and female, respectively. Estimates are calculated for "average" retirees, but may be more or less depending on actual health status, area of residence, and longevity. Figure 2.18 below, displays these values since 2002.

Figure 2.18 Estimate of Amount Needed for Health Care Spending During Retirement

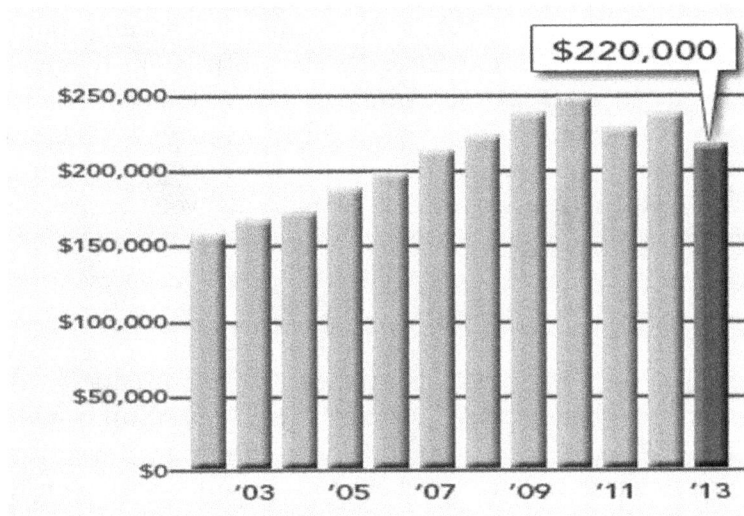

Source: Fidelity Benefits Consulting, 2013

This also assumes individuals do not have employer-provided retiree health care coverage, but qualify for Medicare. The calculation takes into account cost sharing provisions (such as deductibles and coinsurance) associated with Medicare Part A and Part B (inpatient and outpatient medical insurance). It also considers Medicare Part D (prescription drug coverage) premiums and out-of-pocket costs, as well as certain services excluded by Medicare. **This estimate does not include other health-related expenses such as over-the-counter medications, most dental services and long-term care.**

Fidelity's health care cost estimate had decreased only once before. That was in 2011, when the estimate declined

$20,000 due to a one-time adjustment driven by Medicare changes that reduced out-of-pocket expenses for prescription drugs for many seniors. Between 2002 and 2012, the estimate had increased an average of 6% annually. In 2001, Fidelity's estimate was $160,000. Making the wrong choices could have serious consequences as you age and your health changes; stressing family finance's to the limit and altering your retirement lifestyle.

In another report, according to research from EBRI, a 65 year old couple today will need to allocate $238,000 of their retirement pool of money to cover projected out-of-pocket health care expenses during a 25 year retirement period.

HEALTH CARE DEMAND CURVES

The Bureau of Labor Statistics (BLS) produces the Consumer Expenditure Survey (CE) program which consists of two surveys, the Quarterly Interview Survey and the Diary Survey. These surveys provide information on the buying habits of American consumers, including data on their expenditures, income, and consumer unit (families and single consumers) characteristics. The survey asks 5,000 respondents to list all income and expenditures out of their personal budgets for a period of 6 weeks. From sodas, movies and mortgage payments to car, pizza, and insurance expenses - literally anything paid out of the household is recorded. Respondents are then asked demographic questions such age, education, number of children, and where they live. From this data one can see how people spend money at different ages and on what products and services.

Harry S. Dent, Jr. has done some of the best research and analysis I've seen regarding long-term consumer buying habits and demographic trends. In 1988, Dent developed a new long term indicator to predict economic activity based on spending and birth rate patterns. New generations come along every 40 years. In his research

Dent found that as individual's age, they move through predictable earning, spending and productivity cycles.

As you might expect, demand for healthcare is the highest after 50. It begins to creep up from the early 30s to 40s but begins to take a dramatic rise after age 50. From the data Dent has collected from these CE surveys he has created demand curves for multiple products and services. These demand curves simply graph the average age of the household on the x-axis and on the y-axis, graphs the dollars spent per year on a product or service. Several demand curves for select healthcare expenditures are presented next. I've organized them according to the age when a person may be in need of the specific product or service. We're not going to explain each one because they are pretty self-explanatory. What's important to think about is the age where peak demand occurs and when it finally begins to trend lower. The following nine graphs are courtesy of H.S. Dent. If you're interested in more demand curves, you can view the PDF file at Dent's website at www.hsdent.com.

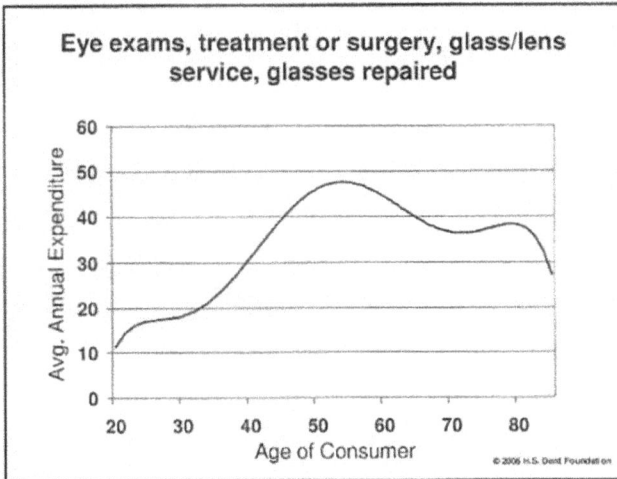

Eye exams, treatment or surgery, glass/lens service, glasses repaired

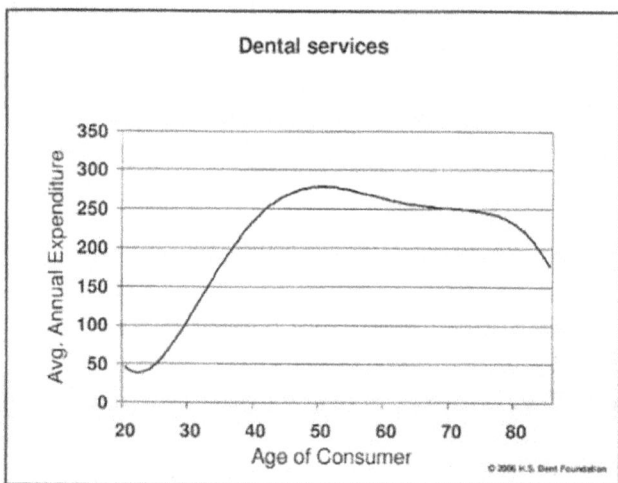

Dental services

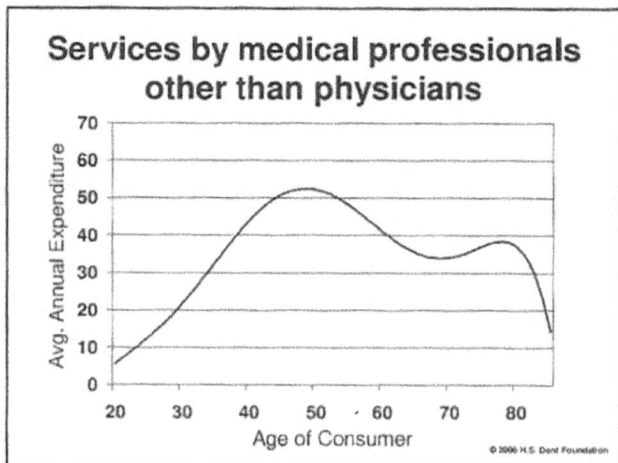

Services by medical professionals other than physicians

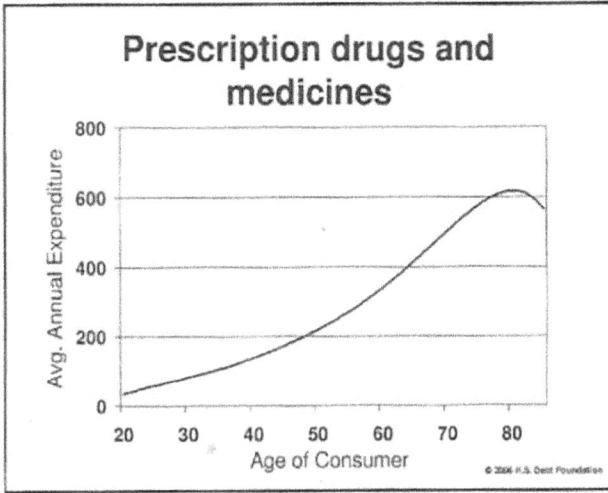

Prescription drugs and medicines

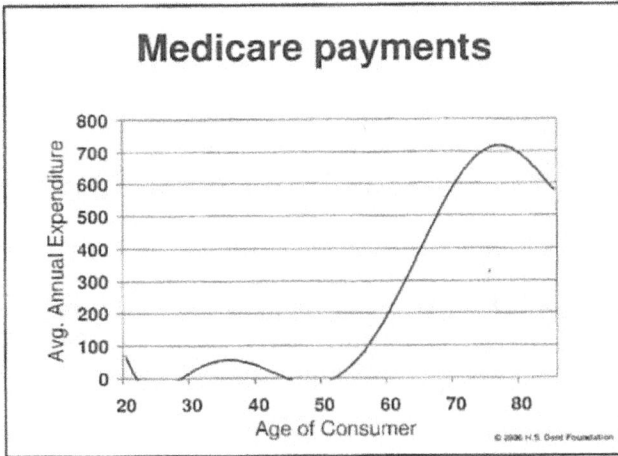

Medicare payments

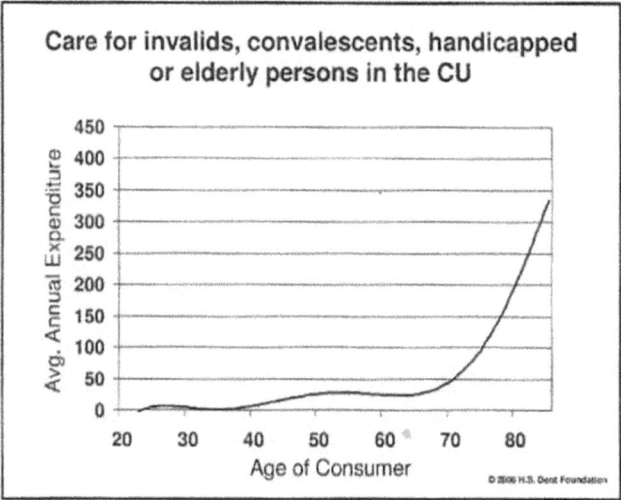

Care for invalids, convalescents, handicapped or elderly persons in the CU

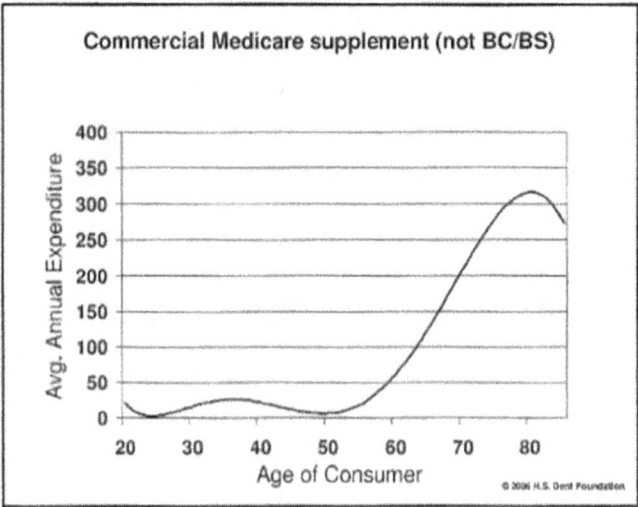

Commercial Medicare supplement (not BC/BS)

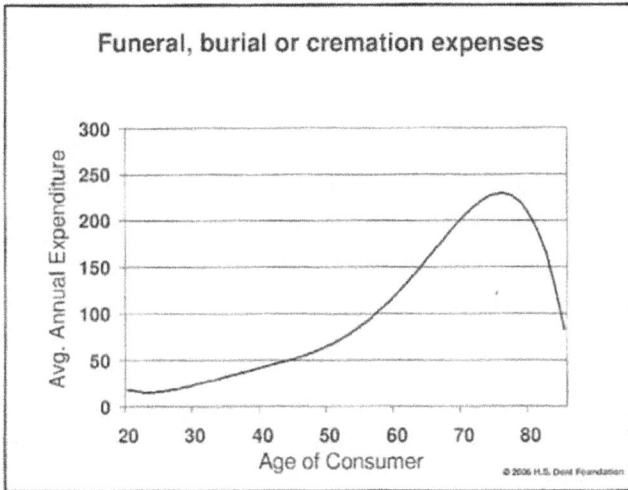

Funeral, burial or cremation expenses

Health care costs have the potential to torpedo many future retirement plans. Individuals and couples need to do some thoughtful planning ahead of time to ensure they are both adequately protected against rising health risks and have the ability to continuing making premium payments to ensure continued coverage and benefits. Otherwise they may face a radically different lifestyle during their later retirement years than they expected. Most would agree baby boomers, an estimated **78,000,000** who were born from 1946 through 1965, will have a profound effect on health care in this country in the years to come. The first boomers were eligible to begin receiving early Social Security benefits in 2008. In 2011, those same boomers became the first wave eligible to qualify for Medicare. It's been estimated that beginning in 2011, 10,000 baby boomers will turn 65 each day and every day for the next 18 years. By 2030, 80 million people may be enrolled in the Medicare program, up from 47 million in 2010. This is a near doubling in just 20 years!

"We can never insure one hundred percent of the population against one hundred percent of the hazards and vicissitudes of life, but we have tried to frame a law which will give some measure of protection to the average citizen and to his family against the loss of a job and against poverty-ridden old age."

Franklin D. Roosevelt
32nd President of the United States of America
Remarks made at the signing of the Social Security Act

44th Governor of New York
Assistant Secretary of the Navy
New York State Senate – 26th District

CHAPTER THREE

SOCIAL SECURITY ACT OF 1935

From 1800 to 1929, Americans lived through 23 recessions and four depressions, one every 4.8 years. The 37th presidential election of 1932 took place at the depths of the Great Recession. That year saw the incumbent, Republican President Herbert Hoover, being challenged by the Democrat, Franklin D. Roosevelt (FDR). With unemployment over 20% in 1932 alone, Roosevelt promised an economic recovery with a New Deal for the American people. With nearly 60% of the vote, Roosevelt won by a landslide in both the electoral and popular vote.

THE NEW DEAL

The New Deal was a series of domestic economic programs focused on relief for the poor, recovery of the economy and reform of the financial system to prevent future depressions. Many aspects of these programs were deemed unconstitutional and the Supreme Court struck down much of the New Deal. FDR responded by gaining new presidential authority from Congress and the New Deal was eventually enacted in the United States between 1933 and 1936. It involved laws passed by Congress as well as presidential executive orders during Roosevelt's first term in office. Many historians now break the New Deal into two programs. The First New Deal (1933–34) dealt with diverse groups, from banking and railroads to industry and farming, all of which demanded help for economic survival. The Federal Emergency Relief Administration provided $500 million for relief operations by states and cities, while the short-lived Civil Works Administration gave localities money to operate make-work projects in 1933-34. The Second New Deal (1935-38) was much more liberal and more controversial. Included in this package of legislation was passage of the Wagner Act to promote labor unions, the Works Progress Administration (WPA) relief program, which made the federal government the largest single employer in the nation, the Social Security Act, and new programs to aid tenant farmers and migrant workers. In 1937, creation of the United States Housing Authority and Farm Security Administration were formed. The Fair Labor Standards Act of 1938 was created which set maximum hours and minimum wages for most categories of workers.

Frances Perkins was a loyal supporter of FDR. After his election to the presidency, she became the 4th U.S. Secretary of Labor and the first woman appointed to a U.S Cabinet position. During her term as Secretary of Labor, Perkins championed many aspects of the New Deal. Her most important contribution came in 1934, as chairwoman of the President's Committee on Economic Security. This was a cabinet-level group appointed by FDR just one year earlier. In this post she was involved in all aspects of the reports including her hand in the creation of the Social Security Act. With the Social Security Act she established unemployment benefits, pensions for the many uncovered elderly Americans, and welfare for the poorest Americans.

The Social Security Act was signed August 14, 1935 by Roosevelt. The Act was a 37 page piece of legislation. The Social Security program began as a measure to implement social insurance during the Great Depression of the 1930s, when poverty rates among senior citizens exceeded 50%. The Act was an attempt to limit what were seen as dangers in the modern American life, including old age, poverty, unemployment, and the burdens of widows and fatherless children. Roosevelt became the first president to advocate federal assistance for the elderly.

Early debates on Social Security's design were centered on how the program's benefits should be funded. While the Act was enacted in 1935, it wasn't until 1937 when payroll taxes were first collected. In 1937 the first benefits under Social Security were paid. These were lump-sum death benefit paid to 53,236 beneficiaries.

SOCIAL SECURITY AMENDMENTS

The provisions of Social Security have been changing since the 1930s, shifting in response to economic worries as well as concerns over changing gender roles and the position of minorities. These changes were implemented as amendments to the original Social Security Act. Below represents some of the provisions which were included in the amendments over time.

Amendments of 1939

The original Social Security Act provided only retirement benefits and only to the worker. The Amendments of 1939 made a fundamental change in the Social Security program. These changes transformed Social Security from a retirement program for workers into a family-based economic security program. These changes included:

- Benefits extended to the spouse and minor children of a retired worker, called dependents benefits.
- Benefits extended to survivors' benefits paid to the family in the event of the premature death of a covered worker.

53

- Increased benefit amounts and accelerated the start of monthly benefit payments to 1940.
- Title VIII taxing provisions taken out of the original Social Security Act and placed in the Internal Revenue Code (IRS). These provisions were renamed the Federal Insurance Contributions Act (FICA) and now referred to as FICA taxes.

Amendments of 1950

- Extended to include domestic labor. Household employees working at least two days a week for the same person were included.
- Nonprofit workers and self-employed also included.
- Extended coverage and liberalize the benefits of the federal old-age and survivors insurance program.
- Broaden and liberalize Federal grants to the States for public assistance and for maternal and child health and child welfare services.

Amendments of 1954

- Hotel workers, laundry workers, all agricultural workers, and state and local government employees became covered.

Amendments of 1956

- Prior to 1956, all individuals had to claim Social Security at age 65.
- Tax rate was raised to 4.0 percent (2.0 percent for the employer, 2.0 percent for the employee) and disability benefits were added.
- Women were allowed to retire at 62 with benefits reduced by 25 percent.
- Widows of covered workers were allowed to retire at 62 without the reduction in benefits.

Amendments of 1961

- Retirement at age 62 was extended to men, and the tax rate was increased to 6.0%.
- Increased the aged widow's insurance benefit by 10% (from 75% to 82½% of the worker's primary insurance amount).

Amendments of 1962

- Changing role of the female worker was acknowledged when benefits of covered women could be collected by dependent husbands, widowers, and children. These individuals had to be able to prove their dependency.

Amendments of 1965

- Established Medicare and Medicaid programs.
- Age at which widows could begin collecting benefits was reduced to 60.
- When divorce, rather than death, became the major cause of marriages ending, divorcées were added to the list of recipients. Divorcées over the age of 65, who had been married for at least 20 years, remained unmarried, and could demonstrate dependency on their ex-husbands received benefits.

Amendments of 1972

- Benefits increased 20% increases for 27.8 million Americans. The average payment per month rose from $133 to $166.
- Set up a cost-of-living adjustment (COLA) to take effect in 1975. An adjustment would be made on a yearly basis if the Consumer Price Index (CPI) increased by 3% or more. A technical error in the

formula caused these adjustments to overcompensate for inflation which became known as double-indexing. The COLAs actually caused benefits to increase at twice the rate of inflation.

- Credits for delaying Social Security beyond the full retirement age were introduced.

Amendments of 1977

- The double-indexing mistake was fixed.
- The tax formulas were altered to raise more money, increasing withholding from 2% to 6.15%.

Amendments of 1983

The 1983 amendments to Social Security were based on the final report from The National Commission on Social Security Reform (NCSSR). This commission was chaired by Alan Greenspan and was charged to investigate the long-run solvency of Social Security. Changes enacted include:

- Enacting a six-month delay in the COLA and changing the tax-rate schedules for the years between 1984 and 1990.
- Proposed an income tax on the Social Security benefits of higher-income individuals that had household incomes in excess of a threshold, which was $25,000 for singles and $32,000 for couple's would become taxable.
- A previously enacted increase in the payroll tax rate was accelerated.
- Additional employees were added to the system.
- The full-benefit retirement age was slowly increased.
- Up to one-half of the value of the Social Security benefit was made potentially taxable income.

- A provision to exclude the Social Security Trust Fund from the unified budget.

For a more in-depth review of the new provisions included in the 1983 amendments, visit the Social Security website at http://www.ssa.gov/history/1983amend.html.

Senior Citizens' Freedom to Work Act of 2000

Though not an amendment to the Social Security Act, President Bill Clinton signed this legislation into law in April 2000. The provisions of the legislation included:

- Eliminates the Social Security retirement earnings test in and after the month in which a person attains full retirement age - currently age 65. Elimination of the retirement test would be effective with respect to taxable years ending after December 31, 1999.
- In the calendar year the beneficiary attains the full retirement age, permanently applies the earnings limit for those at the full retirement age through age 69 ($17,000 in 2000, $25,000 in 2001 and $30,000 in 2002) and the corresponding reduction rate ($1 for $3 offset) to all months prior to attainment of the full retirement age. (In applying the earnings test for this calendar year, only earnings before the month of attainment of full retirement age are considered.)
- Beginning with the month in which the beneficiary reaches full retirement age and ending with the month prior to attainment of age 70, permits the retired worker to earn a delayed retirement credit for any month for which the retired worker requests that benefits not be paid even though he/she is already on the benefit rolls.

Today, the Social Security Act is comprised of 21 different titles.

"We need to build on the success of Social Security by developing bold and innovative ways for Americans to build wealth and save for retirement. I believe we can work together in a bipartisan manner to accomplish these goals."

Debbie Stabenow
Democratic U.S. Senator – Michigan
Chairwoman of the Senate Committee on
Agriculture, Nutrition and Forestry
U.S. House of Representatives – Michigan's 8th
District

CHAPTER FOUR

SOCIAL SECURITY ADMINISTRATION

The Social Security Act created the Social Security Board (SSB) to oversee the administration of the new Social Security program. In 1939, the SSB was merged into the cabinet-level Federal Security Agency (FSA), which included the SSB, the U.S. Public Health Service, the Civilian Conservation Corps (CCC) and other agencies. Then in 1946, the SSB was renamed the Social Security Administration (SSA) under President Harry Truman's Reorganization Plan. In 1953, the FSA was abolished and the SSA was placed under the Department of Health, Education and Welfare, which later became the Department of Health and Human Services (HHS) in 1980. In 1994, President Bill Clinton signed into law legislation returning the SSA to the status of an independent agency in the executive branch of government.

Today, the Social Security Administration is headquartered in Woodlawn, Maryland, just west of Baltimore and is known as the Central Office. The agency includes 10 regional offices, 6 processing centers, approximately 1,260 field offices, and 37 Teleservice

Centers. As of 2013, almost 66,000 people are employed by the SSA. Social Security is currently the largest social welfare program in the United States, constituting 37% of government expenditure and 7% of GDP. From the April 2013 Budget Overview, during fiscal year 2012, the SSA:

- Paid over $800 billion to almost 65 million beneficiaries.
- Handled over 56 million transactions on the National 800-Number Network.
- Received over 65 million calls to field offices nationwide.
- Served about 45 million visitors in over 1,200 field offices nationwide.
- Completed over 8 million claims for benefits and 820,000 hearing dispositions.
- Handled almost 25 million changes to beneficiary records.
- Issued about 17 million new and replacement Social Security cards.
- Posted over 245 million wage reports.
- Handled over 15,000 disability cases in Federal District Courts.
- Completed over 443,000 full medical CDRs.
- Completed over 2.6 million non-medical redeterminations of SSI eligibility.

The SSA has been operating the past couple of years with relatively constrained budgets. Since 2011, the SSA has lost 11,000 employees, about 12% of its workforce, according to Acting Social Security Commissioner Carolyn Colvin. As workloads rise, a greater proportion of the SSA workforce will become eligible to retire. In FY 2015, 33% of SSA's employees will be eligible. While not every employee will, the SSA predicts that 28% to 36% of its workforce will retire over the next 10 years. This means the SSA will be losing some of its most experienced service center and field representatives. These factors are contributing to the efforts by the SSA to incorporate technology solutions for use by consumers.

The Social Security Administration, as a federal government agency, operates on a fiscal year from October 1st through September 30th of the following year. For FY 2014, the SSA submitted a budget request of $12.297 billion. Today, the Social Security Administration has three key programs and is also involved in the collecting premiums for Medicare Part B and in some cases Medicare Part A. These programs will be covered in greater detail in subsequent chapters.

Disability Insurance (DI)

Established in 1956, the DI program provides benefits for disabled workers and their families. In FY 2014, the SSA will pay about $415 billion in DI benefits to approximately 11 million disabled workers and their family members.

At the end of 2003, there were nearly 5.9 million individuals collecting Social Security disability payments. Ten years later, at the end of 2013, there were nearly 9 million individuals collecting disability insurance. This is a 52% increase over ten years of over 3 million individuals.

Supplemental Security Insurance (SSI)

Established in 1972 by Title XVI of the Social Security Act, payments began in 1974. The SSI program is a needs-based program which provides financial support to aged, blind, or disabled adults and children who have limited incomes and resources. It is a Federally-administered program and is funded from general revenues. For FY 2014, the SSA will pay about $59 billion in Federal and State Supplementation benefits to almost 8.5 billion SSI recipients.

Prior to establishing the SSI program, the Social Security Act provided means-tested assistance through three separate programs. These programs were the Old Age

Assistance (originally Title I of the Social Security Act of 1935), Aid to the Blind and Aid to the Permanently and Totally Disabled. In 1973, these assistance programs were renamed and reassigned to SSA. Federal law only establishes broad guidelines. Each state is largely responsible for setting its own eligibility and payment standards.

As a means-tested program, individuals must have income and resources below specified levels to be eligible for benefits. An individual's benefit payment is reduced dollar for dollar by the amount of their "countable income". This is income less all applicable exclusions in a given month. Income in the SSI program includes earned income such as wages and net earnings from self-employment and unearned income such as Social Security benefits, unemployment compensation, deemed income from a spouse or parent and the value of in-kind support and maintenance such as food and shelter.

Medicare

The administration of the Medicare program is the responsibility of the Centers for Medicare and Medicaid Services (CMS), but the SSA is used for determining initial eligibility, some processing of premium payments and for limited public contact information. They also administer a financial needs-based program which supplements Medicare Part D program enrollees. This program may be applied for at any time, even previous to enrollment in Part D. It provides no more than a $40.00 relief for monthly Medicare part D premiums.

Old Age Survivor's Insurance (OASI)

Created in 1935, the OASI program provides retirement and survivors benefits to qualified workers and their families. For FY 2014, the SSA will pay about $709 billion in OASI benefits to approximately 48 million beneficiaries, including about 80% of the population aged 65 and older. The programs are primarily financed by taxes which employers, employees, and the self-insured pay annually.

Social Security Statement

The SSA began mailing out annual estimated benefit statements to workers age 25 and older in 1999. The Social Security Statement is a four page document. Page 2 of *Your Social Security Statement* provides your estimated benefits.

Figure 4.1 Your Estimated Benefits

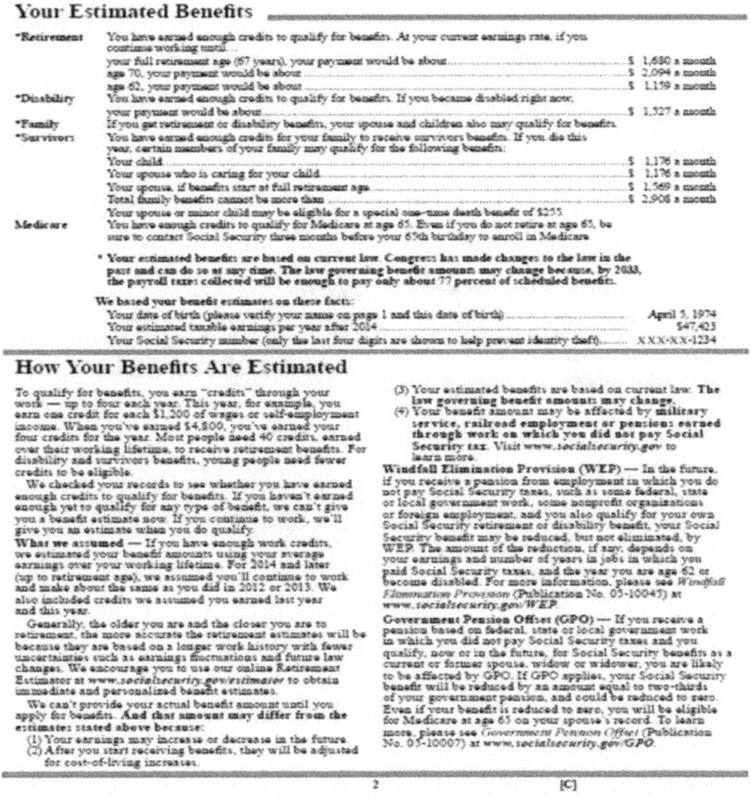

Your Estimated Benefits

*Retirement   You have earned enough credits to qualify for benefits. At your current earnings rate, if you continue working until...

your full retirement age (67 years), your payment would be about.......... $ 1,680 a month
age 70, your payment would be about.......... $ 2,094 a month
age 62, your payment would be about.......... $ 1,159 a month

*Disability   You have earned enough credits to qualify for benefits. If you became disabled right now, your payment would be about.......... $ 1,327 a month

*Family   If you get retirement or disability benefits, your spouse and children also may qualify for benefits.

*Survivors   You have earned enough credits for your family to receive survivors benefits. If you die this year, certain members of your family may qualify for the following benefits:

Your child.......... $ 1,176 a month
Your spouse who is caring for your child.......... $ 1,176 a month
Your spouse, if benefits start at full retirement age.......... $ 1,569 a month
Total family benefits cannot be more than.......... $ 2,906 a month

Your spouse or minor child may be eligible for a special one-time death benefit of $255.

Medicare   You have enough credits to qualify for Medicare at age 65. Even if you do not retire at age 65, be sure to contact Social Security three months before your 65th birthday to enroll in Medicare.

* Your estimated benefits are based on current law. Congress has made changes to the law in the past and can do so at any time. The law governing benefit amounts may change because, by 2033, the payroll taxes collected will be enough to pay only about 77 percent of scheduled benefits.

We based your benefit estimates on these facts:
Your date of birth (please verify your name on page 1 and this date of birth).......... April 5, 1974
Your estimated taxable earnings per year after 2014.......... $47,423
Your Social Security number (only the last four digits are shown to help prevent identity theft).......... XXX-XX-1234

How Your Benefits Are Estimated

To qualify for benefits, you earn "credits" through your work — up to four each year. This year, for example, you earn one credit for each $1,200 of wages or self-employment income. When you've earned $4,800, you've earned your four credits for the year. Most people need 40 credits, earned over their working lifetime, to receive retirement benefits. For disability and survivors benefits, young people need fewer credits to be eligible.

We checked your records to see whether you have earned enough credits to qualify for benefits. If you haven't earned enough yet to qualify for any type of benefit, we can't give you a benefit estimate now. If you continue to work, we'll give you an estimate when you do qualify.

What we assumed — If you have enough work credits, we estimated your benefit amounts using your average earnings over your working lifetime. For 2014 and later (up to retirement age), we assumed you'll continue to work and make about the same as you did in 2012 or 2013. We also included credits we assumed you earned last year and this year.

Generally, the older you are and the closer you are to retirement, the more accurate the retirement estimates will be because they are based on a longer work history with fewer uncertainties such as earnings fluctuations and future law changes. We encourage you to use our online Retirement Estimator at www.socialsecurity.gov/estimator to obtain immediate and personalized benefit estimates.

We can't provide your actual benefit amount until you apply for benefits. And that amount may differ from the estimates stated above because:
(1) Your earnings may increase or decrease in the future.
(2) After you start receiving benefits, they will be adjusted for cost-of-living increases.

(3) Your estimated benefits are based on current law. The law governing benefit amounts may change.
(4) Your benefit amount may be affected by military service, railroad employment or pensions earned through work on which you did not pay Social Security tax. Visit www.socialsecurity.gov to learn more.

Windfall Elimination Provision (WEP) — In the future, if you receive a pension from employment in which you do not pay Social Security taxes, such as some federal, state or local government work, some nonprofit organizations or foreign employment, and you also qualify for your own Social Security retirement or disability benefit, your Social Security benefit may be reduced, but not eliminated, by WEP. The amount of the reduction, if any, depends on your earnings and number of years in jobs in which you paid Social Security taxes, and the year you are age 62 or become disabled. For more information, please see Windfall Elimination Provision (Publication No. 05-10045) at www.socialsecurity.gov/WEP.

Government Pension Offset (GPO) — If you receive a pension based on federal, state or local government work in which you did not pay Social Security taxes and you qualify, now or in the future, for Social Security benefits as a current or former spouse, widow or widower, you are likely to be affected by GPO. If GPO applies, your Social Security benefit will be reduced by an amount equal to two-thirds of your government pension, and could be reduced to zero. Even if your benefit is reduced to zero, you will be eligible for Medicare at age 65 on your spouse's record. To learn more, please see Government Pension Offset (Publication No. 05-10007) at www.socialsecurity.gov/GPO.

2   [C]

Source: Social Security Administration; Sample-Estimated Benefits Page

Page 3 of *Your Social Security Statement* provides your earnings record as displayed in Figure 4.2 below.

Figure 4.2 Your Earnings Record

Source: Social Security Administration; Sample-Earnings Record Page

In mid-2011, the SSA stopped mailing annual benefit statements and switched from paper to digital delivery. By implementing this change, the cost savings to the federal government totaled about $70 million annually in printing and postage. In May 2012, full-fledged digital statements, which include retirement benefits estimated at various ages and a personal earnings history identical to the previous paper statements became available. Your personalized statement also includes estimates of how much you could collect if you became disabled before your full retirement age as well as how much your spouse could collect in survivor benefits following your death.

More than 10 million individuals have currently signed up for a personalized account at the SSA. While this number may seem large, it still only represents about 6% of U.S. workers who have established an account online with the SSA. At the urging of Congress, beginning in September 2014, the SSA will resume mailing paper statements to workers attaining ages 25, 30, 35, 40, 45, 50, 55 and 60 and over who are not receiving Social Security benefits and who are not registered for an online account.

Online Registration

The only way to access this information now is by establishing an online account with the SSA, which can be done at their website, www.ssa.gov/mystatement. You should review your account at least once per year to ensure the SSA is receiving your correct earnings history. If something doesn't look right, corrections can be made with the proper documentation by contacting the SSA.

What if I'm not yet ready to file for Social Security benefits? Should I register online for an account with the SSA? Without a doubt the answer is yes. Anyone who is age 18 or older can sign up for a Social Security account. To complete the registration process you will need:

- Your Social Security number.
- Your mailing address.
- A valid email address.

During the registration process you will be asked some questions. The answers to the questions must match the information on file with Social Security, as well as information from your credit report. Experian, one of the three major credit reporting agencies, oversees Social Security's online verification process. The questions asked could include names of former employers, previous addresses of where you lived and name of credit cards which you may have. I went through the process last year and it took about 15 minutes to complete.

The online account creation doesn't always go smooth for everyone. Those who can't answer the security questions can request a paper statement be mailed to them or they can visit their local Social Security office and present a government-issue ID in order to create an account and gain access to the online version of the statement.

There is one cautionary note to be aware of. Social Security indicates on their website that you cannot create an online account if you have a security freeze, fraud alert or both on your Experian credit report. With the fiasco which occurred at Target, in 2013, with some 40 million American having their credit card information compromised during the holidays, millions of individual have taken step to protect their data and accounts by doing exactly that. To create an account you will either need to lift the security freeze or fraud alert you've placed on your Experian credit report or visit your local Social Security office in person to establish an account.

If you are filing online you can restrict the scope of your application to spousal benefits as long as you are at your full retirement age (FRA), by answering "yes" to the question of whether you want to delay receipt of your retirement benefits on the "when to start retirement benefits" page. Also as long as you are at your FRA, you can specify you want to "file and suspend" your benefits in the remarks section of the online application. The SSA expanded the online menu to include instant benefit verification letters for those currently receiving benefits from Social Security. The letter serves as proof of income to secure loans, mortgages and in applying for state or local benefits. Individuals can also use the letter to prove current Medicare health insurance coverage, retirement or disability status if this is applicable to your situation.

Social Security Card Security

In a 2009 study, conducted by Carnegie Mellon University, they found that it is possible to guess a Social Security number using details easily found from a Facebook profile, such as date of birth and hometown. Researchers were able to accurately guess the first five digits of 44% of Social Security numbers issued after 1988 on their first try, just by using the birthdate and the state the number was issued in. They were able to guess the complete number almost 9% of the time. How did they do it?

The authors of the study used a list of known Social Security numbers from the Social Security Death Master File. This is an index of deaths which have been reported to the SSA. They used the file to find patterns on how the last four digits are assigned. The first five digits are based on the state the Social Security number was issued in. They found they are largely assigned in order based on where the number was issued. In 2011, the SSA implemented a more randomized process for assigning Social Security numbers, making more combinations available in every state. Anyone with a Social Security number issued before then should not list their birthdate and place of birth on any social media site.

Death and Social Security

Not all aspects of the SSA run so efficiently. According to the Centers for Disease Control and Prevention (CDC) every year nearly 2.5 million American die. The latest final data is for 2010. Yet, the SSA receives about 7 million reports each year, often including duplicate records of the same death. Deaths are tracked as follows:

1. When a beneficiary dies the death is recorded and reported to the SSA by state agencies, funeral directors, family members, hospitals or other sources.
2. The SSA is supposed to then cancel a dead individual's benefits and then add the report to a Death Master File.
3. The file is split in two. The first file is the full Death Master File which is shared with key federal agencies responsible for benefits and tax information including the Centers for Medicare and Medicaid Services (CMS), Department of Defense, Department of Veterans Affairs, Internal Revenue Service (IRS) Office of Personnel Management and the Railroad Retirement Board. The second file is a separate public file which only includes about 60% of reported deaths. This file is used by other federal agencies which are blocked from getting the full file by federal rules. These agencies include the Agriculture Department, Department of Homeland Security, Justice Department and the Treasury Department's "Do Not Pay" list.

The problems occur because not all reports are verified by the SSA for accuracy. Data is also incorrect or lost. In addition, there is human error. Finally, the public file doesn't include data sent by some state vital-records agencies which are considered among the most accurate sources. This is because some states do not allow their data to be released to the public by the federal government for privacy and legal restrictions.

David A. Fahrenthold, a reporter with the Washington Post, published an excellent article on this topic back in November 2013. In the story he indicated that over the past few years, Social Security paid $133 million to beneficiaries who were deceased. The federal employee retirement system paid more than $400 million to retirees who had passed away. An aid program spent $3.9 million in federal money to pay heating and air-conditioning bills for more than 11,000 of the dead.

Office of the Inspector General

The *Inspector General Act of 1978* was passed in the wake of the Watergate scandal to ensure integrity and accountability in the Executive Branch of the federal government. The Act created independent and objective units to conduct and supervise audits and investigations relating to Agency programs and operations. The Social Security Administration's Office of the Inspector General (OIG) has the following responsibilities:

- Promotes economy, efficiency, and effectiveness in the administration of SSA programs.
- Prevents and detects fraud, waste, and abuse in SSA programs and operations.
- Informs the SSA and Congress about problems and deficiencies and recommends corrective action.

The Inspector General (IG) is under the general supervision of the Commissioner of the Social Security Administration. The IG may not be prohibited from initiating, carrying out, or completing any audit or investigation, or from issuing any subpoena. The Office of the Inspector General at the Social Security Administration was established on March 31, 1995, pursuant to the Social Security Independence and Program Improvements Act of 1994.

The SSA annually performs the Widow(er)'s Insurance Benefits/Retirement Insurance Benefits operation to identify and notify widows and widowers who are eligible for higher retirement benefits. Most widows and widowers receive two notices. The first notice is when they attain their FRA while the second notice is sent when they attain age 70. However, the SSA does not send similar notices to spouses who may be eligible for higher retirement benefits based on their own earnings.

In a 2008 audit, the OIG found that spouses did not always receive the higher retirement benefits due them. It estimated that 13,580 spouses were eligible for $123.7 million in higher retirement benefits after they attained age 70. In response to that audit, in 2009, the SSA formed a workgroup and identified a population of 18,768 spouses eligible for higher retirement benefits based on their own earnings at age 70. The workgroup developed a notification letter which was to be sent to those beneficiaries. However, according to the SSA, it did not take further action because of limited resources at the time. As a result, these spouses did not receive the higher retirement benefits for which they were eligible.

In March 2014, the OIG issued an audit report titled, *"Spouses Eligible for Higher Retirement Benefits"*, in which they found the SSA still had not taken action to notify spousal beneficiaries of their eligibility to receive higher retirement benefits. Based on this most recent random sample of 250 spousal beneficiaries, the OIG estimated that 26,033 spouses were now eligible for about $195.3 million in higher retirement benefits. These numbers consisted of:

- 12,349 spouses from the OIG's current audit who were eligible for $59.8 million in retirement benefits.
- 13,684 spouses from their prior audit who were eligible for $135.5 million in retirement benefits.

This occurred because the SSA did not identify and notify spouses when they became eligible for higher retirement benefits at age 70 or older and did not apply the deemed filing provision or was unaware of the spouses' eligibility for retirement benefits when they applied for spousal benefits.

The SSA has agreed with the three recommendations which the OIG has offered. Steps for implementing or studying the technology feasibility will take place in fiscal years 2014 and 2015. These are just more reasons individuals need to be vigilant in monitoring their Social

Security accounts to ensure they are receiving the maximum retirement benefit due them.

Contacting Social Security

For more information you can visit the SSA website at www.socialsecurity.gov or call their toll-free number, 1-800-772-1213. For those who may be deaf or hard of hearing, call their TTY number, 1-800-325-0778. Their hours are from 7 am to 7 pm, Monday through Friday. According to Social Security you'll generally have a shorter wait time if you call mid-week after Tuesday. In addition, you may have a local Social Security office nearby which you can visit.

When it comes to getting help, the local SSA representatives are typically mandated to help individuals sign up and apply for benefits. They are not trained in or able to evaluate complicated claiming strategies and long-term projections beyond break-even analysis. The SSA staff members are forbidden to give advice regarding the optimal age to claim retirement benefits and the best claiming strategies to employ. You need to present a specific situation to them before they can discuss it with you.

"The reason to deal with Social Security is that it is a system where we have a tradition and history of making sure it is solidly funded for 75 years. At the moment, we look out and we see it is solidly funded until 2033."

Jacob "Jack" Lew
76th U.S. Secretary of the Treasury
Former White House Chief of Staff
Former Director of the OMB
Former Deputy Secretary of State for Management of Resources
The Obama Administration

CHAPTER FIVE

SOCIAL SECURITY TERMINOLOGY

Some writers will place a terminology section at the end of their book in the appendix or glossary. As you read, if there is a term you don't understand you've got to flip to the back of the book to see if the word and its definition is included there. I opted to include a terminology section as a separate chapter because I believe if you understand the key terminology used in Social Security it will be significantly easier to navigating the process. There are terms unique to Social Security you will not find in other government programs.

Appeal (Appeal Rights): You will receive a letter of explanation whenever Social Security makes a decision regarding your eligibility for Social Security or Supplemental Security Income (SSI) benefits. If you disagree with the decision, you have the right to appeal (ask SSA to review your case). If the SSA decision was wrong, it will be changed.

Average Indexed Monthly Earnings (AIME): The dollar amount used to calculate your Social Security benefit if you attained age 62 or became disabled (or died) after 1978. To arrive at your AIME, we adjust your actual past earnings using an "average wage index," so you won't lose the value of your past earnings (when money was worth more) in relation to your more recent earnings. If you attained age 62 or became disabled (or died) before 1978, we use Average Monthly Earnings (AME).

Average Monthly Earnings (AME): The dollar amount used in calculating your monthly Social Security benefit, if you attained age 62 or became disabled (or died) before 1978. The AME is determined by dividing the total earnings in the "computation years" by the number of months in those same years.

Base Years: The years for computing Social Security benefits are the years after 1950 up to the year of entitlement to retirement or disability insurance benefits. For a survivor's claim, the base years include the year of the worker's death.

Benefits: There are five types of benefits which are paid. These are for retirement, disability, family dependents, survivors and Medicare. The retirement, family (dependents), survivor and disability programs pay monthly cash benefits, and Medicare provides medical coverage.

Benefit Verification Letter: An official letter from Social Security that verifies the amount an individual receives each month in Social Security benefits and/or Supplemental Security Income (SSI) payments. These letters are normally issued following a request from a person receiving benefits or his/her authorized representative.

Child: Include your biological child or any other child who can inherit your personal property under state law or who meets certain specific requirements under the Social Security Act. This would include a legally adopted child, an equitably adopted child, a stepchild, or a grandchild.

Cost of Living Adjustment (COLA): Social Security benefits and Supplemental Security Income (SSI) payments may be automatically increased each year to keep pace with increases in the cost-of-living (inflation).

Computational Years: Computation years are the years with highest earnings selected from the "base years." We add total earnings in the computation years and divide by the number of months in those years to get the AME or the AIME. Your 35 highest years of earnings are used to compute your retirement benefits.

CPI-W: An index prepared by the U. S. Department of Labor that charts the rise in costs for selected goods and services. This index is used to compute cost of living adjustments (COLA) each year.

Credits: As you work and pay taxes, you earn credits that count toward your eligibility for future Social Security benefits. You can earn a maximum of four credits each year. Most individuals need 40 credits to qualify for benefits. Younger individuals need fewer credits to qualify for disability or survivors benefits. This was previously called Quarters of Coverage.

Decision Notice: When you apply for Social Security, SSA decides if you will receive benefits. SSA will send you an official letter explaining their decision and, if benefits are payable, SSA will tell you the amount you will get each month.

Delayed Retirement Credits: Social Security benefits are increased by a certain percentage (depending on date of birth) if a person delays taking retirement benefits beyond their full retirement age. The benefit increase no longer applies after age 70, even if the individual continues to delay taking benefits.

Dependent Benefits: These are also called family benefits. When you're eligible for retirement or disability benefits the following people may receive benefits on your record. These include a spouse if he or she is at least 62 years old (or any age but caring for an entitled child under age 16 or disabled), children if they are unmarried and under age 18, or under age 19 and a full-time elementary or secondary student, children age 18 or older but disabled before age 22 or ex-spouses age 62 or older.

Direct Deposit: This is the standard way to receive Social Security benefits and Supplemental Security Income (SSI). Your money is sent electronically to an account in a financial institution (bank, trust company, savings and loan association, brokerage agency or credit union) each month.

Disability Benefits: You can get disability benefits if you are under full retirement age, have enough Social Security credits and have a severe medical impairment (physical or mental) that's expected to prevent you from doing "substantial" work for a year or more, or have a condition that is expected to result in death.

Documents: Forms and papers such as birth certificates, marriage certificates, W2 forms, tax returns, deeds, etc., submitted by individuals when applying for benefits and services. SSA can only accept originals or copies certified by the agency that has the original document.

Dually Entitled: Social Security beneficiary whose retirement benefit, when based on their earnings record, is lower than the spousal/survivor benefit they are entitled to receive. The dually entitled receives their own benefit plus a spousal/survivor benefit which is equal to the difference between their own benefit and the full spousal/survivor benefit.

Early Retirement: You can start getting Social Security retirement benefits as early as age 62, but your benefit amount will be less than you would have gotten if you waited until your full retirement age. By taking retirement benefits early, your benefit will remain permanently reduced, based on the number of months you received benefits before you reached full retirement age.

Earnings Record: A chronological history of the amount of money you earned each year during your working lifetime. The credits you earned remain on your Social Security record even when you change jobs or have no earnings.

Eligible: Eligible for a benefit means an individual meets all the eligibility criteria but hasn't filed an application.

Entitled: Entitled to a benefit means an individual meets all the eligibility criteria and has filed an application for benefits.

Evidence: The documents you must submit to support a factor of entitlement or payment amount. The individuals in your local Social Security office can explain what evidence is required to establish entitlement and help you to get it.

Family Maximum: The maximum amount of benefits payable to an entire family on any one worker's record.

FICA Tax: FICA stands for Federal Insurance Contributions Act. It's the tax withheld from your salary or self-employment income that funds the Social Security and Medicare programs.

Full Retirement Age: The age at which a person may first become entitled to full or unreduced benefits based on age. For workers and spouses born in 1938 or later and widows/widowers born in 1940 or later, the full retirement age increases gradually from age 65 until it reaches age 67 for those workers and spouses in the year 2027 and widows and widowers in the year 2029. This increase affects the amount of the reduction for persons who begin receiving reduced benefits.

Insured Status: If you worked and earned enough Social Security credits to be eligible for retirement or disability benefits or enable your dependents to be eligible for benefits due to your retirement, disability, or death you have insured status.

Lawful Alien Status: Refers to people admitted to the U.S. who are granted permanent authorization to work by the U. S. Citizenship and Immigration Services (USCIS), formerly called the INS, or admitted to the U.S. on a temporary basis with USCIS authorization to work.

Lump Sum Death Payment: A one-time payment of $255 paid in addition to any monthly survivor's benefits that are due. This benefit is paid only to your widow/widower or minor children.

Maximum Earnings: The maximum amount of earnings SSA can count in any calendar year when computing your Social Security benefit.

Minimum Retirement Age: The minimum age for retirement - age 62 for workers and age 60 for widows or widowers. Individuals can choose a reduced benefit any time before you reach full retirement age.

Month of Election: This usually applies to retirement claims. In certain situations, you can choose the month in which your benefits will start.

Old Age Survivors and Disability Insurance (OASDI): The Social Security programs that provide monthly cash benefits to workers and their dependents when they retire, die or become disabled.

Primary Insurance Amount (PIA): The monthly amount payable if you are a retired worker who begins receiving benefits at full retirement age or if you're disabled and have never received a retirement benefit reduced for age.

Protective Filing Date: The date you first contact SSA about filing for benefits. It may be used to establish an earlier application date than when SSA received your signed application.

Reduction Months: Months beginning with the first month you're entitled to reduced benefits up to, but not including, the month in which you reach full retirement age.

Representative Payee: If you receive Social Security benefits or Supplemental Security Income (SSI) and become unable to handle your own financial affairs, SSA (after a careful investigation) can appoint a relative, a friend, or an interested party to handle your Social Security matters. Representative payees are required to maintain complete accounting records and periodically provide reports to Social Security.

Retirement Age for Full Benefits: Full retirement age was 65 for many years. Beginning with the year 2000 (for workers and spouses born in 1938 or later or widows/widowers born in 1940 or later, the retirement age increases gradually from age 65 until it reaches age 67 in the year 2022.

Retirement Benefit: Money that is payable to you upon retirement if you have enough Social Security credits.

Retirement Earnings Test: If you receive monthly Social Security benefits before your full retirement age and work, your earnings from wages and/or self-employment cannot exceed a certain amount without reducing your monthly benefits.

Retroactive Benefits: Monthly benefits that you may be entitled to before the month you actually apply, if you meet the requirements.

Self-employment Income: An individual is self-employed if you operate a trade, business or profession, either individually or as a partner, and have net earnings of $400 or more in a taxable year.

Social Security Death Index (SSDI): Is a database of death records created from the SSA's Death Master File Extract. Most individuals who have died since 1936 and who had a Social Security number and whose death has been reported to the SSA are listed in the SSDI. For most years since 1973, the SSDI includes 93% to 96% of deaths of individuals aged 65 or older. It is frequently updated with the version of June 22, 2011 containing 89,835,920 records.

Spouse: You are the spouse of the worker if, when he or she applied for benefits and you and the worker were married or you would have the status of a husband or a wife for that person's personal property if they had no will or you went through a marriage ceremony in good faith, which would have been valid except for a legal impediment.

Supplemental Security Income (SSI): A federal supplemental income program funded by general tax revenues, not Social Security taxes. It helps aged, blind, and disabled people who have limited income and resources by providing monthly cash payments to meet basic needs for food, clothing, and shelter.

Survivor's Benefits: Benefits based on your record (if you should die) are paid to your widow/widower age 60 or older, 50 or older if disabled, or any age if caring for a child under age 16 or disabled before age 22, children, if they are unmarried and under age 18, under 19 but still in school, or 18 or older but disabled before age 22 and parents, if you provided at least one-half of their support. An ex-spouse could also be eligible for a widow/widower's benefit on your record.

Wages: All payment for services performed for an employer. Wages do not have to be cash. The cash value of all compensation paid to an employee in any form other than cash is also considered wages, unless the form of payment is specifically not covered under the Social Security Act.

Wage Earner: A person who earns Social Security credits while working for wages or self-employment income.

Widow/Widower: You are the widow/widower of the worker if, at the time he or she died and you and the worker were validly married or you would have the status of a husband or a wife for that person's personal property if he or she had no will or you went through a marriage ceremony in good faith that would have been valid except for a legal impediment. The minimum age for widow/widower's benefits is 60, or 50 if disabled.

"Our country also hungers for leadership to ensure the long-term survival of our Social Security system. With 70 million baby boomers in this country on the verge of retirement, we need to take action to shore up the system."

Kay Bailey Hutchison
Former Republican U.S. Senator – Texas
Treasurer of Texas
Texas House of Representatives

CHAPTER SIX

SOCIAL SECURITY PROGRAMS

"Let me tell you how it will be
There's one for you nineteen for me
'Cause I'm the taxman, yeah, I'm the taxman.
Should five percent appear too small
Be thankful I don't take it all
'Cause I'm the taxman, yeah I'm the taxman...
...Don't ask me what I want it for (Aahh Mr. Wilson)
If you don't want to pay some more (Aahh Mr. Heath)..."

Written by George Harrison. Published by Northern Songs.

For millions of baby boomers who are starting to retire, it may be time to dust off one of those old albums, The Beatles 1966 album, *Revolver.* *"Taxman"* was written by George Harrison and released as the opening track from that album. After the Beatles started to make some money, George wrote the song out of anger after realizing how much he was going to have to pay in taxes.

According to Wikipedia, as their earnings placed them in the top tax bracket in the United Kingdom, the Beatles were liable to a 95% super-tax introduced by Harold Wilson's Labour Party government. Edward Heath was the leader of the other political party, the Conservative Party.

According to the Social Security Administration (SSA), about 58 million individuals receive monthly Social Security benefits. Most beneficiaries, about 41 million, are retirees and their families. When Social Security was envisioned, it was never meant to be the only source of income for individuals when they retire. Social Security replaces about 40% of an average wage earner's income after retiring. Most financial advisors say retirees will need 70% or more of pre-retirement earnings to live comfortably. This means individuals also will need savings, investments and private pensions to complement what they will receive from Social Security to ensure a comfortable retirement.

This chapter will cover the three main programs within Social Security: Disability Insurance, Supplemental Security Income and Old Age and Survivor's Insurance. If you're nearing retirement and have been a government worker or your spouse has been a government worker you may be in for a nasty surprise when you file for Social Security retirement benefits. There are two regulations which could affect those Social Security benefits. These two regulations, which are discussed at the end of this chapter, could reduce or even completely eliminate your benefits.

BENEFITS PAID TO RECIPIANTS

In 1940, benefits paid totaled $35 million. This rose to $961 million in 1950, $11.2 billion in 1960, $31.9 billion in 1970, $120.5 billion in 1980, and $247.8 billion in 1990 (all figures in nominal dollars, not adjusted for inflation). In 2004, $492 billion in benefits were paid to 47.5 million beneficiaries. By 2009, nearly 51 million Americans received $650 billion in Social Security benefits.

According to the Research Notes & Special Studies by the Historian's Office of the Social Security, Ida May Fuller was a legal secretary who retired in November 1939. On

January 31, 1940, Fuller became the first individual to be issued a monthly retirement check in the amount of $22.54. She started collecting benefits in January 1940 at age 65 and lived to be 100 years old, dying in 1975. Ida May Fuller worked for three years under the Social Security program. During the last three years she was covered under Social Security, her covered earnings totaled $2,475. During that time her accumulated taxes paid into Social Security totaled $24.75. The amount she collected during her 35 years (in retirement) while she was receiving Social Security benefits - $22,888.92.

Social Security Basic Facts

According to the National Center for Health Statistics, in 1935, life expectancy in the U.S. was 61.7 years. By 2010 it had increased to 78.7 years. By 2033, the number of older Americans will increase from today's 45.1 million to 77.4 million. There are currently 2.8 workers for each Social Security beneficiary. By 2033, there will be 2.1 workers for each beneficiary.

According to the SSA, an estimated 163 million workers are covered under Social Security. About one in four married couples and nearly half of unmarried individuals rely on Social Security for 90% or more of their retirement income. Other statistics for 2012 include:

- 51% of the workforce has no private pension coverage.
- 34% of the workforce has no savings set aside specifically for retirement.
- SSA paid benefits to about 61.9 million people in 2012.
- Social Security provided at least half the income for 64% of the aged beneficiaries in 2011.
- Social Security benefits were awarded to about 5.7 million people in 2012.

- Women accounted for 55% of adult Social Security beneficiaries in 2012.
- The average age of disabled-worker beneficiaries was 53.2 in 2012.
- Eighty-six percent of SSI recipients received payments because of disability or blindness in 2012.

Social Security provides for more than just retirement benefits:

- Retired workers and their dependents account for 70% of total benefits paid.
- Disabled workers and their dependents account for 19% of total benefits paid.
  - About 91 percent of workers age 21-64 in covered employment in 2011 and their families have protection in the event of a long-term disability.
  - Just over 1 in 4 of today's 20 year-olds will become disabled before reaching age 67.
  - 69% of the private sector workforce has no long-term disability insurance.
- Survivors of deceased workers account for about 11% of total benefits paid.
  - About one in eight of today's 20 year-olds will die before reaching age 67.
  - About 96% of persons aged 20-49 who worked in covered employment in 2011 have survivor's insurance protection for their young children and the surviving spouse caring for the children.

Social Security is a major source of income for most elderly:

- Nine out of ten individuals age 65 and older receive Social Security benefits.
- Social Security benefits represent about 39% of the income of the elderly.

- Among elderly Social Security beneficiaries, 53% of married couples and 74% of unmarried persons receive 50% or more of their income from Social Security.
- Among elderly Social Security beneficiaries, 23% of married couples and about 46% of unmarried persons rely on Social Security for 90% or more of their income.

In 2013, total Social Security expenditures were $1.3 trillion, representing 8.4% of the $16.3 trillion of U.S. GDP (2013) and 37% of the Federal expenditures which were $3.684 trillion.

'Cause I'm the Taxman

Social Security is funded through payroll taxes, the Federal Insurance Contributions Act tax (FICA) and/or Self Employed Contributions Act tax (SECA). According to the SSA, an estimated 165 million workers will pay Social Security taxes in 2014. Total payroll taxes, for which individuals who are considered employees pay, have a total of 7.65% taken out of their paychecks. For the self-employed, they pay a total of 15.3% in payroll taxes. There is also an estimated 10 million Americans who earn more than $100,000 per year. Beginning in 2014, those individuals will pay a larger slice of their income to Social Security and Medicare taxes.

According to a study conducted by the Urban Institute, a non-partisan think tank in Washington D.C., a single man who retired in 1980, at age 65 and having earned an average wage of $44,600 (in 2012 dollars) during his working years, would have paid about $98,000 in Social Security taxes and probably had received $207,000 in lifetime benefits. Consider this analysis today. A single man earning the same average wage today and retiring in 2030, will likely pay $404,000 in lifetime taxes but receive just

$339,00 in lifetime benefits, about 16% less than what he paid in.

FICA Tax

Today, workers now pay nearly double the 3.6% tax rate workers paid in 1965. Employers and employees each pay a 6.2% Social Security tax. This 6.2% portion, which funds Social Security, is only applied up to the taxable wage-based maximum. For 2014, the maximum amount is increased to $117,000. This is 2.9% higher than the $113,700 limit in 2013. In 1965, the maximum amount was $4,800. This would be the equivalent to about $35,400 in 2013 dollars. This means top earners will pay $7,254 in Social Security taxes in 2014, which will be about $200 more than the 2013 maximum of $7,049. Self-employed individuals pay both portions of the tax for a combined rate of 12.4%, with the same taxable wage-based maximum of $117,000 in 2014. Self-employed individuals will pay a maximum of $14,508 but can deduct half of their FICA taxes on their federal tax return.

Medicare Tax

Employers and employees also pay a Medicare tax on all wages with no cap. For 2014, each will pay a 1.45% Medicare tax. The self-employed pay both portions for a combined Medicare tax of 2.9% on all earnings.

Medicare Surcharge Tax

Beginning in 2013, high earning individuals, defined as those with earned income of more than $200,000 who are single or married couples, filing jointly, with incomes of $250,000 or more, pay an additional 0.9% in Medicare taxes to help fund expanded health care coverage under the Affordable Care Act. This tax applies to earned income only.

Table 6.1 below illustrates the threshold amounts based on tax filing status.

Table 6.1 Medicare Surcharge Tax Filing Thresholds

Filing Status	Threshold Amount
Married Filing Jointly	$250,000
Married Filing Separately	$125,000
Single	$200,000
Head of Household	$200,000
Qualifying widow(er)	$200,000

Source: Social Security Administration; Understanding the Benefits

This additional Medicare tax is imposed only on the wages that exceed the applicable threshold levels. It also is only imposed on individual taxpayers and C corporations. Estates and trusts are exempt. For married couples, if one spouse's income exceeds the threshold level for individual taxpayers of $200,000, that spouse's employer is required to withhold the additional 0.9% Medicare tax from the spouse's income in excess of the threshold, even though the couple files jointly and does not exceed the threshold for married couples. In this case, the employee is entitled to claim a credit on their joint federal tax return for any withheld additional Medicare tax which the employee was not liable.

Investment Income Tax

This tax doesn't fund either Social Security or Medicare. It is included here as some individuals confuse this tax with the Medicare surcharge tax because both have the same threshold amounts for taxpayers. The investment income tax is an additional 3.8% tax which is imposed on the lesser of the following:

1. Net investment income or
2. The excess, if any, of the taxpayer's adjusted gross income (AGI) for the year over the applicable threshold amount.

The threshold amount for a single taxpayer is $200,000. For married couples, filing separately, the threshold is $125,000. For married couples, filing jointly, the threshold is $250,000. These threshold amounts are not indexed annually for inflation. The investment income tax applies to unearned income. Unearned income is the sum of the following:

- Gross income from interest, dividends, annuities, rents and royalties which is not derived in the ordinary course of the taxpayer's trade or business.
- Income derived from a trade or business involving a passive activity of the taxpayer or trading in financial instruments or commodities.
- Net gain attributable to the disposition of property other than property held in a trade or business not described in the second bullet point.

The 3.8% rate is added to tax rates currently in effect, subsequently increasing the capital gains and dividend tax rates for many taxpayers. The rate will increase from 20% to 23.8% for taxpayers in the 39.6% income tax brackets and from 15% to 18.8% for taxpayers in lower tax brackets. The investment income tax applies to individuals and to certain trusts and estates.

Example

A married couple has adjusted gross income (AGI) of $425,000 and net investment income (NII) equal to $125,000 for the calendar year 2013. Their AGI exceeds their threshold amount for married couples by $175,000 ($425,000 - $250,000). Since their NII of $125,000 is less than the $175,000 by which their income exceeds the threshold, tax applies to all of their NII of $125,000. Then in 2014, their AGI drops to $300,000, with the same NII of $125,000. Now their AGI only exceeds the threshold amount by $50,000 ($300,000 - $250,000). Since their NII of $125,000 is now more than the $50,000, by which their income exceeds the threshold, the tax applies only to the $50,000 excess. The $125,000 of NII is not subject to the tax on their 2014 federal tax return. Since the investment income tax applies to unearned income and the Medicare surcharge tax applies to earned income, a taxpayer will not be subject to both additional taxes on the same income.

According to the SSA statistics, about 85 cents of every Social Security tax dollar you pay goes to a trust fund which pays monthly benefits to current retirees, their families and to surviving spouses and children of covered workers who have died. The other 15 cents goes to a trust fund which pays benefits to individuals with disabilities and to their families. Less than 1 penny goes towards managing the entire Social Security program.

The entire amount of taxes paid for Medicare goes to a trust fund which pays for some of the costs of hospital and related care of all Medicare beneficiaries. Medicare is managed by the Centers for Medicare & Medicaid Services (CMS). The Medicare program will be covered in depth in chapter thirteen.

When provisional income tops $25,000 for individuals or $32,000 for married couples, 50% of Social Security benefits plus all other income, including tax-exempt income is included in the income calculation. According to the SSA, about 40% of current Social Security beneficiaries pay federal income taxes on their retirement benefits. Reduction in benefits, as a result of exceeding the earnings cap restriction limits, or paying federal income taxes on a portion of your Social Security benefits will be discussed further in a subsequent chapter.

Same- Sex Couples

On June 26, 2013, in a 5-4 majority decision, the Supreme Court ruled in the case *U.S. v. Windsor*, Section 3 of the Defense of Marriage Act (DOMA) as unconstitutional. This case involved a same-sex couple being denied from claiming the federal marital estate tax deduction even though New York had recognized their union. As a result of the Supreme Court decision, Edith Windsor was refunded $363,000 taken from the estate of her late female spouse. With the ruling, couples in states which recognize same-sex marriages gained access to over 1,000 federal benefits, including federal marital income and estate tax deductions and the ability to file joint federal tax returns together.

Also as a result of this decision, Social Security is no longer prevented from recognizing same-sex marriages for purposes of determining entitlements to or eligibility for benefits. Same-sex couples are now entitled to spousal benefits during marriage and survivor benefits after death of one spouse. If they have minor dependent children, at the time one souse claims benefits, the children may also be entitled to dependent benefits. The SSA is working closely with the Department of Justice to develop policies which are legally sound so claims can be processed correctly.

In December 2013, the SSA began processing claims for some retirement, surviving spouse and lump-sum death payments for same-sex marriages, paying benefits where they are due. At the moment the SSA can only pay benefits to same-sex couples who are legally married and reside in a state which recognizes their marriage. Your status in a civil union or other non-marital relationship may affect your entitlement to benefits. You must tell the SSA if you are in a civil union or other non-marital legal relationship. The SSA is also considering same-sex marriages when processing some claims for Supplemental Security Income (SSI).

As of this writing, 19 states and the District of Columbia allow same-sex marriage. These states are:

California, Connecticut, Delaware, Hawaii, Iowa, Illinois, Maine, Maryland, Massachusetts, Minnesota, New Hampshire, New Jersey, New Mexico, New York, Oregon, Pennsylvania, Rhode Island, Vermont and Washington. The Obama administration has been resolute in its policy that it cannot extend Social Security benefits to couples living in states which do not recognize same-sex marriage under current law. However, there is proposed legislation which has been introduced in Congress which would ensure same-sex spouses receive Social Security benefits regardless of where they live. The Justice Department is currently reviewing this also.

The SSA is encouraging retirement age same-sex married couples living in those states, which currently do not recognize same-sex marriage, apply for benefits, if entitled to them, to protect against the loss of any potential benefits. There is no penalty or fine for applying for benefits which the SSA later denies.

Disability Insurance

Disability is not something most individuals want to think about. However, according to the SSA, studies show a 20 year old has a 3-in-10 chance of becoming disabled before reaching their full retirement age. Some individuals may receive benefits from Social Security who cannot work because they have a medical condition which is expected to last at least one year or result in death. Federal law requires a very strict definition of disability.

Social Security's disability rules are different from those of private plans or other government agencies. The fact that you qualify for disability from another agency or program does not mean you will be eligible for Social Security disability benefits. If you receive other disability benefits, Social Security benefits for you and your family may be reduced if you also are eligible for workers' compensation (including payments through the black lung program) or for disability benefits from certain federal, state or local government programs. You must tell the SSA if:

- You apply for another type of disability benefit.
- You receive another disability benefit or a lump-sum settlement.
- Your benefits change or stop.

Under the law, your disability payments cannot begin until you have been disabled for at least five full months. Payments usually start with your sixth month of disability. Benefits are paid each month and the day on which you receive your benefit payment depends on the birth date of the person on whose earnings record you receive benefits. If you receive benefits as a retired or disabled worker, your benefit will determined by your birth date. If you receive benefits as a spouse, your benefit payment date will be determined by your spouse's birth date.

As long as the medical condition you have does not improve and you cannot work, your disability benefits will likely continue. However, your case will be reviewed periodically to make sure you are still disabled.

Benefits for Family Members

Certain members of your family may qualify for benefits under your disability. They include:

- Your spouse, if he or she is age 62 or older.
- Your spouse, at any age if he or she is caring for a child of yours who is younger than age 16 or disabled.
- Your unmarried child, including an adopted child or, in some cases, a stepchild or grandchild. The child must be younger than age 18 or younger than 19 if in elementary or secondary school full time.
- Your unmarried child, age 18 or older, if he or she has a disability which started before age 22. The

child's disability must also meet the definition of disability for adults.

If you have reached age 62, and suddenly health issues force you to retire early, you should apply for disability benefits and also retirement benefits (assuming you need the money) at the same time. If you're approved for disability, your disability check will be larger than your retirement benefit. Disability benefits are based on your full retirement age. If you file for early retirement benefits, they will be reduced by 25% if your age is less than your full retirement age.

There are rules which limit the amount of Social Security benefits that can be paid each month on an individual's earnings record. These rules are called the family maximum benefit rules. Each family member may be eligible for a monthly benefit that is up to half of your retirement or disability benefit amount. However, there is a limit to the total amount of money that can be paid to you and your family. The limit varies, but is generally equal to about 150% to 180% of your retirement or disability benefit. The family maximum rules only come into play when several family members, usually minor children and a spouse who is caring for them, all receive dependent benefits on a worker's earnings record. If an individual becomes ineligible for benefits, that may trigger an increase in benefits for the remaining family members.

Earnings Requirement

To receive disability benefits you must meet two different earnings tests:

1. A "recent work" test based on your age at the time you became disabled; and
2. A "duration of work" test to show that you worked long enough under Social Security.

Certain blind workers only have to meet the duration of work test.

Table 6.2 below, illustrates the rules for how much work you need for the recent work test based on your age when your disability began.

Table 6.2 Recent Work Test

If You Become Disabled	Then You Generally Need
In or during the quarter you turn age 24.	1.5 years of work during the three-year period ending with the quarter your disability began.
In the quarter after you turn age 24 but before the quarter you turn age 31.	Work during half the time for the period beginning with the quarter after you turned age 21 and ending with the quarter you became disabled.
In the quarter you turn age 31 or later.	Work during five years out of the ten-year period ending with the quarter your disability began.

Source: Social Security Administration; Disability Benefits

These rules are based on the calendar quarter in which you turned or will turn a certain age. The calendar quarters for the year are:

- First Quarter: January 1 through March 31
- Second Quarter: April 1 through June 30
- Third Quarter: July 1 through September 30
- Fourth Quarter: October 1 through December 31

Table 6.3, on the next page, displays examples of how much work you need to meet the duration of work test if you become disabled at various selected ages. For the duration of work test, your work does not have to fall within a certain period of time. This table does not cover all situations which may exist.

Table 6.3 Duration of Work Test

If You Become Disabled	The You Generally Need
Before age 28	1.5 years
Age 30	2 years
Age 34	3 years
Age 38	4 years
Age 42	5 years
Age 44	5.5 years
Age 46	6 years
Age 48	6.5 years
Age 50	7 years
Age 52	7.5 years
Age 54	8 years
Age 56	8.5 years
Age 58	9 years
Age 60	9.5 years

Source: Social Security Administration; Disability Benefits

Application Process

To apply for disability benefits, there are two ways in which this can be done.

1. Apply online at www.socialsecurity.gov.
2. Call the toll-free number, 1–800–772–1213, to make an appointment to file a disability claim at your local Social Security office or to set up an appointment for someone to take your claim over the telephone. This disability claims interview can last up to an hour. The TTY number is 1–800–325–0778.

The Adult Disability Report (ADR) needs to be completed as well as an application for Social Security benefits. The ADR application can be completed at the SSA website at www.socialsecurity.gov/disabilityreport. Information which is needed can include:

- Your Social Security number.
- Your birth certificate or baptismal certificate.
- Names, addresses and telephone numbers of the physicians, caseworkers, hospitals and clinics which took care of you and the dates of your visits.
- Names and dosages of all the medicines you take.
- Medical records from your physicians, therapists, hospitals, clinics and caseworkers you already have in your possession.
- Lab and test results.
- A summary of where you worked and the kind of work you did.
- A copy of your most recent W-2 Form or, if you are self-employed, your federal tax return for the past year.

In addition to the basic application for disability benefits there are other forms which will need to be filled out. One form collects information about your medical condition and how it affects your ability to work. Other forms give physicians, hospitals and other health care professionals who have treated you, permission to send the SSA information about your medical condition.

Decision Making Process

Once you have submitted the necessary forms, the SSA will review the application to make sure you meet the basic requirements. If you do the SSA will send your application to the Disability Determination Services office in your state.

The state agency completes the disability decision for the SSA. Information they will be looking at includes:

- What your medical condition is?
- When your medical condition began?
- How your medical condition limits your activities?
- What medical treatments have you received?

The state agency may also ask your physicians for information about your ability to do work-related activities such as walking, sitting, lifting, carrying and remembering instructions. Your physicians will not be asked to decide if you are disabled. A five-step process is used to decide if you are disabled. These steps include:

1. Are you working?
2. Is your medical condition "severe"?
3. Is your medical condition on the List of Impairments?
4. Can you do the work you did before?
5. Can you do any other type of work?

It may take between three and five months to process an application and inform you of the SSA's decision. If your claim is approved the SSA will send you a letter or call you indicating such and will include the amount of your monthly benefit and the effective date. If your application is not approved the letter will explain why and tell you how to appeal the decision if you do not agree with it.

Monthly benefits are based on your average lifetime earnings and your first benefits will be paid at the sixth full month after the date your disability began. For example, if your disability began on March 15th, your first benefits will be paid for the month of September. Since Social Security benefits are paid in the month following the month for which they are due, you will actually receive your first benefit payment in October.

Reviewing your Medical Disability

All individuals receiving disability benefits must have their medical conditions reviewed periodically. Your benefits will continue unless there is strong proof that your condition has improved medically and you are able to return to work. How often your medical condition is reviewed depends on how severe it is and the likelihood it will improve. Your award notice tells you when you can expect your first review.

- *Medical improvement expected:* If your condition is expected to improve within a specific time, your first review will be six to 18 months after you started getting disability benefits.
- *Improvement possible:* If improvement in your medical condition is possible, your case will be reviewed about every three years.
- *Improvement not expected:* If your medical condition is unlikely to improve, your case will be reviewed only about once every five to seven years.

Earnings Limits on Disability Benefits

Special rules make it possible for people receiving Social Security disability benefits or Supplemental Security Income (SSI) to work and still receive monthly payments. There are three options available under these special rules.

1. *Trial work period:* The trial work period allows you to test your ability to work for at least nine months. During your trial work period, you will receive your full Social Security benefits regardless of how much you are earning as long as you report your work activity and you continue to have a disabling impairment. In 2014, a trial work month is any month in which your total earnings are over $770 or if you are self-employed, you earn more than $770

per month (after expenses) or work more than 80 hours in your own business. The trial work period continues until you have worked nine months within a 60-month period.

2. *Extended period of eligibility:* After your trial work period, you have 36 months during which you can work and still receive benefits for any month your earnings are not "substantial." In 2014, earnings over $1,070 per month or $1,800 per month if you are blind are considered to be substantial. No new application or disability decision is needed to receive a Social Security disability benefit during this period.

3. *Expedited reinstatement:* After your benefits stop because your earnings are substantial, you have five years during which you may ask the SSA to start your benefits immediately if you find yourself unable to continue working because of your condition. You will not have to file a new disability application and you will not have to wait for your benefits to start while your medical condition is being reviewed to make sure you are still disabled.

You may also be eligible for other work incentives to help you make the transition back to work. Contact the SSA.

Reaching Full Retirement Age

Once you reach your full retirement age (FRA), your disability benefits end but are automatically converted to Social Security retirement benefits. The monthly benefit amount you receive continues in the same amount. Like retirement benefits, disability benefits are also eligible for cost-of-living adjustments (COLAs).

Upon reaching their FRA, this can sometimes prompt a number of questions by the beneficiary regarding possible claiming strategies (to be discussed later). This assumes a married couple. Can they take advantage of certain claiming strategies since they are now receiving retirement benefits, not disability benefits any longer?

The answer is no. Unfortunately it doesn't work that way in these circumstances. The disability benefits which you had been receiving are based on your own earnings record. Since you filed a claim to receive benefits, you do not have the option to file a restricted claim for spousal benefits only. This strategy is only available to those who file for retirement benefits for the first time at their FRA. Since the individual is now at their FRA and is entitled to their own benefits, that entitlement negates their choice for spousal benefits only.

Compassionate Allowances

The Compassionate Allowances (CAL) program identifies claims where the applicant's disease or condition clearly meets Social Security's statutory standard for disability. By incorporating cutting-edge technology, the agency can easily identify potential Compassionate Allowances and quickly make decisions. To date, almost 200,000 people with severe disabilities have been approved through this fast-track disability process. In January 2014, the SSA announced 25 new Compassionate Allowances (CALs) conditions, including a dozen cancers, bringing the total number of conditions to 225.

The CAL program expedites disability decisions for Americans with the most serious disabilities to ensure that they receive their benefit decisions within days instead of months or years. The new conditions also include disorders that affect the digestive, neurological, immune, and multiple body systems. CALs are a way of quickly identifying diseases and other medical conditions that invariably qualify under the List of Impairments based on minimal objective medical information. CAL conditions are selected using information received at public outreach hearings, comments received from the Social Security and

Disability Determination Services communities, counsel of medical and scientific experts, and the SSA's own research with the National Institutes of Health (NIH). The SSA also considers which conditions are most likely to meet their current definition of disability.

The Compassionate Allowances program is not a separate program from the Social Security Disability Insurance or Supplemental Security Income programs. Social Security has held seven Compassionate Allowances public outreach hearings. The hearings have been on rare diseases, cancers, traumatic brain injury (TBI) and stroke, early-onset Alzheimer's disease and related dementias, schizophrenia, cardiovascular disease and multiple organ transplants and autoimmune diseases.

Rising Number of Disability Claimants

Over the last six years, disability claims have increased by 25%. Just in 2012 alone, 3.2 million Americans applied for either disability insurance or SSI. Along with this dramatic increase in claims and payouts, federal budget cuts have also created a backlog of more than a million overdue follow-up reviews for current recipients.

There could be a number of reasons why these disability claims keep rising. As a result of the large increase in the number of backlog cases, to reduce this administrative judges are required to decide 500 or more cases per year. As a result of this massive workload placed on the judges, some may be awarding more benefits than they would if they had more time to consider each case.

Another interesting take on this issue is, as individuals find ways to get on Social Security disability and thus leave the workforce, this fact is contributing to the decline in the labor force participation rate. According to a recent analysis by Jack Albin, EVP and chief investment officer for BMO Private Bank, during the last 10 years, 30% of Americans leaving the workforce were on Social Security disability. One aspect which may be driving this development and causing beneficiaries to remain on disability benefits for as long as possible is this. If individuals decide to return to full-time employment, they lose their benefits including early access to Medicare. Once you have received disability benefits for 24-months, then in the 25th month you are eligible to apply for Medicare. This could be creating an enormous incentive for those individuals to remain on the employment sideline and not try re-entering the workforce.

Supplemental Security Income

The second program within Social Security is Supplemental Security Income (SSI). SSI pays benefits to disabled adults and children who have limited income and resources. Many individuals who are eligible for SSI may also be eligible for Social Security benefits. In fact, the application for SSI is also an application for Social Security benefits. However, SSI and Social Security are different in many ways.

- Social Security benefits may be paid to you and certain members of your family if you are "insured", meaning you worked long enough and paid Social Security taxes. Unlike Social Security benefits, SSI benefits are not based on your prior work or a family member's prior work.
- SSI is financed by general funds of the U.S. Treasury such as personal income taxes, corporate and other taxes. Social Security taxes withheld under the Federal Insurance Contributions Act (FICA) or the Self Employment Contributions Act (SECA) do NOT fund the SSI program.
- In most states, SSI beneficiaries also can get medical assistance (Medicaid) to pay for hospital stays, doctor bills, prescription drugs, and other health costs.
- Most states also provide a supplemental payment to certain SSI beneficiaries.

- SSI beneficiaries may also be eligible for food assistance in every state except California. In some states, an application for SSI benefits also serves as an application for food assistance.
- SSI benefits are paid on the first of the month.
- To get SSI, you must be disabled, blind, or at least 65 years old and have "limited" income and resources.
- In addition, to get SSI you must:

  o Be a resident of the United States, and
  o Not be absent from the country for a full calendar month or more or for 30 consecutive days or more; and
  o Be either a U.S. citizen or national, or in one of certain categories of qualified non–citizens.

If you are receiving SSI and in a same-sex marriage, you must inform the SSA. In addition, your spouse's income and resources may affect your SSI eligibility or payment amount. By utilizing the *Benefit Eligibility Screening Tool* and taking the 5 to 10 minutes to answer a few questions, you can find out if you are eligible for SSI or other benefits.

Benefits Payable

The basic monthly SSI payment is the same nationwide, though many states do add money to the basic benefit. For 2014 it is:

- Individual: $721
- Couple: $1,082

These amounts are just slightly larger than they were in 2013, when they were $710 for an individual and $1,066 for a couple. Not everyone gets the same amount. Where and with whom you live also makes a difference in the amount of your SSI payment. You could receive more if you live in a state that adds money to the federal SSI payment.

Income Sources

Whether you're eligible to receive SSI depends on your income and assets. Your income is what you receive and includes wages, Social Security benefits and pensions. Income can also include items such as food and shelter. Not all your income is counted by Social Security. The SSA does not count:

- The first $20 dollars a month of most income you receive.
- The first $65 a month you earn from working and half the amount over $65.
- Supplemental Nutrition Assistance Program (SNAP) benefits formerly known as food stamps.
- Shelter you get from private nonprofit organizations.
- Most home energy assistance.

Social Security does not count any wages a blind individual uses for work expenses. If you are married, part of your spouse's income and assets are also included when deciding whether you qualify for SSI. If you are younger than 18, part of your parents' income and assets are included. If you are a sponsored non-citizen, the SSA may also include your sponsor's income and assets. If you are a student, some of the wages or scholarships you receive may not count.

You must report all earned income you receive from wages or self-employment beginning with the date you filed your SSI application. If you or your family has other sources of income, you could receive less in benefits. If you do have income, your monthly benefit will generally be lower than the maximum federal SSI payment. However, your income could be greater than the limits indicated and you may still qualify. Table 6.4 below displays these monthly income limits.

Table 6.4 Monthly Income Limits, 2014 vs 2013

Monthly Income Limits	2013	2104
Individual whose income is only from wages	$1,505	$1,527
Individual whose income is not from wages	$730	$741
Couple whose income is only from wages	$2,217	$2,249
Couple whose income is not from wages	$1,086	$1,102

Source: Social Security Administration; Disability Benefits

Assets and Resources

Assets which count when deciding whether you should receive SSI include:

- Real estate
- Bank accounts
- Cash
- Stocks
- Bonds

An individual may be able to receive SSI if their assets are not worth more than $2,000. A couple may qualify for SSI if their assets are not worth more than $3,000. Assets which are not counted include:

- The house you live in and the land it is on.
- Life insurance policies with a face value of $1,500 or less.
- Your car.
- Burial plots for you and members of your immediate family.
- Up to $1,500 in burial funds for you and up to $1,500 in burial funds for your spouse.

To qualify for SSI you must live in the U.S. or the Northern Mariana Islands and be a U.S. citizen or national. If you are eligible for Social Security or other benefits you should apply for them. You are able to receive SSI and other benefits if you are eligible for both. Information needed when you apply for SSI includes:

- Your Social Security number or a record of your Social Security number.
- Your birth certificate or other proof of age.
- Information about the home where you live such as your mortgage or your lease and landlord's name.
- Payroll slips, bank books, insurance policies, burial fund records and any other information about your home and assets.
- The names, addresses and telephone numbers of the physicians, hospitals and clinics you have been to if you are applying because you are blind of disabled.
- Proof of U.S. citizenship or eligible non-citizen status.
- Your checkbook or other documents which show your bank, credit union or savings and loan account number. If approved for SSI payments you must receive them electronically.

If your application is approved, the SSA will send you a letter indicating when your payments will begin and how much you will get. Your first SSI payment will be made for the first full month after you applied or became eligible for SSI. If you do not agree with a decision made about your SSI you can appeal it.

Old Age and Survivor's Insurance

The third program within the SSA is the Old Age and Survivor's Insurance (OASI) program. OASI provides retirement and survivors benefits to qualified workers and their families. This is the program commonly referred to as

Social Security. Since we're going to cover the various aspects of this program in detail in subsequent chapters, for this section we're going to briefly look at some of the research which has been conducted regarding Social Security beneficiaries, their attitudes towards receiving retirement benefits and saving for retirement.

Depending on the survey you read, between 70% and 74% of Americans are claiming reduced early retirement benefits at age 62. Only about 5% of individuals wait until age 70. According to the SSA, for 2014, average monthly Social Security benefits will be:

- Retired worker: $1,294 or $15,528 per year.
- Retired couple: $2,111 or $25,332 per year.
- Disabled worker: $1,148 or $13,776 per year.
- Disabled worker with a spouse and child: $1,943 or $23,316.
- Widow or widower: $1,243 or $14,916 per year.
- Young widow or widower with two children: $2,622 or $31,464 per year.

For 2014, the maximum Social Security retirement benefit which someone can collect, at their full retirement age of 66 is $2,642 per month. This is $109 more than the maximum benefit of $2,533 in 2013.

The Pension Research Council, a retirement research center affiliated with the University of Pennsylvania's Wharton School, published a study in August 2012 titled, *"How Financial Advisors and Defined Contribution Plan Providers Educate Clients and Participants about Social Security."* Mathew Greenwald, Andrew Biggs and Lisa Schneider conducted a survey of 400 financial advisors, drawn from a variety of different backgrounds including wirehouses, independent advisors, among others. The survey gathered information on advisors' own view of their knowledge levels regarding Social Security claiming decisions, the principal sources they relied on to expand their knowledge, their views regarding educational resources available through the SSA and the financial services companies they work with.

Two of the interesting findings were that much of the client-advisor discussions focus on Social Security's solvency which has little practical impact on those near retirement today. The second was how advisors frame claiming decisions in their conversations with clients. Many advisors use the terms gamble and break-even in discussions concerning claiming benefits. An over reliance on break-even analysis could in turn be causing clients to development a loss aversion mentality leading to benefit claiming mistakes. These are mistakes, which can hit aging widows the hardest in their later years of life, when they need their retirement benefits more than ever.

In 2013, BMO Private Bank conducted a survey of 1,000 individuals. Their findings revealed that 61% of individuals didn't discuss Social Security with anyone when they made the decision to retire and start collecting benefits. For those that did, 75% indicated they had discussed the situation with their spouse.

University of Michigan has been conducting its annual *Health and Retirement* study for most of the last 15 years. It polls over 25,000 individuals over the age of 50. The results of the study are consistent with and have been confirmed by other studies conducted. Individuals who collect guaranteed, annuitized incomes are consistently more satisfied with their lives. This is especially true among families with less wealth.

Earning Credits

Credits are based on the amount of your earnings. For 2014, you receive one credit for $1,200 of earnings up to the maximum of four (4) credits per year. If you are self-employed you earn credits the same way, one credit for each $1,200 in net earnings but no more than four credits per year. Special rules apply if you have net earnings of less than $400. If you serve in the military, you earn credits the same way and in some cases you could get additional earnings credits under certain conditions. There are special rules for other kinds of work which includes:

- Domestic household work.
- Farm work.
- Work for a church or church-controlled organization that does not pay Social Security taxes.

This earnings value can be increased each year by the SSA, but the maximum number of credits received is constant.

The SSA began mailing out annual estimated benefit statements to workers age 25 and older in 1999. In mid-2011, the SSA stopped mailing annual benefit statements and switched from paper to digital delivery. To access your earnings record now, you must establish an online account with Social Security. Why do you want to do this? You want to make sure you verify that the earnings record Social Security has is correct. As mentioned earlier, beginning in September 2014, the SSA will resume mailing paper statements to workers attaining ages 25, 30, 35, 40, 45, 50, 55 and 60 and over who are not receiving Social Security benefits and who are not registered for an online account.

Correcting Earnings Records

Some researchers estimate there could be as high as a 3% error rate on earnings records on Social Security statements. If your earnings record isn't correct you will have to provide proof to correct the deficiencies. That proof is your past IRS federal income tax returns. The IRS recommends saving three to six years of filed returns. This may be fine unless you have an earnings record dispute with Social Security going back further than six years.

Table 6.5, on the next page, illustrates how the time limit operates. An earnings record can be corrected at any time up to three years, three months and fifteen days after the year in which the wages were paid or the self-employment income was derived. After the time limit has passed, the earnings record can be corrected only as explained in the Social Security Handbook, §14-24-1425.

Table 6.5 Once the Time Limit Has Passed

Were paid wages or derived self-employment income in	Period of correction is	Record of wages or self-employment income is final on
Calendar year 2000	1/01/01 through 4/15/04	4/16/04
Taxable year ending 6/30/91	7/01/91 through 10/17/94	10/18/94
Taxable year ending 9/30/92	10/01/92 through 1/16/95	1/17/95

Source: Social Security Administration; Social Security Handbook

A story appeared on MarketWatch in April 2013. It involved an individual who was a teacher. He thought he had enough earnings credits to be eligible for Social Security. He established an online account to review his earnings record. Much to his surprise it indicated he was 2 years short in credits. The SSA was missing data from well over 10 years ago when he had a job outside of the school district he was employed with. He contacted the IRS looking for copies of certain tax years dating back about 20 years ago. He was told by the IRS, not only did they not have copies back that far, they didn't have electronic transcripts going back that far either. Unfortunately, he had shredded those income tax records years earlier. With no proof he paid Social Security taxes during those questionable year's, his only option was to work two more years so he would be eligible for retirement benefits.

Each year your employer sends a copy of your W-2 (Wage and Tax Statement) to Social Security. Social

Security compares your name and Social Security number on the W-2 with their records. If a match, your earnings shown on the W-2 are recorded on your lifelong earnings record with Social Security. How could earnings be missing from your record for earlier years? Any below could apply:

- Your employer reported your earnings using the wrong name or Social Security number.
- Your employer reported your earnings incorrectly.
- You got married or divorced and changed your name, but never reported the change to Social Security.
- You worked using a Social Security number that did not belong to you.

If you have earnings missing from your Social Security record for the most current year or the previous year, no need to worry just yet. The SSA may not have recorded those earnings yet. According to the SSA, if you discover earnings missing from your record the first thing you should do is find proof of those earnings. Proof could be:

- A W-2 form (*Wage and Tax Statement*)
- A tax return
- A wage stub or pay slip
- Your own wage records
- Other documents showing you worked

Don't count on the IRS. Establish an online account with Social Security. Check your earnings record each year. If after three years, your earnings are not yet recorded (i.e. 2013 earnings not recorded after 2016), you probably need to contact the SSA.

Qualifying for Retirement Benefits

With Medicare, an individual needs 40 quarters (10 years of work) in order to be eligible to receive benefits. To receive retirement benefits from Social Security you must have earned 40 credits (10 years of work) during your working career if you were born in 1929 or later. If you stop working, the number of accrued credits you have earned, remain with your Social Security record. However, you will not be able to apply for and receive retirement benefits until you have accrued 40 credits.

Not all employees work in jobs which are covered by Social Security. Some of these employees are:

- Most federal employees hired before 1984 (since January 1, 1983, all federal employees have paid the Medicare hospital insurance part of the Social Security tax).
- Railroad employees with more than 10 years of service.
- Children younger than age 21, who do household chores for a parent, except a child who is age 18 or older who works in the parent's business.

Cost-of-Living Adjustments

Ida May Fuller received her first $22.54 benefit payment in January of 1940, which would be the same amount she would receive each month for the next 10 years. For Ida May Fuller and the millions of other Social Security beneficiaries like her, the amount of that first benefit check was the amount they could expect to receive for life. It was not until the Amendments of 1950 that Congress first passed legislation for an increase in benefits. Current beneficiaries had their payments recomputed and Ida May Fuller, for example, saw her monthly check increase from $22.54 to $41.30. These re-computations were effective for September 1950 and appeared for the first time in the October 1950 checks. A second increase was legislated for September 1952. Together these two increases almost doubled the value of Social Security benefits for existing beneficiaries. From that point on, benefits were increased only when Congress enacted special legislation for that purpose.

With inflation relatively high in the early 1970s, Congress passed legislation as part of the Amendments of 1972 to provide automatic annual cost-of-living adjustment (COLA) allowances based on the annual increase in consumer prices (CPI-W) beginning in 1975. The provision provided for an automatic COLA only if the increase in the CPI-W was at least 3%. This was called the "3-percent trigger" at the time. No longer would beneficiaries have to wait for a special act of Congress to receive a benefit increase and no longer would inflation drain value from Social Security benefits. By the mid-1980s inflation began to wane and in 1986 Congress enacted legislation to eliminate the 3% trigger.

COLAs are based on changes in the Consumer Price Index for Urban Wage Earners and Clerical Workers (CPI-W), which is determined by the Bureau of Labor Statistics (BLS) in the Department of Labor (DOL). The average CPI-W for the third calendar quarter of the previous year is compared to the average CPI-W for the third calendar quarter of the current year. If the increase in the CPI-W is at least one-tenth of one percent (0.1%) there will be a COLA. If the CPI-W increases by less than 0.05% or if it decreases, there will not be a COLA for the upcoming year. COLAs are applied to your primary insurance amount (PIA), beginning with the year you reach age 62, up to the year you start receiving benefits. With COLAs, Social Security and Supplemental Security Income (SSI) benefits keep pace with inflation. Appendix A lists all increases in Social Security benefits since 1950 and yearly COLA increases since 1975.

You are eligible for COLA increases starting with the year you become age 62, even if you do not claim benefits until your FRA or even age 70. Beginning January 1, 2014, monthly Social Security benefits increased by 1.5% as a result of the COLA increase for 2014. Increased payments to SSI beneficiaries will begin on December 31, 2013. This is the smallest increase in benefits since 1975 and is slightly below the COLA increase for 2013, which was 1.7%. Since 1990, the average has been about 2.7%. According to the SSA, the 1.5% benefit increase affects nearly 63 million Americans receiving monthly Social Security and SSI.

Example

What are these COLAs actually worth? A single man is able to collect $2,000 per month in Social Security benefits at his full retirement age, assuming this is age 66. If he decides to collect early retirement benefits, at age 62, the amount he receives is reduced by 25% to $1,500 per month. If he delays until he reaches age 70 and earns his four years of delayed retirement credits, his benefit would now be worth $2,640 per month. This is 132% more than his full retirement age benefit and 76% more than what he collected at age 62.

Since 2000, COLAs have averaged about 2.8%. By waiting until age 70, including COLAs, he would receive a 119% increase in monthly benefits to $3,395 per month. Another way to look at this is if this individual begins collecting his PIA at 66, which is $2,000 per month and he receives a 2% COLA for the year, he receives an annual increase of $480. If he waits until age 70 to collect his maximum benefit of $2,640 and receives the same 2% COLA, he would get a boost to his annual retirement income by about $634.

According to the SSA, for 2014 the average Social Security retirement benefit will increase to $1,294 per month as a result of the COLA increase, up from the 2013 average of $1,275 per month. For retired couples, the average benefit will increase to $2,111 per month, up from $2,080 per month in 2013.

Table 6.6, on the next page, examines the effect which COLAs have on retirement benefits. By the time one reaches the age of 70, COLA increases have added an extra $518 to a retiree's monthly retirement benefit.

Table 6.6 Effect of COLAs on Retirement Benefits

Age at which benefits are claimed	Percent of PIA if FRA is 66	Retirement benefit without COLA	Retirement benefit with COLA	PIA with COLA for FRA at 66
62	75%	$1,500	$1,500	$2,000
63	80%	1,600	1,637	2,046
64	87%	1,732	1,813	2,093
65	93%	1,866	1,998	2,141
66	100%	2,000	2,190	2,190
67	108%	2,160	2,420	2,240
68	116%	2,320	2,659	2,292
69	124%	2,480	2,908	2,345
70	132%	2,649	3,167	2,399

(Assumes PIA is $2,000 per month and an annual 2.3% cost-of-living adjustment)

Source: Social Security Administration

If we extend the illustration past the age of 70, we can see how these COLAs can truly impact retirement benefits as displayed in Table 6.7.

Table 6.7 Cumulative Impact of COLAs Over Time

Benefit at Age	If Claimed at 62	If Claimed at 70	If Claimed at 66
70	$1,799	$3,167	$2,399
75	2,016	3,548	2,688
80	2,259	3,975	3,012
85	2,531	4,454	3,374
90	2,835	4,990	3,780
95	3,177	5,591	4,236
100	3,559	6,264	4,746

(Assumes PIA is $2,000 per month, FRA is 66 and an annual 2.3% cost-of-living adjustment)

Source: Social Security Administration

Using the above assumptions, the amount of money can be substantial. Lifetime benefits over 10 years could be $266,427, over 20 years $600,879 and over 30 years $1,020,725.

Windfall Elimination Provision

Not all workers pay into Social Security. Instead they may pay into another public pension system such as the Civil Service Retirement System, a teacher's pension system or a police or fireman's pension system. If this is the only employment which the worker had they are not eligible for Social Security. However, many workers pay into Social Security for a portion of their career and then a public retirement system for the remainder of their career. These workers may be entitled to both Social Security benefits as well as a public pension. Expecting to receive their full retirement benefit from Social Security, they are surprised by the fact when they are told that their benefit has been reduced by a regulation called the Windfall Elimination Provision (WEP). The SSA does not know if you are entitled to such a pension. Therefore, the estimated benefit statement you see online will not reflect any potential reductions you may be subject to due to this regulation.

Most federal workers hired after 1983 are covered by Social Security. Public-sector employees in 15 states are not. Those include the entire states of:

- Alaska
- California
- Colorado
- Connecticut
- Illinois
- Louisiana
- Maine
- Massachusetts
- Missouri

- Nevada
- Ohio
- Texas

In addition, there are certain local governments in Georgia, Kentucky and Rhode Island which not covered also.

The Congressional Research Service estimates about 1.5 million Social Security beneficiaries are affected by WEP reductions. If you receive a relatively low pension you are protected. The reduction in your Social Security benefit cannot be more than 50% of the amount of your pension. This is based on earnings after 1956 on which you did not pay Social Security taxes. In 2014, the reduction generally cannot exceed $408 per month. The WEP does not apply to spousal and survivor's benefits but another regulation, the Government Pension Offset (GPO) could.

The WEP is a regulation which can affect the benefit received by the worker. It affects how the amount of your retirement or disability benefit is calculated if you receive a pension from work where Social Security taxes were not taken out of your wages. Congress passed the WEP in 1983 to eliminate any advantage a worker might have by being paid from a public pension system and Social Security. Prior to the 1983 changes, those who mainly worked in jobs not covered by Social Security had their retirement benefits calculated as if they were long-term, low-wage workers. They had the advantage of receiving Social Security benefits representing a higher percentage of their earnings plus a pension from a job where they didn't pay Social Security taxes. The WEP does not apply if:

- You are a federal worker first hired after December 31, 1983.
- You were employed on December 31, 1983 by a non-profit organization which did not withhold Social Security taxes from your wages at first but then began withholding Social Security taxes from wages.
- Your only pension is based on railroad employment.

- The only work you did where you did not pay Social Security taxes was before 1957.
- You have 30 or more years of substantial earnings under Social Security.

The WEP only affects the worker collecting retirement or disability benefits on his or her own earnings and may apply if:

- You reached 62 after 1985.
- You became disabled after 1985.
- You first became eligible for a monthly pension based on work where you did not pay Social Security taxes after 1985, even if you are still working.

The actual amount of the WEP reduction is based on a sliding scale depending on the number of years a worker reported wages with Social Security taxes withheld. Under the WEP, the SSA separates your average earnings into three amounts and multiplies those amounts using three factors. For a worker who turns 62 in 2014, the first $816 of average monthly earnings is multiplied by 90%, the next $4,101 in average monthly earnings by 32% and the remainder by 15%. The sum of the three amounts equals the total monthly payment amount.

The 90% factor is reduced in the modified formula and phased in for workers who reach age 62 or became disabled between 1986 and 1989. For those who reach 62 or became disabled in 1990 or later, the 90% factor is reduced to 40%.

There are some limited exceptions to this rule. If an individual has 30 years or more of "substantial" earnings under the Social Security program, the 90% factor is not reduced. The amount that is considered substantial earnings is increased each year. For 2014 it is $21,750. Table 6.7, on the next page, lists the amount of substantial earnings for each year, beginning with 1937.

Table 6.7 Substantial Earnings by Year

Year	Substantial Earnings	Year	Substantial Earnings
1037-1954	$900	1990	$9,525
1955-1958	$1,050	1991	$9,900
1959-1965	$1,200	1992	$10,350
1966-1967	$1,650	1993	$10,725
1968-1971	$1,950	1994	$11,250
1972	$2,250	1995	$11,325
1973	$2,700	1996	$11,625
1974	$3,300	1997	$12,150
1975	$3,525	1998	$12,675
1976	$3,825	1999	$13,425
1977	$4,125	2000	$14,175
1978	$4,425	2001	$14,925
1979	$4,725	2002	$15,750
1980	$5,100	2003	$16,125
1981	$5,550	2004	$16,275
1982	$6,075	2005	$16,725
1983	$6,675	2006	$17,475
1984	$7,050	2007	$18,150
1985	$7,425	2008	$18,975
1986	$7,875	2009-2011	$19,800
1987	$8,175	2012	$20,475
1988	$8,400	2013	$21,075
1989	$8,925	2014	$21,750

Source: Social Security Administration; Windfall Elimination Provision

If the individual has fewer years of substantial earnings than 30, the percentage of the first $816 which is paid in benefits could be reduced to as little as 40%. If you have 21 to 29 years of substantial earnings, the 90% factor is reduced to between 45% and 85%. Table 6.8 below illustrates these percentages.

Table 6.8 Years of Substantial Earnings under the Windfall Elimination Provision

Years of Substantial Earnings	Percentage
30 or more	90%
29	85%
28	80%
27	75%
26	70%
25	65%
24	60%
23	55%
22	50%
21	45%
20 or less	40%

Source: Social Security Administration; Windfall Elimination Provision

Since dependent benefits are derived from the worker's benefit, the WEP can affect your dependents as well. For example, if a worker is affected by the WEP benefit formula and receives a reduced Social Security benefit of $700 per month, his wife would receive a maximum spousal benefit of $350 per month, 50% of the worker's WEP benefit amount. However, when the worker dies, the WEP reduction is removed and the surviving spouse's benefit is re-calculated by the SSA using the regular benefit formula. The spouse will collect the full benefit regardless of how much of a WEP had been applied during his lifetime.

WEP Examples

An individual is 65 years old. He worked as a teacher for 18 years where he paid no Social Security taxes. He was also employed in another career for 20 years where he did pay Social Security taxes. His FRA is 66 and his current Social Security benefit statement estimates his PIA to be $980 per month. For 2014, his approximate reduction due to WEP would be the maximum of $408 because 50% of $980 would be $490. Thus, his actual retirement benefit from Social Security would be $572 ($980 - $408) per month.

In another situation a worker has a teacher's pension benefit of $600 per month. He is also entitled to an estimated retirement benefit from Social Security of $1,250 per month upon reaching his FRA from employment of 20 years when he did pay Social Security taxes. In this scenario, the maximum WEP reduction would be $300 (50% of $600), not the $408 regardless of how few years he paid Social Security taxes. His retirement benefit would be reduced to $950 ($1,250 - $300) per month plus his teacher's pension benefit of $600 each month for a total of $1,250 per month, not the $1,850 each month.

How might the WEP reduction affect his spouse? Let's look at the first situation where the husband is entitled to a retirement benefit of $980 per month at his FRA. If his wife waited until her FRA to begin collecting her spousal benefit, she would normally be entitled to 50% of her husband's PIA at his FRA, which in this case would be $490 per month. However, since the husband is impacted by the WEP regulation, his benefit was reduced to $572 per month. This also causes his spouse's retirement benefit from Social Security to be reduced by 50% to $286 each month. Now if his spouse decided to collect early retirement benefits, her benefit would be further reduced due to the early filing. Survivor benefits for a spouse are not affected by the WEP provision.

The SSA has a WEP Online Calculator, which consumers can use if the WEP is applicable to them. The online calculator is accessible by following the link at www.socialsecurity.gov/retire2/anyPiaWepjs04.htm or you can download their Detailed Calculator at www.socialsecurity.gov/OACT/anypia/anypia.html.

Government Pension Offset

The Government Pension Offset (GPO) is a regulation which applies to spousal and survivor benefits which can affect spouses, widows and widowers. If you receive a pension from a federal, state or local government, a public school system or some other retirement plan where you did not pay Social Security taxes for the work you did, your spousal or survivor benefit from Social Security may be reduced or even eliminated by the GPO rule. This rule applies to Social Security benefits, both as a spouse or survivor. If you are subject to the GPO rule, your Social Security benefits will be reduced by two-thirds of your government pension. Workers in the same states previously mentioned in the WEP section are also affected by the GPO.

GPO Example

A spouse receives a monthly civil service pension of $600 per month. Her husband's FRA benefit from Social Security is $2,000 per month. At her FRA she would normally be eligible for a spousal benefit of $1,000 per month (50% of $2,000). However, in this example, her spousal benefit is reduced by $400 (two-thirds of $600) because of the GPO rule. Her adjusted spousal benefit will only be $600 per month.

Using the same values for a survivor benefit example, the spouse would normally be entitled to a 100% survivor benefit of $2,000 at her FRA. Because she is subject to the GPO rule, her survivor benefit would be reduced by the $400 to $1,600 per month. By not being aware of this rule and its impact, this monthly reduction of $400 could have severe, unintended consequences for retirement planning and income needs over their remaining lives.

You cannot bypass the GPO rule by electing to receive a lump-sum annuity payout of your government pension. The SSA will calculate the reduction as if you chose to get a monthly benefit from your government pension. Generally, Social Security benefits, as a spouse, widow or widower will not be reduced by the GPO rule if you:

- Are receiving a government pension which is NOT based on your earnings.
- Are a federal, including Civil Service Offset, state or local government employee whose government pension is based on a job where you were paying Social Security taxes and
  - You filed for and were entitled to spouse's, widow's or widower's benefits before April 1, 2004 or
  - Your last day of employment, which your pension is based on, is July 1, 2004 or
  - You paid Social Security taxes on your earnings during the last 60 months of government service.

How can you quickly determine if you may be possibly affected by either of these two regulations? Pull out your Social Security benefit statement. If you see a lot of zeroes for annual income on page 3 of *Your Social Security Statement*, this could be a warning sign that you may see a reduction in anticipated retirement benefits. Remember, these regulations apply to where you earned the income, not where you currently live. So if you were a teacher in Illinois and have since moved to Florida to retire, you're most likely subject to the regulations. The bottom half of page 2 on *Your Social Security Statement* also has a disclosure regarding these two regulations as illustrated in Figure 6.1, on the next page.

Figure 6.1 How Benefits Are Estimated

How Your Benefits Are Estimated

To qualify for benefits, you earn "credits" through your work — up to four each year. This year, for example, you earn one credit for each $1,200 of wages or self-employment income. When you've earned $4,800, you've earned your four credits for the year. Most people need 40 credits, earned over their working lifetime, to receive retirement benefits. For disability and survivors benefits, young people need fewer credits to be eligible.

We checked your records to see whether you have earned enough credits to qualify for benefits. If you haven't earned enough yet to qualify for any type of benefit, we can't give you a benefit estimate now. If you continue to work, we'll give you an estimate when you do qualify.

What we assumed — If you have enough work credits, we estimated your benefit amounts using your average earnings over your working lifetime. For 2014 and later (up to retirement age), we assumed you'll continue to work and make about the same as you did in 2012 or 2013. We also included credits we assumed you earned last year and this year.

Generally, the older you are and the closer you are to retirement, the more accurate the retirement estimates will be because they are based on a longer work history with fewer uncertainties such as earnings fluctuations and future law changes. We encourage you to use our online Retirement Estimator at www.socialsecurity.gov/estimator to obtain immediate and personalized benefit estimates.

We can't provide your actual benefit amount until you apply for benefits. And that amount may differ from the estimates stated above because:

(1) Your earnings may increase or decrease in the future.
(2) After you start receiving benefits, they will be adjusted for cost-of-living increases.

(3) Your estimated benefits are based on current law. The law governing benefit amounts may change.
(4) Your benefit amount may be affected by military service, railroad employment or pensions earned through work on which you did not pay Social Security tax. Visit www.socialsecurity.gov to learn more.

Windfall Elimination Provision (WEP) — In the future, if you receive a pension from employment in which you do not pay Social Security taxes, such as some federal, state or local government work, some nonprofit organizations or foreign employment, and you also qualify for your own Social Security retirement or disability benefit, your Social Security benefit may be reduced, but not eliminated, by WEP. The amount of the reduction, if any, depends on your earnings and number of years in jobs in which you paid Social Security taxes, and the year you are age 62 or become disabled. For more information, please see Windfall Elimination Provision (Publication No. 05-10045) at www.socialsecurity.gov/WEP.

Government Pension Offset (GPO) — If you receive a pension based on federal, state or local government work in which you did not pay Social Security taxes and you qualify, now or in the future, for Social Security benefits as a current or former spouse, widow or widower, you are likely to be affected by GPO. If GPO applies, your Social Security benefit will be reduced by an amount equal to two-thirds of your government pension, and could be reduced to zero. Even if your benefit is reduced to zero, you will be eligible for Medicare at age 65 on your spouse's record. To learn more, please see Government Pension Offset (Publication No. 05-10007) at www.socialsecurity.gov/GPO.

Source: Social Security Administration; Sample of a Social Security Statement

If you are subject to these regulations, do not underestimate the impact they could have on your retirement income cashflows, particularly in your later years. Portfolios typically do not fail in the earlier years of retirement. They fail in the later years of retirement due to poor planning and when options are severely constrained due to age and health conditions.

According to the Congressional Research Service, more 500,000 Social Security beneficiaries have had their benefits reduced by the GPO formula. Even if you review your latest Social Security estimated benefits you might get caught off guard because the SSA records don't indicate if you may be subject to either of the two regulations above or do they reduce the estimated benefit which appears on your Social Security benefit statement.

Social Security and the Law

The income from Social Security is protected by the law from most creditors. This does NOT include debts owed to the IRS, federal student loans or other government claimants and from alimony or child support payments. You could be prosecuted as a criminal for fraud if you knowingly:

- Furnish false information as to your identity in connection with the establishment and maintenance of Social Security records.
- For the purpose of increasing your payment under Social Security or any other Federally funded program or for the purpose of obtaining such payment:
    1. Use a Social Security number obtained on the basis of false information.
    2. Falsely represent a number to be your Social Security number.
- Make or cause to be made a false statement or misrepresentation of a material fact for use in determining your rights to Social Security or SSI benefits.
- Make or cause to be made any false statement or representation as to:
    1. Whether wages were paid to you, the period during which wages were paid, or the amount of your wages.
    2. Whether you have net earnings from self-employment, the amount of your earnings, or the period during which you earned the money.

127

- Conceal or fail to report any event affecting the initial or continued right to payment received or to be received by you personally or on behalf of another.
- Use payment received on behalf of another for any purpose other than the use for the benefit of that person.

Other penal provisions contained in the Social Security Act or in the Federal Criminal Code may also apply to offenses affecting the Social Security program. The SSA will prosecute even if a fraudulent act is discovered before wrongful payments are made by the Government. The penalty can range from a fine of not more than $500, imprisonment of one year or both, up to a fine of not more than $10,000, imprisonment of not more than 15 years, or both. The amount of the penalty and/or imprisonment will depend upon the specific law violated.

No Benefits in Jail

Husbands or wives who kill their spouses CANNOT collect benefits on them. Neither can children who kill their parents. If someone goes to jail, any benefits which would have come due during that jail time are lost. However, as long as your spouse and/or children are not in there with you, they can continue receiving benefits.

Rights to Representation

You are entitled to have a representative help you when you do business with Social Security if you so choose. This representative can be an attorney or other qualified individual to represent you. You can also have more than one representative. However, you cannot have someone who has been suspended or disqualified from representing others before the Social Security Administration or who may not, by law, act as a representative. The SSA will work with your representative, just as they would with you. For your protection, in most situations, your representative cannot charge or collect a fee from you without first getting written approval from the SSA. However, your representative may accept money from you in advance as long as it is held in a trust or escrow account. Both you and your representative are responsible for providing the SSA with accurate information. It is illegal to furnish false information knowingly or willfully. If you do, you may face criminal prosecution.

After you choose a representative, you must inform the SSA, **in writing**, as soon as possible. To do this, get Form SSA-1696-U4, Appointment of Representative, from the SSA's website at www.socialsecurity.gov or from any Social Security office. Once you appoint a representative, they can act on your behalf before Social Security by:

- Getting information from your Social Security file.
- Helping you obtain medical records or information to support your claim.
- Coming with you, or for you, to any interview, conference or hearing you have with the SSA.
- Requesting a reconsideration, hearing or Appeals Council review.
- Helping you and your witnesses prepare for a hearing and questioning any witnesses.

To charge you a fee for services, your representative must first file either a fee agreement or a fee petition with the SSA. Your representative **cannot** charge you more than the fee amount authorized by the SSA. If you or your representative disagree with the fee authorize, either of you can ask the SSA to look at it again. A representative who charges or collects a fee without the authorization of the SSA, or charges or collects too much, may be suspended or disqualified from representing anyone before the Social

Security Administration and also may face criminal prosecution. The amount of the fee the SSA decides your representative may charge is the most you owe for their services even if you agreed to pay your representative more. However, your representative can charge you for out-of-pocket expenses, such as medical reports, without the SSA's approval. If an attorney or non-attorney whom Social Security has found eligible for direct payment represents you, the SSA will usually withhold 25% (but never more) of your past-due benefits to pay toward the fee. The SSA pays all or part of the representative's fee from this money and will send you any money left over. Your representative will receive a copy of any decision(s) the SSA makes on your claim(s).

CHAPTER SEVEN

COLLECTING SOCIAL SECURITY RETIREMENT BENEFITS

The Social Security Handbook has over 2,700 rules. Explanations of these rules are found in the Program Operating Manual System (POMS). It is these rules and guidelines which define how Social Security operates and how benefits are calculated and paid. Envision the following information on a timeline. In many cases, it is not "what" you need to know but rather "when" you need to know it.

Social Security benefits can be claimed at any age between 62 and 70. The SSA's, *Annual Statistical Supplement 2013,* reveals the most popular age to start benefits is still 62. According to the SSA, 37.5% of men and 42.4% of women claim at 62. These numbers are down from approximately 50% ten years ago. The decrease in early filings appears attributable to an increase in the number of individuals who wait until their FRA with 31.5% of men and 25.2% of women waiting until then to claim benefits. Only 6% of men and 5% of women waited until age 70 to claim benefits. There are special situations where benefits can be claimed as early as age 60, as in survivor benefits or age 50 if you are disabled. The difference between claiming reduced early retirement benefits at age 62 and waiting until age 70 to claim the maximum benefit amount you'll be eligible for will result in a retirement benefit which is 76% larger. Your Social Security benefits are one of your most important retirement income vehicles you have. These benefits provide a combination of inflation protection, longevity protection, investment risk protection and spousal/survivor coverage.

When and How Benefits Are Paid

If you receive benefits based on your own earnings record, when you receive your benefit payment will be determined by your birth date. If you receive benefits based on your spouse's earnings record, your benefit payment date will be determined by your spouse's birth date.

Table 7.1 Benefit Payment Dates

Date of Birth	Benefits Paid Each Month on
1st – 10th	Second Wednesday
11th – 20th	Third Wednesday
21st – 31st	Fourth Wednesday

Source: Social Security Administration; What You Need To Know When You Get Retirement or Survivor Benefits

Benefits are paid in the following month of when you receive them. Your October benefit will actually be received in November. If you receive both Social Security and SSI benefits, your Social Security payment will arrive on the third day of the month and your SSI payment will arrive on the first day of the month. Payments from the Social Security Administration (SSA) are now done electronically, either as a direct deposit, a deposit made to your Direct Express card program or to an electronic transfer account.

Calculating Retirement Benefits

Your Social Security benefit is a percentage of your average lifetime earnings. Your actual earnings are adjusted or indexed to account for changes in average wages since the year the earnings were received. Low-income workers receive a higher percentage of their average lifetime earnings than those in the upper income brackets. A worker with average earnings can expect a retirement benefit that replaces about 40% of their average lifetime earnings.

The SSA takes a worker's top 35 years of earnings, adjusts all earnings for inflation and then replaces a percentage of the worker's average monthly wage. The first step is to adjust or "index" his or her earnings to reflect the change in general wage levels that occurred during the worker's years of employment. Such indexation ensures that a worker's future benefits reflect the general rise in the standard of living that occurred during his or her working lifetime. Next, those 35 years with the highest indexed earnings are chosen and the values are summed. Then the total amount is divided by the total number of months in those 35 years which is 420 months. The resulting average amount is rounded down to the next lower dollar amount. This is average indexed monthly earnings (AIME). How is this calculation done?

An insured worker becomes eligible for retirement benefits when he or she reaches age 62. Those workers born in 1952 become eligible for retirement benefits in 2014. The SSA always indexes an individual's earnings to the average wage level two years prior to the first year of eligibility. If 2014 were the year of eligibility, the SSA would divide the national average wage index for 2012 ($44,321.67) by the national average wage index for each year prior to 2012 in which the worker had earnings. These ratios are the index factors for each year. Then, each index factor is multiplied by the worker's earnings for that year. A worker's earnings value cannot exceed the maximum earnings level set by the SSA each year. For 2013, maximum earnings are $113,700.

This is also called the benefit base. So if you had earnings in 2013 of $135,000, only $113,700 would be your earnings value for that year. These calculations provide the worker's indexed earnings for each year prior to 2012. The SSA would consider any earnings after 2012 at face value. Then, the SSA computes the AIME and uses this amount in computing the worker's primary insurance amount (PIA) for 2014.

The PIA is the sum of three separate percentages of portions of the AIME. To compute the PIA, the replacement ratio is calculated in the following way. Social Security replaces 90% of the first $816 of AIME, 32% of AIME between $816 and $4,917 and then 15% of AIME over $4,917. These dollar amounts, called "bend points," govern the portions of the AIME. While the percentages are fixed by law, the numerical values can change each year.

Let's apply all this. An individual eligible to retire in 2014 has as their 35 highest earnings years, which after applying all index factors to each year, cumulative indexed earnings of $2,500,823. This value is then divided by 420 months to arrive at an AIME of $5,954. From this AIME and the 2014 bend points $816 and $4,917, their PIA at their FRA would be $2,378.50 (.9 x 816 + .32 x [4,917 − 816] + .15 x [5,954 − 4,917]). If this individual claimed at age 62, they would receive a reduced benefit of $1,783.89 (2,378.50 x .75) per month.

In today's workforce it is not uncommon for some workers to have gaps in their employment record. This is another reason for establishing your online account with Social Security to review your personal statement. Figure 7.1, on the next page, displays page 2 of *Your Social Security Statement*. There is a section titled, "*We based your benefits estimate on these facts.*" It contains a line for estimated earnings after [a specific year will be listed]. If your future earnings vary significantly from these earnings estimates it could significantly skew the benefit estimates listed on your benefit statement.

Figure 7.1 Your Estimated Benefits

Your Estimated Benefits

*Retirement	You have earned enough credits to qualify for benefits. At your current earnings rate, if you continue working until...	
	your full retirement age (67 years), your payment would be about	$ 1,680 a month
	age 70, your payment would be about	$ 2,094 a month
	age 62, your payment would be about	$ 1,159 a month
*Disability	You have earned enough credits to qualify for benefits. If you became disabled right now, your payment would be about	$ 1,527 a month
*Family	If you get retirement or disability benefits, your spouse and children also may qualify for benefits.	
*Survivors	You have earned enough credits for your family to receive survivors benefits. If you die this year, certain members of your family may qualify for the following benefits:	
	Your child	$ 1,176 a month
	Your spouse who is caring for your child	$ 1,176 a month
	Your spouse, if benefits start at full retirement age	$ 1,569 a month
	Total family benefits cannot be more than	$ 2,908 a month
	Your spouse or minor child may be eligible for a special one-time death benefit of $255.	
Medicare	You have enough credits to qualify for Medicare at age 65. Even if you do not retire at age 65, be sure to contact Social Security three months before your 65th birthday to enroll in Medicare.	

* Your estimated benefits are based on current law. Congress has made changes to the law in the past and can do so at any time. The law governing benefit amounts may change because, by 2033, the payroll taxes collected will be enough to pay only about 77 percent of scheduled benefits.

We based your benefit estimates on these facts:

Your date of birth (please verify your name on page 1 and this date of birth)	April 5, 1974
Your estimated taxable earnings per year after 2014	$47,423
Your Social Security number (only the last four digits are shown to help prevent identity theft)	XXX-XX-1234

How Your Benefits Are Estimated

To qualify for benefits, you earn "credits" through your work — up to four each year. This year, for example, you earn one credit for each $1,200 of wages or self-employment income. When you've earned $4,800, you've earned your four credits for the year. Most people need 40 credits, earned over their working lifetime, to receive retirement benefits. For disability and survivors benefits, young people need fewer credits to be eligible.

We checked your records to see whether you have earned enough credits to qualify for benefits. If you haven't earned enough yet to qualify for any type of benefit, we can't give you a benefit estimate now. If you continue to work, we'll give you an estimate when you do qualify.

What we assumed — If you have enough work credits, we estimated your benefit amounts using your average earnings over your working lifetime. For 2014 and later (up to retirement age), we assumed you'll continue to work and make about the same as you did in 2012 or 2013. We also included credits we assumed you earned last year and this year.

Generally, the older you are and the closer you are to retirement, the more accurate the retirement estimates will be because they are based on a longer work history with fewer uncertainties such as earnings fluctuations and future law changes. We encourage you to use our online Retirement Estimator at www.socialsecurity.gov/estimator to obtain immediate and personalized benefit estimates.

We can't provide your actual benefit amount until you apply for benefits. And that amount may differ from the estimates stated above because:

(1) Your earnings may increase or decrease in the future.
(2) After you start receiving benefits, they will be adjusted for cost-of-living increases.

(3) Your estimated benefits are based on current law. The law governing benefit amounts may change.
(4) Your benefit amount may be affected by military service, railroad employment or pensions earned through work on which you did not pay Social Security tax. Visit www.socialsecurity.gov to learn more.

Windfall Elimination Provision (WEP) — In the future, if you receive a pension from employment in which you do not pay Social Security taxes, such as some federal, state or local government work, some nonprofit organizations or foreign employment, and you also qualify for your own Social Security retirement or disability benefit, your Social Security benefit may be reduced, but not eliminated, by WEP. The amount of the reduction, if any, depends on your earnings and number of years in jobs in which you paid Social Security taxes, and the year you are age 62 or become disabled. For more information, please see Windfall Elimination Provision (Publication No. 05-10045) at www.socialsecurity.gov/WEP.

Government Pension Offset (GPO) — If you receive a pension based on federal, state or local government work in which you did not pay Social Security taxes and you qualify, now or in the future, for Social Security benefits as a current or former spouse, widow or widower, you are likely to be affected by GPO. If GPO applies, your Social Security benefit will be reduced by an amount equal to two-thirds of your government pension, and could be reduced to zero. Even if your benefit is reduced to zero, you will be eligible for Medicare at age 65 on your spouse's record. To learn more, please see Government Pension Offset (Publication No. 05-10007) at www.socialsecurity.gov/GPO.

2   [C]

Source: Social Security Administration; Sample-Estimated Benefits Page

How large of an effect this can be depends on the number of years already worked and the degree of the discrepancy?

Collecting Social Security and Unemployment Benefits

According to a Department of Labor report, about 11% of individuals who collected unemployment benefits in 2012 were 60 and older. Receiving unemployment benefits does NOT affect your Social Security benefits because the SSA does not count unemployment benefits as earnings. Thus, you don't need to worry about earnings cap reductions, which will be discussed in the next section. However, the reverse isn't always true when collecting unemployment.

Unemployment benefit programs are administered by the various states. If you are receiving unemployment compensation and you become entitled to Social Security benefits on your earnings record or the earnings record of another individual such as a widow or spouse, your unemployment compensation may be reduced. State laws, where you live in which benefits are received, will determine the reduction of unemployment benefits if any.

In recent years, states have been changing their rules to allow individuals to qualify for more unemployment benefits. According to the National Employment Law Project in Ann Arbor, MI only Illinois, Louisiana, Minnesota and South Dakotas reduce unemployment benefits for this reason. Contact your state's unemployment agency to find out full details of jobless benefits which may be available to you.

Earnings Cap Reductions

If you continue to work while receiving retirement benefits, prior to reaching your FRA, you could be subject to a reduction in those retirement benefits. The Social Security earnings cap restriction applies only to gross wages and/or salaries. An employee's contribution to a pension or retirement plan, such as a 401(k) contribution, is included if the contribution amount is included in the employee's gross wages. If you work for wages, income counts when it is earned, not when it is paid. If other family members receive benefits based on your work history, your earnings from work you do after you start receiving retirement benefits could reduce their benefits also.

The earnings cap does not apply to unearned income such as other governmental benefits, investment earnings, interest, dividends, pensions, annuities and capital gains. Individuals who work and receive disability or SSI payments have different earnings rules. These individuals must immediately report all of their earnings to Social Security no matter how much they earn. Earnings cap restrictions are covered in the next chapter.

Basic Reduction Formulas for Claiming Early

For the most part the earliest Social Security benefits can be claimed is age 62. The exceptions to this include being disabled, being a widow/widower or having dependent children. There are specific rules which apply to each of these exceptions which are discussed throughout the book. By claiming early, your benefits are reduced a fraction of a percent for each month before reaching your FRA. **This reduction is permanent.** There are four basic reduction formulas.

1. A retirement insurance benefit is reduced by 5/9ths of 1% (0.0056) for each month of entitlement before reaching their FRA.
2. A wife/ husband's insurance benefits are reduced by 25/36ths of 1% (0.0069) for each month of entitlement before reaching their FRA up to 36 months.
3. Retirement insurance benefits and spouse's benefits are then reduced by 5/12ths of 1% (0.0042) for each month of reduction in excess of 36 months. This applies to individuals whose FRA is after age 65. A spouse can choose to retire as early as age 62, but doing so may result in a benefit as little as 32.5% of the wage earners' primary insurance amount (PIA).

4. Widow/widower's insurance benefits are reduced for each month of entitlement between age 60 and their FRA. The amount of reduction each month is derived from dividing 28.5% by the number of possible months of early retirement. An individual who's FRA is 65 could be entitled up to 60 (12 x 5) months before reaching their FRA. In this example, each month is 28.5% divided by 60 and would be reduced by 0.00475 (.285 / 60). If their FRA is 66 the reduction is 0.00396 (.285 / 72). The most your benefits can be reduced is 28.5% of the wage earners' PIA. If you wait until your FRA to start receiving your widow/widower's benefit and your deceased spouse had claimed early and was receiving reduced benefits, your widow/widower's benefit will always be reduced. A widow/widower's benefit payable before age 60, based on disability, is not further reduced for months before age 60.

Key Ages as you Near Retirement

These are key ages at which specific events occur. As you near retirement you should be aware of the events which occur at these periods of your life.

Age 59½ – Early Withdrawal Penalty Goes Away

This is the earliest you can begin withdrawals from tax advantage retirement accounts without restrictions and without the 10% penalty. This would include traditional IRAs, Roth IRAs, 401(k)s and similar retirement plans.

Age 60 – Early Survivor Benefits

Once a spouse passes away, the earliest a surviving spouse can begin to claim a survivor's benefit is at age 60. If they do claim this early, the benefit will be reduced based on the number of months remaining until the survivor reaches their full retirement age. They must also be unmarried at the time they file for the benefit.

Age 62 – Early Retirement Benefits

This is the earliest age at which you can begin to receive retirement benefits from Social Security. However, if you begin collecting benefits at this age, you will qualify for reduced benefits. At age 62, your benefit would be about 25% lower than what it would be if you waited until you reached your FRA. Your benefit is reduced by about one-half of 1% for each month you start receiving Social Security before your FRA. In other words, you will receive 75% of your primary insurance amount (PIA) if you claim early benefits and your FRA is 66. Also, if you decide to claim and continue working, your benefits may be subject to the earnings cap restriction. For workers born 1955 and later, the early retirement benefit is less than 75%. The reduction will be greater in future years as the full retirement age increases. The minimum is 70%.

Age 62 is also the earliest a spouse can receive a spousal benefit. The benefit will typically be 35% of the worker's FRA benefit. For those born in 1955 or later the spousal benefit is less than 35%. The minimum is 32.5%.

Age 65 – Medicare

This is the age when you are first eligible to apply for Medicare Part A and Part B. You have a 7-month window; 3 months before your birth month, your birth month and 3 months after your birth month. Although the full retirement age is rising, you should still apply for Medicare during your Initial Enrollment Period, if you have no creditable health insurance coverage. If you wait to enroll, you may have late penalties and your Medicare medical insurance (Part B) and prescription drug coverage (Part D) may cost you more money. If you are already receiving Social Security benefits when you turn age 65, you will automatically be enrolled in Part A and given the option to enroll in Part B. The SSA will normally deduct your Medicare Part B premium from your Social Security benefit amount, so you will see a decrease in your monthly Social Security check when this occurs. This benefit decrease could be significant for those who are high income earners.

There is one rule you need to know regarding Social Security and Medicare benefits. If you turn your FRA at 66 and then decide you want to file and suspend your Social Security benefits, in order to trigger spousal benefits while allowing your own benefit to earn delayed retirement credits, your Medicare premiums CANNOT be paid automatically from your Social Security benefits. Medicare premiums will need to be paid out-of-pocket. You need to be sure you are getting billed properly by CMS and paying your Part B premiums timely. Otherwise, the SSA will revoke your file and suspension claim in order to garner the funds to pay the Medicare premium. You won't know this has happened and you will have forgone retirement benefits for four years and not have earned delayed retirement credits. **Social Security doesn't need to inform you they have done this.**

If you are at least age 65 and also collecting Social Security benefits, you must enroll in Medicare Part A. By law Social Security benefits and Medicare are linked together. By implementing a file and suspend strategy it will trigger your Part A coverage, making you ineligible to continuing making tax-deductible contributions to a health savings account (HSA). You can't opt out of Medicare Part A even if you want to.

Medicare Part B premium increases are limited by Congress to the increase in Social Security benefits in a given year. If you are deferring collecting Social Security benefits and Part B premiums increase significantly, you'll be paying it. For example, if you are already collecting Social Security benefits, the most your Part B premiums could be increased in 2014 would be limited to the 1.5% COLA increase for 2014.

Age 66 – Full Retirement Age

To receive 100% of your earned PIA benefit, you must wait until you reach your FRA before you begin collecting benefits. Age 66 is also the age when a spouse can collect a maximum 50% spousal benefit and the age where file and suspend, along with restricted claim strategies can be implemented. Age 66 is also the age when reductions in benefits, due to an earnings cap restriction disappear.

Table 7.2 below, displays how an individual's FRA is phased in for those born from 1955 to 1959. The intervals increase throughout age 66 until age 67. If you were born in 1942, or earlier, you are already eligible to receive your full Social Security benefit. Those born between 1943 and 1954, reach their FRA at age 66. Those individuals born in 1960 and later reach the full retirement age at 67.

Table 7.2 Ages to Reach to Receive Full Social Security Benefits

Year of Birth	Full Retirement Age
1943 - 1954	66
1955	66 and 2 months
1956	66 and 4 months
1957	66 and 6 months
1958	66 and 8 months
1959	66 and 10 months
1960 and later	67

Note: **Individuals who are born on January 1st of any year should refer to the previous year.**

Source: Social Security Administration; Understanding the Benefits

Ages 66 to 70 – Delayed Retirement Benefits

You may choose to work beyond your full retirement age. Once you reach your FRA, any earnings are no longer subject to the earnings cap restriction. Depending on what you earn though, you could be subject to additional federal income taxes. Each year you work adds another year of earnings to your Social Security record. Higher lifetime earnings may mean higher benefits when you retire.

Your benefit will increase automatically by a specific percentage from the time you reach your FRA until you reach age 70. This percentage varies depending on your year of birth. Covered workers who reach their FRA in 2009 or later earn delayed retirement credits worth two-thirds of 1% per month for each month they delay collecting Social Security benefits up to age 70. For those born between 1943 and 1954, the SSA will add 8% per year to your benefit for each year you delay signing up for Social Security beyond your full retirement age. By waiting until age 70, you will increase your benefit to 132% of whatever your PIA was at age 66. As an example, your PIA at age 66 is $1,000 per month. By waiting the four years until you reach age 70, your retirement benefit would increase to $1,320 ($1,000 x 1.32) per month. Delayed retirement credits are not compounded annually and are effective in January of the following year.

For those born after 1954, the FRA is higher starting at 66 and 2 months for those born in 1955 and gradually increasing to age 67 for those in 1960 or later. This means for those with an FRA of 67, maximum delayed retirement credits are worth 24% (8% x 3 years).

Prior to 1982, delayed credits were worth 1% per year. Beginning in 1982 they were increased to 3%. Starting in 1990, they were increased in 0.5% increments every two years until they reached the statutory cap of 8% in 2009.

Age 70 – No More Advantages

Once you reach age 70 there is no benefit to waiting any longer to collect your Social Security benefits. You will have earned your maximum retirement benefit.

Age 70½ – Required Minimum Distributions

You must begin taking specific required minimum distributions (RMDs) from tax-deferred retirement accounts such as traditional IRAs and 401(k)s. You actually have until April of the following year in which you turn age 70 1/2 to take your first distribution. After that your RMDs must be taken by December 31st of each year.

Summary of Benefit Amounts Received Based on Age

Figure 7.2 below provides an example of how your monthly benefit amount can vary based on the age at which you decide to start collecting retirement benefits. This assumes a full retirement age of 66.

Figure 7.2 Variance of Monthly Benefit Based on Age

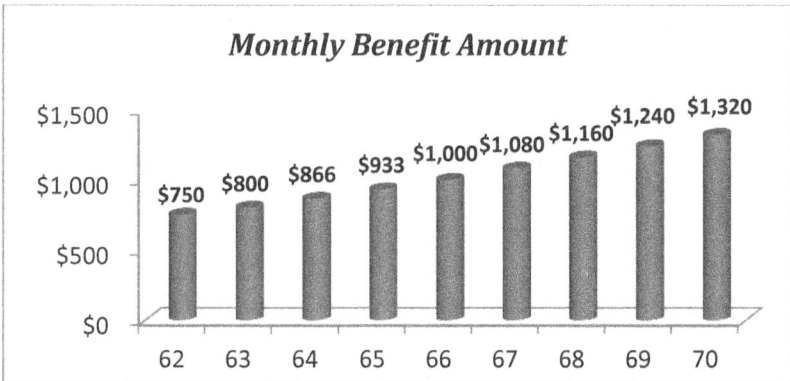

Source: Social Security Administration; When To Start Receiving Retirement Benefits

Looking at the information from the chart above, based on percentages, you receive the following percentage of your PIA at the following ages when you claim your retirement benefits.

- Age 62 – 75%
- Age 63 – 80%
- Age 64 – 87%
- Age 65 – 93%
- Age 66 – 100%
- Age 67 – 108%
- Age 68 – 116%
- Age 69 – 124%
- Age 70 – 132%

(Percentages above rounded, which may result in a slightly different benefit amount than what Social Security may calculate.)

Lump-Sum Payouts

There are three ways in which a beneficiary could claim a lump-sum payout. One is by filing for retroactive retirement benefits. Another is by requesting reinstatement of voluntarily suspended benefits. The third is a death benefit.

1. Filing for Retroactive Retirement Benefits

If you are older than your FRA when you first claim Social Security benefits, you may be entitled up to six months of retroactive benefits, which are paid as a lump-sum benefit. This retroactive period begins six months before filing the application to claim Social Security benefits. For example, an individual turns their FRA in September 2012. They decide to file their claim to begin collecting their Social Security benefits, one year later in September 2013. They would be entitled to retroactive benefits beginning six months earlier from March 2013.

These retroactive benefits for months prior to reaching their FRA are not payable to a retired worker, spouse, widow or widower if this results in a permanent reduction of their monthly benefit. For example, if an individual's FRA is age 66 and they claim benefits at 66 and 3 months, they would not be entitled to six months retroactive benefits. This is because they only reached their FRA 3 months earlier. They could request a lump-sum payment for 3 months of retroactive benefits.

If you have passed your FRA but not yet claimed retirement benefits AND you don't intend to wait until age 70 to collect your maximum benefits, this lump-sum retroactive benefit can be an option if you need cash. This strategy can be used if one needs emergency funds or anticipates a shortened lifespan. An individual could take these funds and roll them into a financial product which can meet a need such as a deferred annuity which begins payments at age 80 for longevity protection or long-term care. Or it could be used to pay for a large vacation or home remodeling project. It may be a better alternative than dipping into your savings or investments to pay for a large vacation or home remodeling project.

Example 1

Let's take a look at the following example. It has a little twist on what we just covered. Both the husband and wife turned age 66 in the current year.

- Husband's FRA: 66
- Wife's FRA: 66
- Husband's PIA: $2,200 per month
- Wife's PIA: $650 per month

The couple did nothing when they reached their FRAs. Now one year has passed. What options are now available? In this example, it makes since for the wife to claim spousal benefits as soon as possible. Her spousal benefit is worth 50% of her husband's PIA since she has reached her FRA. She is entitled to collect $1,100 (50% of $2,200) per month. This is more than if she even waits to age 70 and collects four years of delayed retirement credits. At 70, her retirement benefit would only be worth $858 ($650 x 1.32) each month.

145

The husband can file a retroactive claim to file and suspend his benefits so it triggers spousal benefits for his wife. He can file going back six months. Once he files, he can then voluntarily suspend his benefit during any period beginning with the first month of entitlement. Now that he has done this, his wife can apply for spousal benefits, retroactively going back to his first month of entitlement. She would get a lump sum payment of $6,600 ($1,100 x 6) for the six months. This strategy preserves the husband's ability to continue earning his delayed retirement credits. You might be wondering that since they waited a year, shouldn't the husband's benefit include one year of delayed retirement credits and be worth $2.376 ($2,200 x 1.08). Half of that is $1,188. Yes and no. Yes the husband earns that one year credit but spousal benefits do not include delayed retirement credits. Only survivor benefits earn them.

2. Reinstatement of Voluntarily Suspended Benefits

If you implement a file and suspend claiming strategy, with the intention of collecting a larger benefit later, you have the choice to change your mind and collect a lump sum payment retroactively back to the point of your initial filing. This can be done even if that is longer than six months. You're not requesting a retroactive payment when you file and suspend because you have already triggered a claim. You're asking Social Security to reinstate a retirement benefit which you have voluntarily suspended. This benefit can be reinstatement at any time during the suspension period and provides an individual with a hedge if they should decide to change their mind later. This provides a degree of protection.

Example 2

Let's examine a scenario where a husband has filed and suspended his benefits so his wife could collect spousal benefits. Both are 66 years of age.

- Husband's FRA: 66
- Wife's FRA: 66
- Husband's PIA: $2,200 per month
- Wife's PIA: $600 per month

Since the wife has reached her FRA, she three choices. She can begin collecting her full PIA of $600 per month, she can delay claiming and earn her delayed retirement credits until age 70, when her benefit would then increase to $792 ($600 x 1.32) per month or she can now collect a spousal benefit worth 50% of her husband's PIA, which in this case is $1,100 per month. It's obvious the third choice is the best.

To continue, two years have now passed and the husband decides he wants to change his mind. He now wants reinstatement of his voluntarily suspended benefits so he can collect his retirement benefits. What options does the husband have now that two years have passed?

The husband has two choices he can make. First, now that he is 68, he has earned two years of delayed retirement credits worth 8% each year. The husband can just claim his larger benefit of $2,5 ($2,200 x 1.16) per month from now on. Secondly, he could request 24 months of retroactive benefits worth $50,400 ($2,100 x 24) in a lump sum. If he chooses the lump sum payout, the husband would collect his FRA benefit of $2,100 per month from that point forward. There is no longer an opportunity to earn any more delayed retirement credits because he has now filed to claim his retirement benefits.

A word of caution regarding these first two options discussed. These Social Security benefits may be taxable and a lump sum payment could boost the amount of retirement benefits which are taxable. A discussion of provisional income is detailed in the next chapter. It could also increase Medicare premiums.

3. Death Benefit

A lump sum death benefit of $255 is payable upon the death of a person who had worked long enough to be eligible for Social Security benefits. The benefit is payable to a surviving spouse. If there is no surviving spouse, the lump sum benefit can be paid to a child who is eligible for benefits on the deceased parent's record at the time of death.

When visiting your local Social Security office, to file a claim for either of these lump sum benefits, a few things to keep in mind include:

- Booking an appointment online could preserve extra benefits, even if your actual in-person appointment is weeks away.
- Bring a photo ID.
- Bring your marriage certificate.
- Bring your divorce decree if filing for benefits as a divorced spouse.
- Bring your spouse's death certificate.

Qualifying for Survivor's Benefits

To be eligible for a survivor benefit, the spouse must have been married to the covered worker for at least nine months at the time of death unless one of the following exceptions is met. These exceptions include:

- Worker's death was an accident
- Worker's death occurred in the line of duty as an actively serving member of a uniformed service.

Certain members of the family may be eligible for survivor's benefits when an individual who has worked and paid Social Security taxes dies. To be eligible for benefits, up to 10 years of work is needed, depending on the person's age at the time of death. Under a special rule, if you have worked for only 1½ years in the three years just before your death, benefits can be paid to your minor children and your spouse who is caring for those children. Survivor's benefits can be paid to:

- A widow or widower. Full benefits at their full retirement age (FRA) or reduced benefits as early as age 60.
- A disabled widow/widower as early as age 50.
- A widow/widower of any age who takes care of the deceased's child who is younger than 16 or disabled and receiving Social Security benefits.
- Divorced spouses under certain circumstances.
- Unmarried children younger than age 18 or up to age 19 if they attend elementary or secondary school full time. Under certain circumstances benefits can be paid to stepchildren, grandchildren or adopted children.
- Children who were disabled before age 22 and remain disabled.
- Dependent parents age 62 or older.

You can file up to three months before you want your benefit payments to begin. If you are receiving widow's or widower's benefits, you can switch to your own retirement benefits as early as age 62, assuming your retirement benefit is more than the amount you receive on your deceased spouse's earnings.

Table 7.3, on the next page, lists full retirement ages for survivors based on their year of birth. The example in the table is for an age 62 survivor benefit based on a monthly benefit of $1,000 at FRA. The chart can be accessed at, http://www.socialsecurity.gov/survivorplan/survivorchartre d.htm.

Table 7.3 Full Retirement Ages for Survivors Based on Year of Birth

Year of Birth[1]	Full (survivors) Retirement Age[2]	At age 62[3], a $1,000 survivors benefit would be reduced to	Months between age 60 and FRA	Monthly percentage reduction[4]
1939 or earlier	65	$829	60	.475
1940	65 and 2 months	$825	62	.460
1941	65 and 4 months	$822	64	.445
1942	65 and 6 months	$819	66	.432
1943	65 and 8 months	$816	68	.419
1944	65 and 10 months	$813	70	.407
1945-1956	66	$810	72	.396
1957	66 and 2 months	$807	74	.385
1958	66 and 4 months	$805	76	.375
1959	66 and 6 months	$803	78	.365
1960	66 and 8 months	$801	80	.356
1961	66 and 10 months	$798	82	.348
1962	67	$796	84	.339

1. If the survivor was born on January 1st of any year, use the information for the previous year.
2. If someone was born on the 1st of the month, the SSA determines the benefit and FRA as if their birthday was in the previous month.
3. The $1,000 benefit would be reduced to $715 for anyone who started receiving survivor's benefits at age 60.
4. Monthly reduction percentages are approximate due to rounding. The maximum benefit is limited to what the worker would receive if they were still alive. Survivors benefits which start at age 60 are always reduced by 28.5%

Source: Social Security Administration

Each year of birth can be clicked on to find out how much the benefit will be reduced if someone begins receiving survivor's benefits between age 60 and their FRA. It should be noted that if the worker started receiving retirement benefits before their FRA, the SSA will not pay the full retirement age benefit amount on their record. The survivor benefit will be further reduced. The maximum survivor's benefit is limited to what they would have received if they were still alive.

Social Security and Women

The importance of Social Security to women should not be underestimated, especially as they enter the later stages of their lives. Statistically, since women tend to outlive men, every woman should have at least considered their financial situation once their spouse passes.

From the 2013 Current Population Survey (CPS), in 2012, the median earnings of working-age women who worked full-time, year round were $38,000, compared to $48,362 for men. In a report from the Employee Benefit Research Institute (EBRI), in 2012, women had IRA accounts with an average balance of $81,700, compared with men who had balances of $139,467.

According to the SSA and the Office of Retirement Policy (ORP), out of 36.4 million beneficiaries age 65 and older in 2012, 20.3 million or 56% were women. Of those aged 85 and older, 67% of beneficiaries were women. In 2012, for unmarried women, including widows aged 65 and older, Social Security comprises 50% of their total income. This compares to only 36% for unmarried men and only 30% of elderly couples' income. For all elderly unmarried women receiving Social Security, 50% relied on their benefits for 90% or more of their income. In 2010, only 23% of unmarried women aged 65 and older were receiving their own private pension. Elderly women tend to have a higher poverty rate because they did not earn enough which results in not enough paid into Social Security to ensure comfortable benefits when they retire. SSA research shows twice as many women as men are poor: 11% of women compared to 6.6% of men.

Social Security Calculators

The SSA provides a number of calculators, available for consumers to use at their website, www.ssa.gov/estimator/. The Retirement Estimator gives estimates based on your actual Social Security earnings record. These are just estimates and Social Security can't provide your actual benefit amount until you apply for benefits. That amount may differ from the estimates provided because:

- Earnings may increase or decrease in the future.
- After you start receiving benefits, they will be adjusted for cost-of-living increases.
- Your estimated benefits are based on current law. The law governing benefit amounts may change because, by 2033, the payroll taxes collected will be enough to pay only about 77 cents for each dollar of scheduled benefits.
- Your benefit amount may be affected by military service, railroad employment or pensions earned through work on which you did not pay Social Security tax.

You can use the Retirement Estimator if:

- You have enough Social Security credits at this time to qualify for benefits and
- You are not:
  - Currently receiving benefits on your own Social Security record;
  - Waiting for a decision about your application for benefits or Medicare;
  - Age 62 or older and receiving benefits on another Social Security record; **or**

- Eligible for a Pension Based on Work Not Covered By Social Security.

If you cannot use the Retirement Estimator **or** you want a survivors or disability benefit estimate, you can use one of Social Security's other benefit calculators at www.ssa.gov/planners/benefitcalculators.htm.

- *Quick Calculator:* This calculator gives you a simple, rough estimate when you input your date of birth and this year's earnings. The Quick Calculator does not include reduction for WEP.
- *Online Calculator:* Input your date of birth and your complete earnings history to get a benefit estimate. You may project your future earnings until your retirement date.
- *WEP Online Calculator:* If you are eligible for a pension based on work that was not covered by Social Security, your benefit amount may be reduced by the Windfall Elimination Provision (WEP) or Government Pension Offset (GPO).
- *Detailed Calculator:* This calculator provides the most precise estimates. It must be downloaded and installed on your computer. It includes reduction for WEP. There is also a Mac version of the Detailed Calculator.
- *Earnings Limit Calculator:* If you are currently working and are eligible for retirement or survivors benefits this year, you can learn how your earnings may affect your benefit payments.

In addition, there are a number of other free calculators which individuals can use to run various Social Security claiming scenarios. The mutual fund company, T. Rowe Price, has a calculator available called the Social Security Benefits Evaluator and is available at www.troweprice.com/socialsecurity. Financial Engines also has a free tool at www.corp.financialengines.com.

"Each of the three legs of our traditional retirement stool - personal savings, pensions and Social Security – is wobbling. If we do nothing, each of the three will likely cease to exist as we know them well before my generation enters retirement."

Marco Rubio
Republican U.S. Senator – Florida
Remarks before the National Press Club – May 13, 2014

Speaker of the Florida House of Representatives
Florida House of Representatives – 111th District
West Miami City Commissioner

CHAPTER EIGHT

RECEIVING SOCIAL SECURITY BENEFITS WHILE WORKING

This can be a confusing topic for many individuals. The confusion can be in the terminology used when discussing what effects continuing to work will have on the Social Security benefits you are receiving or planning to receive. There are two issues which you need to be concerned with. The first is earnings cap restrictions, which can affect your retirement benefits received from Social Security. The impact is dependent on the amount of wages you have earned during the year. Second are your federal income taxes. Some of your Social Security benefits can be subject to federal income taxation depending on the total income you have received for the year.

How does working affect the benefits you receive from Social Security? How are my benefits affected if I claim early or wait until I reach my full retirement age to file while I am still working? Does it matter if I claim early and I'm not working but then decide to return to work at a later date?

You can file and claim retirement benefits, spousal benefits or survivor benefits and also be employed at the same time. If your age is less than your full retirement age (FRA) and you claim benefits early, those benefits received will be reduced. If you earn more than certain threshold amounts your benefits will be reduced even further. Benefits lost because of the earnings cap are not truly lost but are deferred to a later time. Your retirement benefit will increase at your FRA to account for those benefits withheld due to earlier earnings. It is based on the number of months of benefits forfeited. This is called the adjustment to redactor factor. However, spouses and survivors who receive benefits because they have minor or disabled children in their care do not receive increased benefits at their FRA if benefits were withheld because of work.

Social Security Benefits and Earnings Cap Restrictions

If you file and claim Social Security benefits before you reach your FRA, some or all of the retirement benefits you receive from the SSA could be reduced or completely eliminated. The amount will be dependent on the wages/salaries you have for the year. There are a variety of rules which come into consideration when discussing earnings cap restrictions which we'll cover next.

Income Which Counts as Earnings

The earnings cap restriction applies to only gross wages and/or salaries. It does not include other income such as other government benefits, investment earnings, interest, pensions, annuities and capital gains. An employee's contribution to a pension or retirement plan, such as a 401(k) contribution, is included if the contribution amount is included in the employee's gross wages. If you work for wages, income counts when it is earned, not when it is paid. Accumulated sick or vacation pay and bonuses are

156

examples of earnings which might be earned in one year yet paid and received in another year.

If you are self-employed, the SSA only counts net earnings from self-employment. Income counts when you receive it not when you earn it, unless it is paid in a year after you become entitled to Social Security and earned it before you became entitled to benefits. The SSA also considers how much work you do in your business to determine if you are retired. In general, if you work more than 45 hours a month in self-employment, you are not retired. If you work less than 15 hours a month, you are retired. If you work between 15 and 45 hours a month, you will not be considered retired if it is in a job which requires a lot of skill or you are managing a sizable business. If other family members receive benefits based on your work history, your earnings from work you do after you start receiving retirement benefits could also reduce the benefits they are receiving.

Under federal law, individuals who are receiving Social Security benefits, who have not reached their FRA are entitled to receive all of their benefits as long as their earnings are under the earnings cap limits.

Earning Cap Restrictions – Before Full Retirement Age

If you were born from January 2, 1943 through January 1, 1955, your full retirement age is 66. Once you reach age 66, and are still working, you may keep all your benefits no matter how much you earn. However, anyone who collects Social Security benefits before they reach their FRA, while continuing to work will have their retirement benefits subject to an earnings cap restriction. This earnings cap penalizes individuals who collect any kind of Social Security benefits, whether retirement, spousal or survivor before their full retirement age while they continue to work. For 2014, you will lose $1 in benefits for every $2 earned over $15,480. This is $360 more than the 2013 earnings cap of $15,120. Income limits can change annually.

Example 3

A woman has turned age 62 in 2014 and is still working. She expects her salary for the year to be about $45,000. She wants to know if she now begins to collect early reduced retirement benefits, how much will be lost due to the earnings cap restriction. Since her salary is expected to be $45,000 for the year, which is $29,520 above the earnings cap restriction of $15,480 for 2014, she loses $1 in benefits for every $2 earned above this limit. Her lose in benefits is $14,760 for 2014. The calculation done is straight-forward ($45,000 - $15,480 = $29,520 / 2 = $14,760). If her reduced benefit is $1,230 or less each month, she will receive no Social Security payments because of the earnings cap.

Example 4

This is an example of someone who is turning age 62 and will be collecting Social Security benefits. A man files for Social Security benefits at age 62 in January 2014 and will receive a benefit of $600 per month or $7,200 for the year. During 2014, he expects to earn $20,800, which is $5,320 above the $15,480 earnings cap limit. Social Security would withhold $2,660 of his Social Security benefit, $1 for every $2 earned over the limit of $15,480 ($20,800 - $15,480 = $5,320 / 2 = $2,660). He would now only receive $4,540 (7,200 – 2,660) in benefits for the year. How is this done?

Social Security withholds all benefit payments until the full earnings cap reduction is satisfied. To do this Social Security would withhold all his benefit payments from January 2014 to May 2014. This is $340 over the amount which should be withheld. Beginning with June 2014, he will receive his $600 per month Social Security benefit for the remainder of the year. In January 2015, the excess $340 which was withheld in May 2014 will be repaid. The following table provides an idea of how much you will receive for the year 2014, based on your monthly benefits and estimated earnings.

158

Table 8.1 Individuals Less Than Full Retirement Age

Individuals Less Than Full Retirement Age During the
Entire Year

Your Monthly Social Security Benefit is	Your Earnings Are	You Will Receive Yearly Benefits of
$700	$15,480 or less	$8,400
$700	$16,000	$8,400
$700	$20,000	$6,140
$900	$15,480 or less	$10,800
$900	$16,000	$10,540
$900	$20,000	$8,540
$1,100	$15,480 or less	$13,200
$1,100	$16,000	$12,940
$1,100	$20,000	$10,940

Source: Social Security Administration; How Work Affects Your Benefits

Benefits forfeited due to the earnings cap are not lost
forever to the beneficiary. Those lost earnings are merely
deferred. Benefits will be increased at their FRA to account
for benefits which were withheld due to the earnings cap.
However, spouses and survivors who receive benefits
because they have minor or disabled children in their care
and are working and lose benefits due to the earnings test
will not get the adjustment to the reduction factor.

*Earning Cap Restrictions – The Calendar Year You Reach
Full Retirement Age*

A more generous earnings cap applies in the calendar year
you reach full retirement age and then disappears
completely once you cross that threshold of age 66. From
January 1st of the year in which you will turn 66, up to your
birthday, a Social Security beneficiary can earn up to
$41,400 in 2014. During this period you will lose $1 in

benefits for every $3 earned over the cap of $41,400. This is a $1,320 increase from the 2013 earnings cap of $40,080. At that point, you can continue to work while receiving Social Security benefits with no restrictions on earnings.

Example 5

This is an example of a woman who is not yet at her full retirement age at the beginning of the year but will reach it in October 2014 when she will turn age 66. We'll assume she filed for early Social Security benefits at age 65 in January 2014 and will receive a benefit of $600 per month or $7,200 for the year. Social Security determines she will earn $43,580 in the nine months from January to September. This is $2,180 over the more generous earnings cap. During this period Social Security will withhold $726.67 ($43,580 - $41,400 = $2,180 / 3) in benefits. Social Security withholds all benefit payments until the full earnings cap reduction is satisfied. To do this Social Security will withhold benefits for January and February 2014. Beginning in March 2014, she will receive her $600 per month Social Security benefit for the remainder of the year. In January 2015, the additional $473.33 ($600 + $600 - $726.67) that was withheld will be repaid. Benefits forfeited to the earnings cap are not lost forever to the beneficiary. Those lost earnings are merely deferred. Benefits will be increased a full retirement age to account for benefits which were withheld due to the earnings cap.

Recalculated Benefits at Full Retirement

If some of your retirement benefits were withheld during previous years because of your earnings, your monthly benefit will increase starting at your FRA. The SSA will recalculate your benefits once you reach your full retirement age to account for those deferred benefits. For example, you claim retirement benefits upon turning 62 in 2014 and your benefit payment from Social Security is $750 per month. You then return to work and have 12 months of benefits withheld due to the earnings cap restrictions. In four years, assuming your full retirement age is reached at 66, the SSA will recalculate your retirement benefit and pay you $800 per month (in today's dollars). Let's assume you earned so much during those four years, from 62 to 66, all benefits were withheld. In this case the SSA would pay you $1,000 per month starting at age 66.

Example 6

Let's now look at one last example and carry it completely through. Tom began collecting reduced retirement benefits at age 63, three years before he reaches his FRA. Three years have now passed and Tom decides to return to work. At this point he should contact the SSA and inform them he is planning to return to work and to estimate how much he will earn so his benefits can be adjusted if necessary. Tom will reach his FRA during the year and will turn 66 in November 2014.

Tom expects to earn $60,000 during the first 10 months of 2014. This is $18,600 ($60,000 − $41,400) over the $41,400 earnings limit for 2014. Let's assume Tom's retirement benefit has been $1,000 per month. In this example, the SSA would withhold $6,200 ($60,000 - $41,400 = $18,600 / 3 = $6,200) in benefits during 2014.

Social Security withholds all benefit payments until the full earnings cap reduction is satisfied. To do this Social Security would withhold all benefit payments from January to July 2014 ($1,000 x 7 months = $7,000). Beginning in August, Tom would receive his regular $1,000 Social Security benefit each month for the remainder of 2014. In January 2015, he will receive the excess $800 ($7,000 - $6,200) that was withheld from his benefits during 2014.

Once Tom reaches his full retirement his full retirement age of 66, the SSA will recalculate his benefits to give him credit for any months in which he did not receive some benefits because of his earnings. In addition, if Tom continues to work it could increase his future benefits if the most recent year of earnings replaces one of his lower earnings years. Social Security bases benefits on a worker's top 35 years of earnings during their working years.

In this example Tom's monthly retirement benefit in 2015 would be increased to reflect the fact that he forfeited seven months of benefits. As indicated earlier, Tom started collecting reduced benefits at age 63. Going forward, the SSA would recalculate his benefits as if he began collecting benefits at 63 and seven months, which would increase his primary insurance amount (PIA) by nearly 4% (7 months x 5/9ths = 3.8%). The percentage reduction for collecting retirement benefits early is 5/9ths of 1% per month for the first 36 months and then 5/12ths of 1% for each additional month before full retirement age.

Special Rule for the First Year You Retire

What happens if you decide to retire in mid-year and you already have earned more than the annual earnings limit? There is a special rule which applies to earnings for one year, which is usually the first year of retirement. Under the rule, a Social Security beneficiary can get a full benefit check for any whole month you are retired, regardless of your yearly earnings prior to claiming retirement benefits.

For 2014, a person younger than their full retirement age for the entire year is considered retired if monthly earnings are $1,290 or less. This is 1/12th of the monthly limit of the 2014 annual earnings limit of $15,480. For example, a man retires at age 62 on October 30, 2014, after he has earned $48,000 through October. He takes a part-time job in November and earns $700 per month. Although his earnings for the year were substantially above the earnings cap limit of $15,480, he will receive a Social Security benefit payment for November and December because his earnings in those last two months are less than $1,290, the monthly limit for individuals younger than full retirement age. Beginning in 2015, only the yearly limit would apply to him. Had he earned more than $1,290 in either of the two months he would not have received a benefit payment for the month.

Would the same logic apply if you were to retire during the calendar year in which you reach your full retirement age? The answer is yes, though the monthly limit is different. In this case you would take 1/12th of the monthly limit for the more generous earnings cap limit of $41,400 for 2014. This would be $3,450. The SSA would compute the individual's payments using both the annual and monthly limits. The individual will be paid using whichever method results in the best payment to him.

Increasing Benefits When You Work

Each year the SSA reviews the earnings records for all Social Security beneficiaries who work. If the most recent year worked turns out to be one of the highest years, the SSA will recalculate your benefit and pay you any increase due. This is an automatic process and those benefits are paid in December of the following year. For example, in December 2014, you should get an increase for your 2013 earnings, assuming you worked in 2013 and the amount earned replaced a lower earnings value from a previous year within the 35 years the SSA uses to calculate your benefits. The increase would be retroactive to January 2014.

Social Security Benefits and Federal Taxation

Once you reach your FRA, the earnings cap penalty completely disappears. At this point you are able to earn whatever income you want without that income affecting the monthly retirement benefit amount you receive from Social Security. We've also shown that depending on what your earnings history looks like, continuing to work after you begin receiving benefits could also increase the future benefits you might receive. However, when it comes to determining if your Social Security benefits are subject to federal taxation, the *Taxman* never disappears.

Provisional Income and Taxable Benefits

According to the SSA, about 40% of current Social Security beneficiaries pay taxes on their retirement benefits. Some individuals are exempt from having their benefits taxed. U.S. citizens who are residents of the following countries are exempt from the U.S. tax on their benefits.

- Canada
- Egypt
- Germany
- Ireland
- Israel
- Italy (must also be a citizen of Italy for the exemption to apply)
- Romania
- United Kingdom

Whether a beneficiary pays federal income tax on their retirement benefits depends on how much additional income the individual receives above and beyond the Social Security benefit. This additional income includes:

- Wages, salaries, tips, etc.
- Taxable and tax-exempt interest
- Dividends
- Pension benefits
- Investment income
- Other income
- 50% of the Social Security benefit

In other words, the IRS includes everything in determining your total income. Use Figure 8.1, on the next page, to refer to income line items which may be discussed.

Figure 8.1 IRS 2013 Federal Tax Form 1040

Form **1040** Department of the Treasury—Internal Revenue Service (99)
U.S. Individual Income Tax Return 2013 OMB No. 1545-0074 IRS Use Only—Do not write or staple in this space.

For the year Jan. 1–Dec. 31, 2013, or other tax year beginning , 2013, ending , 20 | See separate instructions.

Your first name and initial | Last name | Your social security number

If a joint return, spouse's first name and initial | Last name | Spouse's social security number

Home address (number and street). If you have a P.O. box, see instructions. | Apt. no. | ▲ Make sure the SSN(s) above and on line 6c are correct.

City, town or post office, state, and ZIP code. If you have a foreign address, also complete spaces below (see instructions).

Foreign country name | Foreign province/state/county | Foreign postal code

Presidential Election Campaign
Check here if you, or your spouse if filing jointly, want $3 to go to this fund. Checking a box below will not change your tax or refund. ☐ You ☐ Spouse

Filing Status

Check only one box.

1 ☐ Single
2 ☐ Married filing jointly (even if only one had income)
3 ☐ Married filing separately. Enter spouse's SSN above and full name here. ▶
4 ☐ Head of household (with qualifying person). (See instructions.) If the qualifying person is a child but not your dependent, enter this child's name here. ▶
5 ☐ Qualifying widow(er) with dependent child

Exemptions

6a ☐ **Yourself.** If someone can claim you as a dependent, **do not** check box 6a
b ☐ **Spouse**
c **Dependents:**

(1) First name Last name	(2) Dependent's social security number	(3) Dependent's relationship to you	(4) ✓ if child under age 17 qualifying for child tax credit (see instructions)
			☐
			☐
			☐
			☐

If more than four dependents, see instructions and check here ▶ ☐

d Total number of exemptions claimed

Boxes checked on 6a and 6b
No. of children on 6c who:
• lived with you
• did not live with you due to divorce or separation (see instructions)
Dependents on 6c not entered above
Add numbers on lines above ▶

Income

Attach Form(s) W-2 here. Also attach Forms W-2G and 1099-R if tax was withheld.

If you did not get a W-2, see instructions.

7 Wages, salaries, tips, etc. Attach Form(s) W-2 — 7
8a **Taxable** interest. Attach Schedule B if required — 8a
b **Tax-exempt** interest. **Do not** include on line 8a — 8b
9a Ordinary dividends. Attach Schedule B if required — 9a
b Qualified dividends — 9b
10 Taxable refunds, credits, or offsets of state and local income taxes — 10
11 Alimony received — 11
12 Business income or (loss). Attach Schedule C or C-EZ — 12
13 Capital gain or (loss). Attach Schedule D if required. If not required, check here ▶ ☐ — 13
14 Other gains or (losses). Attach Form 4797 — 14
15a IRA distributions — 15a — b Taxable amount — 15b
16a Pensions and annuities — 16a — b Taxable amount — 16b
17 Rental real estate, royalties, partnerships, S corporations, trusts, etc. Attach Schedule E — 17
18 Farm income or (loss). Attach Schedule F — 18
19 Unemployment compensation — 19
20a Social security benefits — 20a — b Taxable amount — 20b
21 Other income. List type and amount — 21
22 Combine the amounts in the far right column for lines 7 through 21. This is your **total income** ▶ — 22

Adjusted Gross Income

23 Educator expenses — 23
24 Certain business expenses of reservists, performing artists, and fee-basis government officials. Attach Form 2106 or 2106-EZ — 24
25 Health savings account deduction. Attach Form 8889 — 25
26 Moving expenses. Attach Form 3903 — 26
27 Deductible part of self-employment tax. Attach Schedule SE — 27
28 Self-employed SEP, SIMPLE, and qualified plans — 28
29 Self-employed health insurance deduction — 29
30 Penalty on early withdrawal of savings — 30
31a Alimony paid b Recipient's SSN ▶ — 31a
32 IRA deduction — 32
33 Student loan interest deduction — 33
34 Tuition and fees. Attach Form 8917 — 34
35 Domestic production activities deduction. Attach Form 8903 — 35
36 Add lines 23 through 35 — 36
37 Subtract line 36 from line 22. This is your **adjusted gross income** ▶ — 37

For Disclosure, Privacy Act, and Paperwork Reduction Act Notice, see separate instructions. Cat. No. 11320B Form **1040** (2013)

Source: Internal Revenue Service; 2013 Form 1040

The percentage of the Social Security benefit, on which the federal income tax is applied, is based on a sliding scale depending on how much outside income the individual or couple has beyond their benefit(s). If the combined income for a single individual is between $25,000 and $34,000, up to 50% of the Social Security benefit is subject to tax. Your base amount is $25,000. If the amount is more than $34,000, up to 85% of the benefit is taxable.

For a married couple filing jointly, if the combined income limit is between $32,000 and $44,000, up to 50% of the benefits are taxable. Your base amount is $32,000. Above $44,000, up to 85% of the benefits are taxable.

Taxes are never applied on all their Social Security benefits no matter how much an individual earns. The maximum amount ever subject to income tax is 85% of the benefit.

Taxability of your Social Security Benefits

To determine if any of your Social Security benefits may be taxable, you need to compare your base amounts for your filing status with the total of:

1. 50% of your Social Security benefits, plus
2. All your other income, including tax-exempt interest.

When making this comparison, do not reduce any of your other income by exclusions, including those for:

- Interest from qualified U.S. savings bonds.
- Employer-provided adoption benefits.
- Foreign earned income or foreign housing.
- Income earned by bona fide residents of American Samoa or Puerto Rico.

Use the Table 8.2, on the next page, to figure the amount of income to compare with your base amounts listed previously. This provides a quick check to see whether some of your benefits may be taxable.

Table 8.2 Taxable Benefit Worksheet

	Check if Your Benefits May Be Taxable	Amounts
A	Enter the amount from **Box 5** of all Forms SSA-1099 and RRB-1099. Include the full amount of any lump-sum benefit payments received in 2013, for 2013 and earlier years	
B	Enter 50% of the amount on line A.	
C	Enter your taxable income. Include taxable pensions, wages, interest, dividends and other taxable income.	
D	Enter any tax-exempt interest income plus exclusions from income.	
E	Add lines B, C and D.	

Source: Internal Revenue Service; Publication Form 1040

Compare the amount on line E, to your base amount for your filing status. If the amount on line E equals or is less than the base amount for your filing status, none of your benefits are taxable this year. If the amount on line E is more than your base amount, some of your benefits may be taxable and you'll need to complete another worksheet to determine the amount to include on your federal income tax return.

NOTE: Below is a template of Worksheet 1 from the IRS Publication 915. This worksheet does NOT work in all situations. If you received a lump-sum in 2013 that was for an earlier year, you will need to also complete Worksheet 2 or 3 and Worksheet 4 to see if you can report a lower taxable benefit. **Always consult with your tax professional.**

Before you begin:

- If you are married filing separately and you lived apart from your spouse for all of 2013, enter "D" to the right of the word "benefits" on Form 1040, line 20a, or Form 1040A, line 14a.
- Do not use this worksheet if you repaid benefits in 2013 and your total repayments (box 4 of Forms SSA-1099 and RRB-1099) were more than your gross benefits for 2013 (box 3 of Forms SSA-1099 and RRB-1099). None of your benefits are taxable for 2013. For more information, see Repayments More Than Gross Benefits.
- If you are filing Form 8815, Exclusion of Interest From Series EE and I U.S. Savings Bonds Issued After 1989, do not include the amount from line 8a of Form 1040 or Form 1040A on line 3 of this worksheet. Instead, include the amount from Schedule B (Form 1040A or 1040), line 2.

1. Enter the total amount from box 5 of ALL your Forms SSA-1099 and RRB-1099. Also enter this amount on Form 1040, line 20a, or Form 1040A, line 14a **1.** _____

2. Enter one-half of line 1 . . . . **2.** _____

3. Combine the amounts from:

- **Form 1040:** Lines 7, 8a, 9a, 10 through 14, 15b, 16b, 17 through 19, and 21
- **Form 1040A:** Lines 7, 8a, 9a, 10, 11b, 12b, and 13. . . . . **3.** _____

4. Enter the amount, if any, from Form 1040 or 1040A, line 8b . . . . **4.** _____

5. Enter the total of any exclusions/adjustments for:

- Adoption benefits (Form 8839, line 28),
- Foreign earned income or housing (Form 2555, lines 45 and 50, or Form 2555-EZ, line 18), and
- Certain income of bona fide residents of American Samoa (Form 4563, line 15) or Puerto Rico . . . . **5.** _____

6. Combine lines 2, 3, 4, and 5 . . . . **6.** _____

7. Form 1040 filers: Enter the amounts from Form 1040, lines 23 through 32, and any write-in adjustments you entered on the dotted line next to line 36.
Form 1040A filers: Enter the amounts from Form 1040A, lines 16 and 17 . . . . **7.** _____

8. Is the amount on line 7 less than the amount on line 6?
No. STOP None of your social security benefits are taxable. Enter -0- on Form 1040, line 20b, or Form 1040A, line 14b.
Yes. Subtract line 7 from line 6 . . . . **8.** _____

9. If you are:

- Married filing jointly, enter $32,000
- Single, head of household, qualifying widow(er) or married filing separately and you lived apart from your spouse for all of 2013, enter $25,000. . . . . **9.** _____

Note. If you are married filing separately and you lived with your spouse at any time in 2013, skip lines 9 through 16; multiply line 8 by 85% (.85) and enter the result on line 17. Then go to line 18.

10. Is the amount on line 9 less than the amount on line 8?
No. STOP None of your benefits are taxable. Enter -0- on Form 1040, line 20b, or on Form 1040A line 14b. If you are married filing separately and you lived apart from your spouse for all of 2013, be sure you entered "D" to the right

of the word "benefits" on Form 1040, line 20a, or on Form 1040A, line 14a.

Yes. Subtract line 9 from line 8 . . . . **10.** _____

11. Enter $12,000 if married filing jointly; $9,000 if single, head of household, qualifying widow(er), or married filing separately and you lived apart from your spouse for all of 2013 . . . . **11.** _____

12. Subtract line 11 from line 10. If zero or less, enter -0- . . . . **12.** _____

13. Enter the smaller of line 10 or line 11 . . . . **13.** _____

14. Enter one-half of line 13 . . . . **14.** _____

15. Enter the smaller of line 2 or line 14 . . . . **15.** _____

16. Multiply line 12 by 85% (.85). If line 12 is zero, enter -0- . . . . **16.** _____

17. Add lines 15 and 16 . . . . **17.** _____

18. Multiply line 1 by 85% (.85) . . . . **18.** _____

19. Taxable benefits. Enter the smaller of line 17 or line 18. Also enter this amount on Form 1040, line 20b, or Form 1040A, line 14b . . . . **19.** _____

Which Worksheet to Use

A worksheet which can be used to figure your taxable benefits is in the instructions for Form 1040 or 1040A. You can use either that worksheet or Worksheet 1 in IRS Publication 915, unless any of the following situations applies to you.

1. You contributed to a traditional individual retirement arrangement (IRA) and you or your spouse is covered by a retirement plan at work. In this situation you must use the special worksheets in Appendix B of Publication 590 to figure both your IRA deduction and your taxable benefits.
2. Situation (1) does not apply and you take an exclusion for interest from qualified U.S. savings bonds (Form 8815), for adoption benefits (Form 8839), for foreign earned income or housing (Form 2555 or Form 2555-EZ), or for income earned in American Sa-moa (Form 4563) or Puerto Rico by bona fide residents. In this situation, you must use Worksheet 1 in this publication to figure your taxable benefits.
3. You received a lump-sum payment for an earlier year. In this situation, also complete Worksheet 2 or 3 and Worksheet 4 in this publication.

See IRS Publication 915, *Social Security and Equivalent Railroad Retirement Benefits* at www.irs.gov/pub/irs-pdf/p915.pdf for a further detailed explanation of the associated tax implications. Within the publication there are several situational examples which can be reviewed.

"Today, middle class and low-income seniors rely on Social Security for the majority of their retirement income, while workers 50 to 64 are increasingly unprepared for retirement."

Sherrod Brown
Democratic U.S. Senator – Ohio
U.S. House of Representatives – Ohio's 13th District
47th Secretary of State – Ohio
Ohio House of Representatives – 61st District

CHAPTER NINE

SOCIAL SECURITY IN A ZIRP WORLD

I entered the investment industry, specifically the fixed income side, during the early 1980s. At the time bank money market rates were in the low 20% range, U.S. Treasury bonds were in the mid-teens and mortgage rates were in the high teens. Inflation rates were near 10% and the economy was in recession, struggling to find a footing.

Fast-forward nearly thirty years later to 2008. Bear Sterns had a shotgun wedding with JP Morgan Chase. Fannie Mae and Freddie Mac were essentially nationalized by the U.S. Government. Lehman Brothers, once one of the premier investment banks in the world failed and it appears Merrill Lynch was shoved into the arms of Bank of America, which at the time was struggling with its Countrywide Financial merger, the largest mortgage lender in the U.S. The U.S. financial system was on the verge of a meltdown and the contagion had spread to Europe. Was the global financial system coming to an end as we know it? Well we all know how the story ended – or do we? A little more than five years have now passed, but for many the recovery and the American economy just don't feel right.

U.S. Treasury Yields in a ZIRP Environment

In response to an escalating crisis at hand, the Federal Reserve adopted two monetary policy measures which hadn't been used before in dealing with previous financial stresses in the economy. One tool was to engineer a significant reduction in interest rates by implementing ZIRP. ZIRP stands for Zero Interest Rate Policy, a method of stimulating economic growth by keeping interest rates close to zero. Under this policy, the Federal Reserve maintains a 0% or close to zero nominal interest rate. Japan was to first to use this measure to deal with its own sustained long-term deflation issues.

The second tool is QE. QE stands for Quantitative Easing, whereby the Federal Reserve expands its own balance sheet by purchasing U.S. Government and mortgage-backed securities, providing liquidity to the banking system. In the nearly 6 years, the Federal Reserve's balance sheet has grown from $906 billion, at the beginning of September 2008, to just over $4.4 trillion at the end of July 2014. The Fed has continued with these two policy measures since the end of 2008, though they have begun to taper their bond purchases.

It's beyond the scope of this book to provide a deep analysis of the success of these tools since the Great Financial Recession. As a result of the Fed pursuing this monetary policy, long-term interest rates have fallen to historic lows and have now remained near historic lows for an extended period of time. During this period we have seen real interest rates at zero percent and for brief periods even negative. The real interest rate is the rate of interest an investor expects to receive after allowing for inflation. It is the nominal interest rate minus the inflation rate. During most of 2013, real interest rates have hovered between 1% and 1.5%. The following charts are yields of selected U.S. Treasury securities and the Consumer Price Index.

Figure 9.1 2-Year Constant Maturity Rate

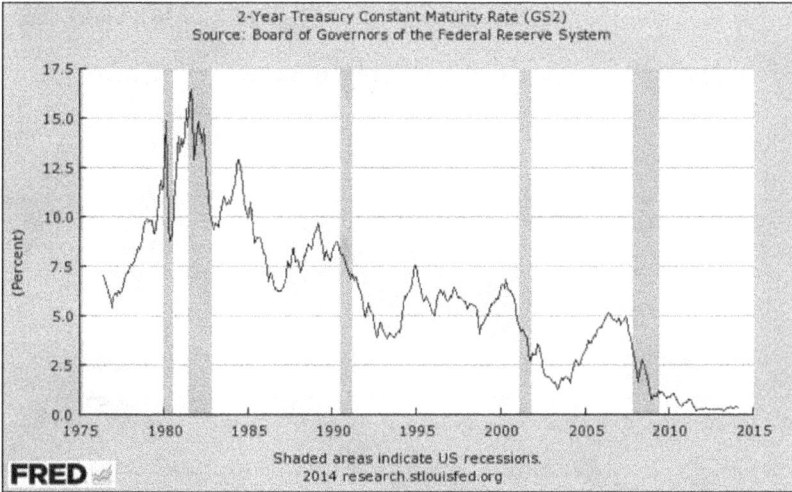

Source: Federal Reserve Bank of St. Louis; H15 Selected Interest Rates

Figure 9.2 10-Year Constant Maturity Rate

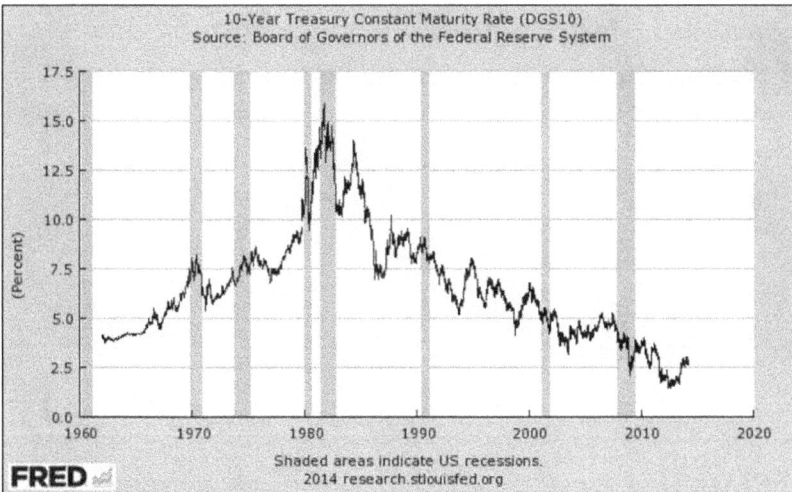

Source: Federal Reserve Bank of St. Louis; H15 Selected Interest Rates

Figure 9.3 CPI: All Urban Consumers

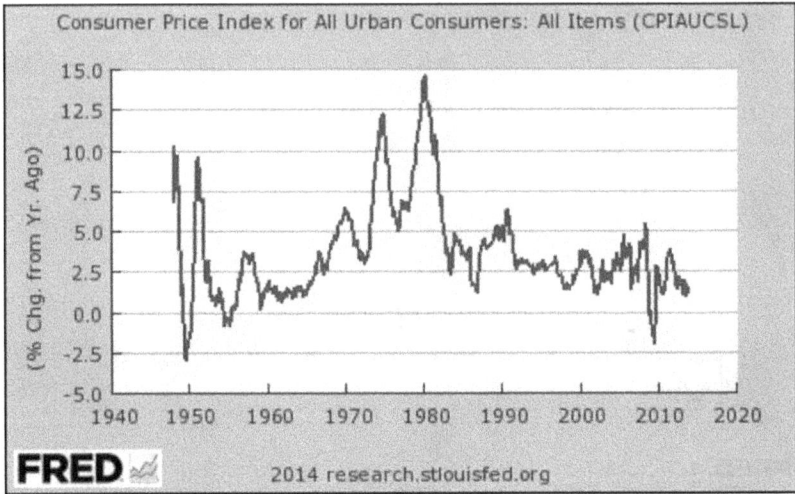

Source: Federal Reserve Bank of St. Louis; All Urban Consumers Index

Figure 9.4 5-Year Treasury Inflation-Index Security

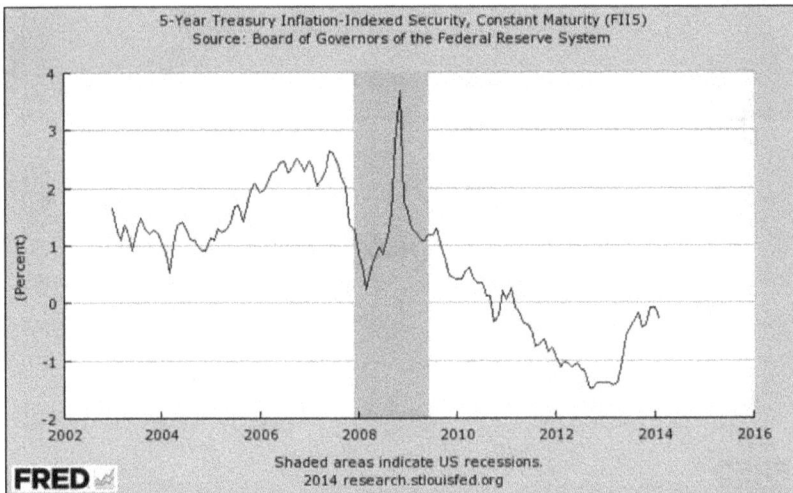

Source: Federal Reserve Bank of St. Louis; H15 Selected Interest Rates

Figure 9.5 10-Year Treasury Inflation-Indexed Security

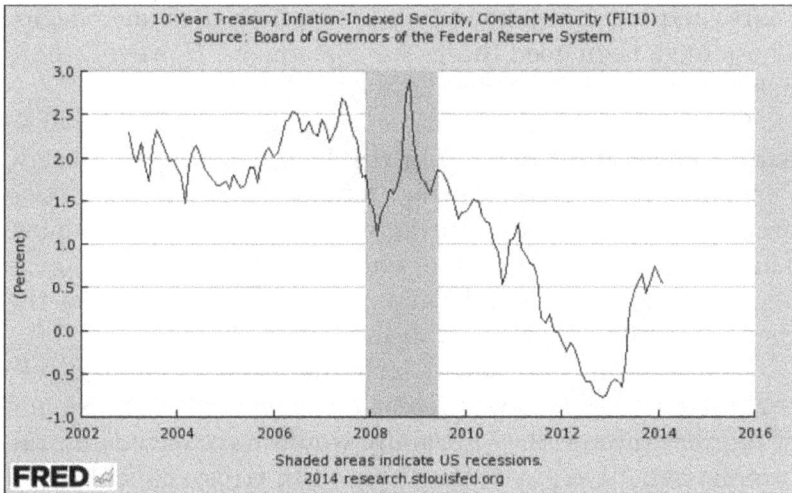

Source: Federal Reserve Bank of St. Louis; H15 Selected Interest Rates

Figures 9.4 and 9.5 display the 5 and 10 year charts of Treasury Inflation-Indexed Securities (TIPS), respectively. TIPS provide protection against inflation. TIPS principal increases with inflation and decreases with deflation, as measured by the Consumer Price Index. When TIPS mature, you are paid the adjusted principal or original principal, whichever is greater. TIPS pay interest twice a year, at a fixed rate. The rate is applied to the adjusted principal so, like the principal, interest payments rise with inflation and fall with deflation.

The Dark Side of ZIRP

Monetary stimulus is supposed to bolster the economy through several channels. With lower interest rates businesses and individuals should borrow and spend more on large ticket items. Low interest rates, in theory, should drive the value of the dollar lower international, making American made products cheaper relative to foreign ones. Mortgage rates have fallen dramatically over the last 5 years, helping many households refinance their mortgages. These have been good things for consumers. However, there has been a downside to living in a ZIRP world.

On the institutional side, current monetary policy has had a devastating impact on the long-term care industry. Portfolio yields are down, forcing insurers to raise premiums dramatically during the 2012-2013 time frames. This is occurring at a time when our aging population is beginning to grow rapidly and chronic diseases are on the rise, especially neurological degenerative disorders.

On the retail side, savers have just been hammered over the last few years. Low interest rates have deprived savers of interest income they normally would have earned on the interest-sensitive assets they hold. Bill Gross, co-founder of PIMCO and manager of the world's largest bond fund calls what the Fed's monetary policy is doing to America's retired as "financial repression". In July 2011, William F. Ford, Ph.D., professor of macroeconomics and monetary economics at Middle Tennessee State University and a former President of the Federal Reserve Bank of Atlanta, published a paper titled, "The Downside of Monetary Easing". The paper discussed the negative impact low interest rates could potential have on savers and in turn, the economy. By Ford's most conservative estimate, by the end of the second quarter of 2010, the volume of interest sensitive assets directly held by U.S. households totaled about $9.9 trillion. If you then add in what life insurance companies and pensions own in interest-sensitive assets, the pool of assets was estimated to be $18.8 trillion.

Table 9.1 illustrates Ford's estimates of the possible losses in spending power, output and employment generated by the Fed's artificially low interest rates, which he calls lost opportunities. The average yield on Treasury's in June 2010 was 2.14% compared to an average of 7.07% in the previous nine recoveries, a difference of 4.93%.

Table 9.1 Lost Opportunities, Estimated Annual Effect of
Low Yields on Savers and the Economy

Measures of total assets sensitive to the Treasury yield curve.	Gains resulting from a 1 percentage point increase in yields.	Gains resulting from increasing yields by 4.93 percentage points to the average level observed in the last nine past recoveries.
Lower bound $9.9 trillion	$52 billion of consumption 0.35% of GDP 493,000 jobs	$256 billion of consumption 1.75% of GDP 2.4 million jobs
Midpoint $14.35 trillion	$75 billion of consumption 0.51% of GDP 715,000 jobs	$371 billion of consumption 2.53% of GDP 3.5 million jobs
Upper bound $18.8 trillion	$99 billion of consumption 0.67% of GDP 936,000 jobs	$587 billion of consumption 3.32% of GDP 4.6 million jobs

Source: Ford, William F.; The Downside of Monetary Easing

According to Ford's estimates, the projected annual impact
of this loss of interest income on just $9.9 trillion of
interest-sensitive assets translates into $256 billion of lost
consumption, a 1.75% loss of GDP and about 2.4 million
fewer jobs. The first column shows the estimated effect on
the economy for every one percentage point reduction in
interest rates. If rates drop by two percentage points, the
effect would be double that presented in column one.

Rethinking the Retirement Dilemma

Individuals and couples now have to rethink the entire
retirement planning process. Generating near risk-free
income in a ZIRP world is much more challenging. Let's
begin with the following situation which highlights what
was just discussed. I'm going to keep this very simple, back
of an envelope simple.

Before the year 2000, someone who was just about to retire could be relatively assured they could get a return of 6% - 8% annually without taking a great deal of investment risk. For someone with $500,000 in savings, that would generate an income stream of $30,000 to $40,000 of interest income each year without withdrawing any principal. For a couple, add in another $24,000 in Social Security benefits and you now have a simplified income stream of $54,000 to $64,000 each year. If you had $1,000,000 in savings, the income stream generated would be $84,000 to $104,000 annually, including the same amount of Social Security benefits. Not too bad for taking relatively little interest rate risk in your portfolio.

How things have now change. For nearly the last five years, living in a ZIRP world for many retirees has been nothing short of a nightmare. What do those same numbers look like now? Today, you might be hard pressed to get 1% without taking some investment risk. For someone with the same $500,000 in savings, that would now generate an income stream of just $5,000 of interest income without withdrawing any principal. For the couple, add in the same $24,000 in Social Security benefits and your annual income stream now is just a paltry $29,000. If you had $1,000,000 in savings, the income stream generated would be $34,000, including the same level of Social Security benefits! Assuming neither couple still works, the first couple has lost between $25,000 and $35,000 of interest income. That's a 46% to 55% decline in household income. The second couple has lost between $50,000 and $70,000 of interest income. That's a 59% to 67% decline in household income. Is it any wonder why so many middle-class Americans are struggling and unsure about their future retirement?

The New Retirement Paradigm

We've been conditioned to believe that in accumulating assets for retirement, we should put as much money as we can into tax-deferred investment vehicles such as 401(k)s and traditional IRAs and worry about the tax consequences later when we're told we'll be in a lower tax bracket. Then when you get to retirement you're told to try to defer those tax-deferred investment withdrawals as long as possible to avoid paying the federal income taxes.

Living in a ZIRP world has turned traditional retirement income planning upside down. Today, this may be the exact wrong advice to be following at this particular point in history. Optimizing retirement income cashflows requires an integration of tax planning which is absolutely essential in extending the longevity of these cashflows while in retirement. The goal is to extend your portfolio longevity. Trying to accomplish this without fully understanding Social Security benefits and integrating various claiming strategies into your retirement plan could just be hazardous to your financial health. Unfortunately, most individuals don't fully appreciate the importance of what Social Security planning can do for them BEFORE they claim. As we have seen earlier, the importance of Social Security for a growing portion of retirees has become significant. For many it is now the foundation of their financial plan, not just a supplement to it any longer.

Rethinking this traditional process postulates the fact that tapping these tax-deferred accounts to fund the initial years of retirement and delaying Social Security benefits until they are worth more could translate into smaller taxes payable in the later years of retirement when positive cashflows can be the greatest concern for most retirees, especially women due to the fact they live longer, on average. It requires a balancing act.

The threshold income amounts discussed in the previous chapter are not indexed for inflation, meaning more Social Security benefits are taxed each year due to COLA increases. If an individual is withdrawing from a pool of money which was tax-deferred, in addition to their Social Security benefits, a retiree in the 25% tax bracket could pay a 46.25% marginal rate on each dollar of income above these threshold amounts of $34,000 for singles and

$44,000 for married couples, for 2014. That translates into less real American dollars for you to do with as you choose.

By delaying Social Security benefits, many individuals may pay little to no taxes when a combination of higher Social Security benefits and a smaller IRA withdrawal, replaces the same level of needed retirement income. Only 50% of Social Security income counts in the provisional income formula while all traditional IRA income and even tax-exempt municipal bond interest income is included. A married couple could have up to $64,000 of Social Security benefits count as only $32,000 in the provisional income formula before they would cross the first threshold which renders up to 50% of their Social Security benefits subject to federal income taxes.

Example 7

Assume a retired couple claims their Social Security benefits early. They collect $45,000 in benefits and withdrawing $45,000 from their traditional IRAs for a total income stream of $90,000. Based on the provisional income formula, they would have taxable income of $70,975.

What happens if they rely on their savings to initial fund their retirement and delay Social Security until age 70. By collecting delayed retirement credits and COLA increases, their benefit level is now $70,000. They would need just $20,000 from IRAs to fund the needed $90,000. With the preferential inclusion of Social Security benefits, their taxable income will be just $35,350. When considering both federal and state taxes, many retirees could see a 75% reduction in taxes paid.

Actuarial Nature of Social Security

When the U.S. Government set up the structure of the Social Security system, their original intent was to provide actuarially fair adjustments. What this means is individuals can expect to receive the same present value of

182

benefits regardless of when they claim. Those who don't expect to live a long time would benefit by claiming their retirement benefits early while those who expect to live a long time would be better off delaying.

It has been many years since these factors were updated for changes in interest rates or mortality rates. Since 1950, male and female mortality has increased by six years and interest rates which were typically 2% to 3% are now close to 1% to 2%. As a result, these mortality improvements and a lower interest rate environment have turned adjustments, which used to be actuarially fair, into strong incentives to delay Social Security benefits. For now at least, living in a ZIRP world has changed the dynamics of Social Security planning as we will see in the following sections.

Commercial Annuities

Many individuals cringe at the thought of the word annuity because they envision an insurance product which they don't understand and which they think costs too much. We're going to use the term commercial annuity, synonymously with any annuity which you can buy from a life insurance company. When buying an annuity, it's also extremely important to understand the financial strength of the insurance company who issues the annuity. The guarantee is only as good as the financial health of the insurance company which issues it, not who sells it to you.

When you make an investment in an annuity, the annuity makes payments to you immediately, on a future date or on a series of dates. The income you receive from the annuity can be monthly, quarterly, annually or even in a lump sum. The size of your income payments are determined by a variety of factors, including the initial amount of your investment, any subsequent amounts you add and the length of your payment period. This could be for a set number of years or the rest of your life and that of a surviving spouse. The last item which affects income payments is whether you want a guaranteed payout, as in a fixed annuity, or a payout stream which is determined by the performance of an underlying investment as in a variable annuity.

The investment you make in a non-qualified annuity grows tax-deferred. Unlike other tax-deferred investments such as 401(k)s and traditional IRAs, there are no annual contribution limits for investing in them. When you begin to take withdrawals, the amount you originally contributed is not taxed but the earnings are taxed as ordinary income. Each income payment received is composed of two payments. One is considered a return of capital, which is non-taxable and the other is considered earnings on income, which is taxable at ordinary rates. The formula for determining the non-taxable portion of each year's payment is as follows: investment in the contract / expected return. This formula is called the exclusion ratio.

For example, assume a 60 year old individual purchases an annuity. His investment in the contact is $12,000. Assume his expected return is $19,200. The exclusion ratio is 62.5% ($12,000 / $19,200 x 100%). If he receives $100 per month from the annuity, $62.50 is a return of capital and is non-taxable while the remaining $37.50 is considered earnings and is taxable as ordinary income. If the investment in the contract equals or exceeds the expected return, the full amount of each payment is received tax-free. However, if the **contract was purchased after December 31, 1986**, the excludable amount is limited to the investment in the contract. Once that amount is fully recovered all future annuity payments are considered taxable as ordinary income.

As it relates to Social Security, we're going to only discuss two basic types of fixed annuities: immediate and deferred. As individuals get closer to retirement, these annuities have become attractive in generating a guaranteed monthly income stream.

With a single premium immediate annuity (SPIA), you begin to receive payments soon after you make the initial lump-sum investment. You can choose between a single-life or joint-life annuity. With single-life you receive income payments for as long as you live. With joint-life, the annuity guarantees income payments as long as either of the two individuals is alive. You can choose guaranteed income payments for a fixed period of time or some annuities have a refund option. With the refund option if the payments over your lifetime total less than the amount of your annuity purchase, your beneficiaries get the remaining balance paid in a lump-sum. Annuities usually also offer inflation-adjusted payments which move up or down based on changes in the Consumer Price Index (CPI-U).

With a deferred income annuity (DIF) the money is invested for a period of time until you're ready to begin making withdrawals. During this period, both the interest rate and your principal are guaranteed by the insurance company which issues the annuity. Earnings are tax-deferred as long as there are no withdrawals.

There can be disadvantages to investing in annuities which increase their costs. Annuities from life insurance companies have to factor in marketing, management and risk-bearing costs into the prices they change investors. Some of these are easy to find while others can be buried in the fine print. Fees for variable annuities are usually higher than they are for fixed annuities. These fees include:

- Commissions
- Surrender charges
- Annual insurance charge
- Annual investment management fees
- Insurance riders

When added up they can range from 2% to 3% each year. Issuers can also adjust their annuity terms. This can include making payouts less generous when mortality improves, which increases the expected payout by the issuer or when interest rates fall, which decreases the investment returns the issuer can earn on the funds which generate income streams to the consumers who purchase them. Fees are always something investors need to be aware of. Like any service or product you buy, you need to do a cost/benefit analysis. Is what you're paying worth the benefit you are receiving? An annuity is an insurance contract. What's disclosed in the contract is very important to understand, as an investor in any insurance product.

Yet despite all the negatives investors speak of and the low interest rates which are being paid, LIMRA just released data in February 2014, which showed for the full year 2013, annuity sales were $230.1 billion, a 5% increase over 2012. Demand for pure income annuity products are at record levels. Total fixed annuities sales grew 17 percent in 2013, totaling $84.8 billion. Deferred income annuity (DIF) sales grew to $2.2 billion, more than double 2012 results, up 113%. Sales of single premium immediate annuities (SPIA) hit a record $8.3 billion, which is 8 percent higher than in 2012. Variable annuities had sales of $145 billion in 2013, marking a decline from 2012.

The Annuity Dilemma

One of the biggest fears among those who have either retired or are nearing retirement is the fear of running out of money. The parallel which many individuals do not understand is that Social Security is the forgotten annuity.

Let's say I briefly describe a product with the following features and benefits to you. The issuer is the federal government, it allows you to claim a benefit at different ages, it has a step-up earnings adjustment which allows you to earn an extra 8% for up to four additional years at no cost to you, it guarantees an income for life, it has built in inflation protection at no cost to you and comes with a survivor option. What would you think? Most individuals would probably want to ask more questions but for the most part you would probably think this is a pretty good product. What is it you may ask?

Well, I just broadly described Social Security to you. Social Security has many attributes like that of an annuity, which is sold by a life insurance company. How much you get in income depends on how much you have in your earnings record, if you continue to work and when you decide to claim benefits. Yet, many individuals make significant mistakes when it comes to claiming their benefits because they don't look at it as though it were an annuity, which co-exists in your portfolio of other investment products you own to generate income for you when you retire. These mistakes can include:

- Claiming reduced early benefits.
- Underestimating the value of those benefits.
- Improperly integrating their benefits as a married couple.
- Not understanding the tax implication associated with working and/or receiving benefits.

Some planners or advisors may try to allocate Social Security's cashflows as part of a bond-like investment. I don't favor that approach because a bond, unless it is issued in perpetuity, has a finite maturity date. You can sell a bond before maturity you can't sell your Social Security benefits. A bond has no survivor option while Social Security does.

When looking at it from the perspective of an annuity, Social Security adjustments are based on the life expectancy of an average individual. Many annuities tend to have above-average life expectancy and the cost of providing the yearly income is priced accordingly. The reality is your Social Security retirement benefit is really a *hybrid* inflation-adjusted immediate annuity with a survivor option. I use the term hybrid, mainly because of the taxation differences and the way the survivor benefit is structured between Social Security and a commercially available annuity. While the differences between Social Security and annuities may seem subtle, in a ZIRP world they can be quite significant.

Buy the Social Security Annuity NOT the Commercial Immediate Annuity in a ZIRP Environment

This section deviates into the world of academia for the moment. Some readers may find the research analysis and math involved boring and even confusing. If so, you can skip to the summary section near the end of this chapter.

Over the last four years, there have been several well written research papers. These papers make very cogent arguments as to the value of delayed retirement credits, when looked at in terms of investment returns and especially when compared to the returns on immediate annuities in today's low interest rate environment. We should all know by now the value of delaying your retirement benefits until you reach age 70. For each year you wait, after reaching your FRA, you earn delayed retirement credits worth 8% each year, not compounded, until you turn age 70. For someone with an FRA at 66, this is an additional 32% increase in retirement benefits over the four years, not including any COLA's received. Those investors who are choosing to buy a commercial immediate annuity in today's ZIRP world may be making an investment decision which does not optimize their annuity cashflows. In other words, it may be a poor use of your investible assets.

1. Research by William Meyer and Dr. William Reichenstein, Ph.D., CFA

In March 2010, Bill Meyer, founder and CEO of Social Security Solutions and Bill Reichenstein, Ph.D., CFA, investment professor at Baylor University and also head of research at Social Security Solutions, published a paper in the Journal of Financial Planning titled, "*Social Security: When to Start Benefits and How to Minimize Longevity Risk*".

In the paper, the authors examine strategies for singles and couples utilizing two criteria. The first is which

188

starting date or dates maximize the present value of retirement benefits through life expectancies. The second objective analyzed was which starting date or dates will minimize longevity risk. This is the risk of outliving your resources.

The authors conclude from their research, for single taxpayers with average life expectancies, who will not be subject to earnings cap restrictions, the present value of retirement benefits is approximately the same no matter when retirement benefits begin. Those with short life expectancies should considering claiming early while those with longer than average life expectancies should consider delay claiming of retirement benefits. For couples creating a strategy, which maximizes Social Security retirement benefits and is sensitive to longevity risk, this can generate a larger cumulative income stream in retirement. The relevant life expectancy for the claiming decision involving the spouse with the higher primary insurance amount (PIA) and earnings record should be the lifetime of the second spouse to die. The relevant life expectancy for the claiming decision involving the spouse with the lower PIA and earnings record should be the lifetime of the first spouse to die. If it is the husband who has the highest earnings record and PIA and if at least one spouse lives well beyond the age that the husband turns age 80, then the couples cumulative lifetime benefits will be higher if he delays retirement benefits until age 70.

2. Research by Dr. John B. Shoven, Ph.D. and Dr. Sita Nataraj Slavov, Ph.D.

John Shoven is an economics professor at Stanford University. Nataraj Slavov is an economist and researcher at the American Enterprise Institute. In 2012, the pair published two excellent working papers which delve into the theory of how low interest rates change the perception many individuals have regarding the claiming of Social Security benefits.

In their first paper, published February 2012, in the Bureau of Economic Research, titled "*The Decision to Delay Social Security Benefits: Theory and Evidence*", the authors investigate the actuarial fairness of the adjustment Social Security makes when a beneficiary makes the decision to delay claiming benefits past their FRA. The simulations which were completed suggest that delaying is actuarially advantageous for a large segment of individuals, particularly for real interest rates of 3.5% or lower. The gains from delaying are greater for lower interest rates, for married couples relative to singles, for single women relative to single men and for two-earner couples relative to one-earner couples.

The authors also used panel data from the Health and Retirement Study to investigate whether individuals' actual claiming behavior appears to be influenced by the degree of actuarial advantage to delaying. They found no evidence of a consistent relationship between claiming behavior and factors that influence the actuarial advantage of delay, including gender and marital status, interest rates, subjective discount rates, or subjective assessments of life expectancy.

In the second paper published July 2012, also in the Bureau of Economic Research, titled "*When Does it Pay to Delay Social Security? The Impact of Mortality, Interest Rates and Program Rules*", their work illustrates the concept that for many retirees, in a low interest rate environment, funding the early stages of retirement with divestures from 401(k) and traditional IRA account balances, while delaying Social Security benefits will generate a higher retirement income level over their lifetime.

The authors draw the conclusion from their work that in a ZIRP environment, retirement benefits are not actuarially fair but by delaying the claiming of those benefits it is actuarially advantageous for a very large subset of the population. The authors examined the actuarial advantage or disadvantage of delaying for individuals whose life expectancy differs from the average. In addition, they looked at the benefits of delaying for single males, single females, one-earner couples and three two-earner couples from different race and education groups, using mortality rates that were differentiated by race and education. By delaying the primary earners benefit, it is equivalent to purchasing a second-to-die or joint life annuity. Whereas, for a single individual who delays claiming retirement benefits it is the equivalent of purchasing a single life annuity.

The authors say the results of their work have important implication for retirement financing. Many financial advisors advocate a parallel income generating strategy as part of developing a retirement plan. That is, retirement savings are used to purchase an immediate annuity which generates a monthly income stream. Both Social Security and the immediate annuity income streams are "consumed" in parallel to fund retirement expenses. However, in today's ZIRP environment, this strategy may be suboptimal for many retirees. This sub-optimization arises as a result of the current low interest rates available on financial products. Delaying Social Security benefits are more generous than the terms for purchasing a commercial annuity. Social Security benefits are entitled to COLA increases, delaying these benefits buys an annuity whose payments remain constant in real term, something which is difficult to find in the commercial market.

3. Research by Dr. Steven A. Sass, Ph.D.

In May 2012, Steven Sass published a research paper titled, *"Should You Buy an Annuity from Social Security"*. Sass is the Program Director of the Financial Security Project at the Center for Retirement Research at Boston College. In the paper, Sass calculates the price of waiting in terms of buying additional monthly income through an annuity. The savings used during the period before collecting Social Security benefits is the "price" and the increase in benefits as the annuity which a retiree can "buy" from Social Security. You cannot buy annuities from the SSA so this is an implied purchase as if you could. The following results are very interesting.

From the paper, the following example is used. A retiree could claim $12,000 a year, in retirement benefits at age 65 or $12,860 at age 66, $860 more in retirement benefits. If he delays claiming benefits for that one year and uses $12,860 from his savings to pay the household expenses he needs to for the 12 month period, that $12,860 is the "price" for the extra $860 in Social Security income. The annuity rate, which is the additional annuity income as a percentage of the purchase price, would be 6.7% ($860 / $12,860; see Table 9.3 on the next page).

Table 9.2 below, displays various inflation-protected annuity rates as a percentage of the purchase price. These rates were obtained from Vanguard. For a couple the wife is 2 years younger than the age displayed.

Table 9.2 Inflation-Protected Annuity Rates; Vanguard Annuity Calculator, January 2012

Age	Men	Women	Couples
62	4.5%	4.1%	3.4%
63	4.7	4.2	3.5
64	4.9	4.4	3.6
65	5.1	4.6	3.7
66	5.3	4.7	3.9
67	5.5	4.9	4.0
68	5.7	5.1	4.2
69	5.9	5.3	4.3

Source: Sass, Steven A.; Should You Buy an Annuity from Social Security; Center for Retirement Research at Boston College

As can be seen from the previous table, at the time, this 6.7% rate was higher than the 5.1% annuity rate a 65 year old man could get if he purchased an inflation-protected immediate income annuity from Vanguard and higher than 3.7% rate which a couple could purchase.

Retirement benefits can be claimed at any time from age 62 to age 70, though the amount received from Social Security will vary. Table 9.3 below illustrates the percentage increase in monthly benefits a beneficiary would receive by delaying benefit claiming to a later age. For example, from the table, monthly retirement benefits would be 7.1% higher if claimed at age 66 and not at age 65. By delaying until age 70, instead of age 65, monthly benefits would be 41.4% higher. If monthly benefits were $1,000 per month, if claimed at age 65, they would be $1,071 if claimed at age 66 and $1,410 if claimed at age 70.

Table 9.3 Increase in Inflation-Adjusted Monthly Social Security Benefits if a Retiree Delayed Claiming

	To Age							
Delay From Age	63	64	65	66	67	68	69	70
62	6.7%	15.6%	24.4%	33.3%	44.0%	54.7%	65.3%	76.0%
63		8.3	16.7	25.0	35.0	45.0	55.0	65.0
64			7.7	15.4	24.6	33.8	43.1	52.3
65				7.1	15.7	24.3	32.9	**41.4**
66					8.0	16.0	24.0	32.0
67						7.4	14.8	22.2
68							6.9	13.8
60								6.5

Source: Sass, Steven A., Author's Calculations; Should You Buy an Annuity from Social Security; Center for Retirement Research at Boston College

Table 9.4, on the next page, illustrates annuity rates for using retirement savings to delay claiming retirement benefits. From the previous illustrated example, the annuity rate, which is the additional annuity income as a percentage of the purchase price, was 6.7% ($860 / $12,860)

for an individual who delayed from age 65 to age 66. These rates were uniformly higher than the current rates on commercial inflation-protected annuities as displayed in Table 9.2, especially for couples.

Table 9.4 Annuity Rates Using Savings to Delay Claiming Social Security Benefits

	To Age							
Delay From Age	63	64	65	66	67	68	69	70
62	6.2%	6.7%	6.5%	6.3%	6.1%	5.9%	5.6%	5.4%
63		7.7	7.1	6.7	6.5	6.2	5.9	5.6
64			7.1	6.7	6.6	6.3	6.0	5.7
65				**6.7**	6.8	6.5	6.2	5.9
66					7.4	6.9	6.5	6.1
67						6.9	6.5	6.1
68							6.5	6.1
60								6.1

Source: Sass, Steven A., Author's Calculations; Should You Buy an Annuity from Social Security; Center for Retirement Research at Boston College

4. Research by Joseph A. Tomlinson, FSA, CFP®

In February 2014, Joe Tomlinson, founder of Tomlinson Financial Planning, published a paper in Advisor Perspectives titled, *"Providing Better Social Security Advice for Clients"*. Tomlinson is both an actuary and a CFP®.

According to the SSA, an individual who has always earned at least the Social Security maximum over a full working career would be entitled to a monthly PIA of $2,641 at age 66 in 2014. Claiming at age 62, they would be entitled to 75% of that or $1,981 per month. If they delay to age 70, they would be entitled to 132% of that PIA, which would be $3,486 per month.

To examine the value of delaying Social Security retirement benefits from age 62 to age 70, a comparison was done against giving up $1,981 per month for eight years to receiving an additional $1,505 ($3,486-$1,981) for the remainder of life. Life expectancy is the critical variable in the analysis.

To measure the delayed benefit he did an internal rate-of-return (IRR) analysis with the age 62-70 reductions as outflows and the increases after age 70 as inflows lasting for the assumed life expectancy. Tomlinson calculated real rates of return for both males and females using customized mortality estimates he developed from a variety of actuarial studies and the real risk-free yield of 10-year Treasury inflation-protected securities (TIPS), which in January 2014 was 0.62%. He then calculated the comparative real return of delaying Social Security benefits until age 70.

Table 9.5 Implied Returns from Delaying Social Security

Gender	Life Expectancy (years)	Implied Real Return	Premium over 10-Year TIPS @ 0.62%
Male age 62	24 to age 86	3.58%	2.96%
Female age 62	27 to age 89	4.57%	3.95%
Last-to-die M/F	30 to age 92	5.24%	4.62%

Source: Tomlinson, Joseph A.; Providing Better Social Security Advice for Clients, Advisor Perspective, February 2014

The implied real returns were 3.58% for men, 4.57% for women and 5.24% for the last spouse to die. Given the inflation adjustments in Social Security, a comparison can be made using 10-year TIPS. This maturity is roughly comparable in duration to the lifetime benefits for a 70 year old. As can be seen in the table above, these implied real returns are significantly better when compared to the real yields from TIPS, especially for women who have a longer life expectancy.

Investment Returns

David Blanchett, CFA, CFP® and head of retirement research for Morningstar's Investment Management division, published a paper in the Journal of Personal Finance in the 2012, volume 11, issue 2 edition titled, *"When to Claim Social Security Retirement Benefits"*. In his paper, from the research he conducted, Blanchett concludes that the larger, later benefits exceed the potential return that most investors earn by starting benefits earlier and investing the difference.

An individual investor who takes reduced early retirement benefits at age 62 must achieve investment returns of 7% or higher in retirement in order to be better off than someone who delays claiming benefits to their FRA of 66, assuming average life expectancy. An investor, waiting to claim retirement benefits at their FRA of 66 would need an investment return of only 4.6% or higher to be better off than someone who delayed claiming retirement benefits until age 70.

According to Blanchett, delaying Social Security benefits is cheaper than buying an annuity in the current low interest rate environment. For example, an individual who collects benefits early at age 62 and invests the proceeds will not have to earn 31.7% a year to buy an annuity four years later that will match Social Security benefits at their FRA.

Summary of Conclusions

Creation of a ZIRP world, by the Federal Reserve Bank, has been a monumental penalty for retirees who have long favored a strategy of having fixed income securities as a significant allocation of assets during retirement. A by-product of this monetary policy has been to force some retirees and near-retirees into moving further out on the risk spectrum in search of higher returns, which translates into higher retirement account balances. This has worked so far in the short run as stock market indices are higher now than they were in the fall of 2007.

Academic research doesn't always happen in reality. As said many times throughout this book, if your financial circumstances are truly constrained, you should begin claiming benefits when you can. Receiving benefits might relieve much stress in your life which in turn could be good for your health and that of your spouse. However, if you have the financial resources, which allows you to delay claiming Social Security retirement benefits, thus earning the delayed retirement credits available, the previously discussed research clearly demonstrates the advantages to doing this. Coupled with the current abnormally low interest rate environment we've been in for several years now, these delayed retirement credits create an actuarial advantage for beneficiaries who are able to delay claiming retirement benefits. The conclusions:

- Life expectancies have a significant impact on present values when claiming retirement benefits.
- Generally speaking, individuals with shorter than average life expectancies should consider claiming retirement benefits earlier, while those with above average life expectancies should consider delaying the claiming of retirement benefits until a date after their FRA.
- For couples the issues are more complex. In general, if there is a wide gap in the PIAs of the spouses, as long as there are no earnings cap restrictions involved, the present value of benefits is maximized when the lower earnings spouse claims benefits early while the higher earning spouse delays claiming benefits until age 70.

- Interest rates also have a significant impact on determining when to claim retirement benefits at different ages. The lower the *real rate of interest*, the more advantageous it is to delay claiming retirement benefits.
- While the benefits of private commercial annuities have been adjusted downward in recent years due to improving life expectancy and a declining interest rate environment, the terms for delaying claiming of Social Security benefits have largely been left unchanged for half a century.
- Within a ZIRP environment it may be more advantageous for beneficiaries to spend down retirement income source to delay the claiming of Social Security benefits rather than consume these income streams in parallel.

Long-term interest rates reached their lows in 2012, with the 10-year U.S. Treasury note reaching a level of about 1.38%. Since then, 10-years have risen by about 125 basis points over the past 24 months, still low by historical standards. Even though long-term interest rates have risen, recent research indicates the advantages still favor delaying claiming retirement benefits. The advantage is just not as great as it was twenty-four months ago.

CHAPTER TEN

STRATEGIES FOR SINGLES

If you read the strategies contained in all three chapters, you will find that some overlap, depending on marital status. When it comes to maximizing Social Security benefits, married couples do have the most flexibility when applying the different rules in coordinating their claiming strategies.

The strategies discussed in this chapter define a person as being single **if no one else can receive Social Security benefits based on that individual's earnings record**. For those "single individuals" who are either widowed, divorced, divorced and then remarried again or have any children who may be able to receive dependent benefits, the rules and strategies for these situations will be discussed in a subsequent chapter. These "single individuals" may have many more claiming strategies.

It is critically important for married couples to coordinate their Social Security strategies to take full advantage of retirement, spousal and survivor benefits to increase their income over their joint lifetimes. However, many individuals do not think there are parallel strategies for those who are single, to employ, to boost their Social Security income. The general assumption is that claiming strategies for singles are straightforward.

Best Age to Start

What is the best age for someone who is single to file and claim their Social Security retirement benefits? Most would assume this is an easy question to answer for someone who is single. Decide how long you think you are going to live, then determine the break-even age. The break-even age is that age at which total retirement benefits received, by delaying to receive a higher monthly benefit, surpasses the total retirement benefits received by starting as early as possible and receiving lower monthly payments.

Is that going to be age 62, 66 (assuming this is their full retirement age), 70, some age in between those or some age later than 70? At age 62, someone who is single can claim early reduced benefits and receive 75% of their primary insurance amount (PIA), which they would receive at their full retirement age (FRA) of 66. This assumes they would not be subject to any earnings cap restrictions, which would apply if they continue to work. Alternatively, once they reach age 66, they could file for benefits and receive 100% of whatever their PIA is. Or they could wait until age 70 to file and claim benefits. By delaying they would be entitled to collect their maximum benefit which is equal to 132% of their PIA at their FRA. By delaying they would receive four years of delayed retirement credits worth 8% per year, not compounded.

Break-Even Age

The break-even age for a single individual is just over age 80. This also happens to be close to the age of average mortality, assuming average health. This implies the individual would have to live at least until that age to make it worthwhile to delay retirement benefits until age 70. The theory implies that whether the individual starts collecting early and receives a smaller reduced benefit amount, for a greater number of years, or starts collecting later and receives a larger benefit for a fewer number of years; the individual will receive close to the same dollars either way. However, William Meyer and William Reichenstein of Social Security Solutions say it's more complicated than that.

As we saw in the previous chapter, Meyer and Reichenstein have written extensively, from the analytical perspective, about claiming Social Security retirement benefits. In that March 2010 published paper in the Journal of Financial Planning titled, "*Social Security: When to Start Benefits and How to Minimize Longevity Risk*", the authors discuss the monthly payoffs from claiming Social Security benefits at ages 62, 66 and 70 from a present value standpoint for a single beneficiary.

In the example which follows, a single individual would be able to collect a retirement benefit of $2,000 per month, if they waited until they reached their FRA to collect. If they claimed at 62, the beneficiary would see their PIA cut by 25%. At their FRA, the benefit would be worth 100% of their PIA. By waiting until age 70 to claim retirement benefits, they would receive another 32% in monthly benefits. The individual lives 22 years and dies at age 84. From the calculations done the authors conclude, assuming average life expectancy and no reduction in benefits resulting from earnings cap restrictions, the present values are approximately the same no matter when benefits begin. In other data which was calculated, if you assume a 20-year life expectancy for a male at age 62 and a 23-year life expectancy for a female at age 62, the male can maximize the present value of benefits by beginning benefits at age 65 while the female can maximize benefits by beginning benefits at age 68. Table 10.1, on the next page, illustrates the results from Meyer's and Reichenstein calculations from their published paper.

Table 10.1 Monthly Payoffs from Social Security for a
Single Individual

Age	Years	Strategy A	Strategy B	Strategy C
62	1	$1,500		
63	2	$1,500		
64	3	$1,500		
65	4	$1,500		
66	5	$1,500	$2,000	
67	6	$1,500	$2,000	
68	7	$1,500	$2,000	
69	8	$1,500	$2,000	
70	9	$1,500	$2,000	$2,640
...	...	...	...	...
83	22	$1,500	$2,000	$2,640
PV, dies at 84		$308,044	$319,094	$311,311
PV Relative, dies at 84		96.5%	100%	97.6%
PV Relative, dies at 75		100%	87.8%	61.3%
PV Relative, dies at 95		83.5%	92.7%	100%

The discount rate is 0.2% per month or 2.43% per year. Since Social Security payments are indexed to inflation, the payments are constant in real terms. Therefore, the appropriate discount rate is the real yield on long-term Treasury Inflation Protected Securities (TIPS). In June 2009, this rate was about 2.43%.

Source: Meyer, William and Reichenstein, William; Social Security: When Should You Start Benefits and How to Minimize Longevity Risk; Journal of Financial Planning, March 2010

In the October 2012 edition of The Retirement Income Industry Association's (RIIA) publication, *Retirement Management Journal*, they expanded on their previous work in an article titled, "*Social Security Claiming Strategies for Singles*". If a beneficiary has a spouse and/or other dependents, there are lots of factors to consider when deciding to claim retirement benefits. For a single person, the primary consideration is the way the monthly increases are calculated. The author's assumed the break-even age would increase progressively for each year you delay. They ran break-even analysis year-over-year and discovered they do not increase at an even rate. What they uncovered were what they call "lumpy" results due to the way the SSA calculates benefits:

- Between age 62 and 63, monthly benefits increase 0.42% of the PIA per month.
- Between age 63 and 66, monthly benefits increase 0.56% of the PIA per month.
- Between age 66 and 70, monthly benefits increase 0.67% of the PIA per month.

As a result of these uneven increases, it creates an opportunity to optimize these retirement benefits. Assuming a FRA of 66, the break-even age for delaying benefits from 62 to 63 is 78 years. However, the break-even age for delaying benefits from 63 to 64 actually goes down to 76 years. It then climbs, if benefits are delayed until late in the 66th year, when the break-even age drops again for a few months. It then climbs again for each delay in receiving benefits until the individual reaches age 70.

Based on the author's research, their conclusion; to maximize the present value of retirement benefits a single person should never claim retirement benefits between age 62 and one month and age 63 and 11 months. Also, they shouldn't claim between age 65 and five months through age 66 and seven months. By claiming at the end of these two periods, an individual will receive not only larger monthly benefits but also greater lifetime benefits IF they live beyond their normal life expectancy.

In May 2013, Randle Spiegelman, V.P., CPA, CFP® with Charles Schwab, in their Schwab Center for Financial Research, released a study titled, *"When Should You Take Social Security"*. By claiming Social Security benefits early, it reduces the amount you will receive. It also means you'll receive monthly checks for a longer time. By claiming Social Security later, it will result in fewer checks received during your lifetime but the amount of those checks will be larger. What age will you break-even and begin to come out ahead if you delay Social Security? That break-even age depends on the amount of your retirement benefits, the assumptions you use to account for taxes and the opportunity cost of waiting (investment return you could have made, inflation, etc.). For example, if you're a top wage earner turning 62 this year, your monthly retirement benefits (in today's dollars) at ages 62 and one month, 66 and 70 are $1,923, $2,591 and $3,447, respectively. Break-even ages are as follows and illustrated in Figure 10.1 below:

- 62 (early) vs. 66 (FRA): Between ages 77 and 78.
- 62 (early) vs. 70 (late): Between ages 80 and 81.
- 66 (FRA) vs. 70 (late): Between ages 83 and 84.

Figure 10.1 Break-Even Ages

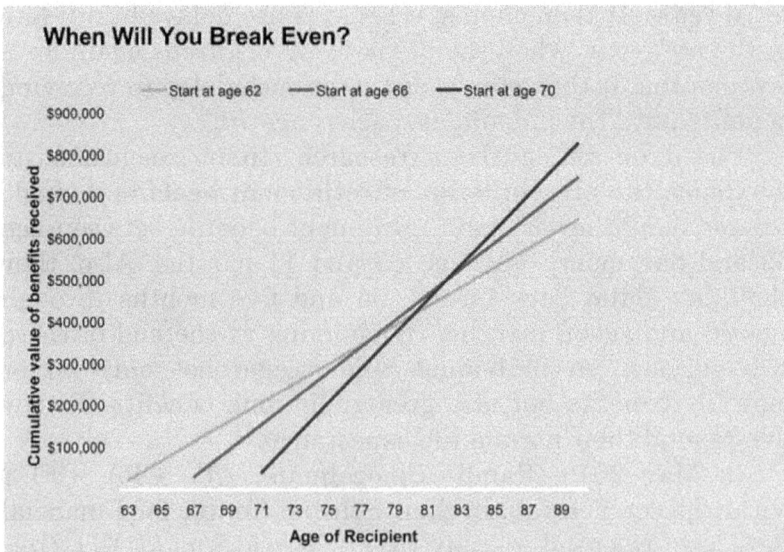

Source: Charles Schwab, Schwab Center for Financial Research

In the example on the previous page, if you wait until age 66 to take Social Security instead of taking it at age 62, you would come out ahead as long as you live to at least age 77-78. The break-even age goes up the longer you wait.

Retirement Benefit Do-Over Strategy

If you are already receiving Social Security retirement benefits, there is an obscure provision which allows you to repay the benefits you've collected and then reapply for retirement benefits later. This can be done interest- and penalty-free. However, in December 2010, the SSA changed the rule. Most retirees who have been collecting benefits no longer have the option of repaying those collected benefits and then restarting their benefits at a higher amount later. As a result of this rule change, using a golf term, the Social Security mulligan is not as attractive as it was before the rule change.

Based on the new rule, you now have a once-in-a-lifetime opportunity to change your mind and repay your benefits. Now it must be within the first twelve months of claiming them. When you restart your benefits at a later date they will be based on your age at the time of the new filing, resulting in a higher benefit. Maybe you decided to file and begin claiming early retirement benefits because you didn't know how long you might live and now you regret making that decision. One note though in implementing this strategy. **If your spouse or minor dependent children received benefits on your earnings record, you would have to repay those benefits also.**

You must file IRS Form 521, *Request for Withdrawal of Application*, at your local Social Security office. Your benefits will stop in a relatively short period of time. The SSA will send you a letter explaining how much you need to repay, including any spousal and/or dependent benefits. You are also entitled to claim an itemized deduction or tax credit, whichever is more beneficial to you, for the taxes you may have paid on those Social Security benefits in the year you repay them. See IRS Publication 915, *Social Security and Equivalent Railroad Retirement Benefits*, for details.

Voluntary Suspension of Benefits Strategy

There is another option for those beneficiaries who decide to change their minds, regarding the best age to claim Social Security benefits, after the twelve month window has closed. Can someone who collects early reduced retirement benefits at age 62, suspend those benefits at a later date and still earn delayed retirement credits? The answer is yes.

You can voluntarily suspend your Social Security benefits at any time and still be eligible to earn delayed retirement credits. For example, you made the decision to collect early retirement benefits beginning at age 62. Had you waited until your FRA of 66, your retirement benefit would have been worth $2,000 per month. Since you filed for early benefits, those benefits were reduced by 25%, allowing you to collect $1,500 per month. You collect those benefits from age 62 through 66 but during that time you wish you had waited for the bigger payout because you really didn't need the money anyway. At your FRA, you tell Social Security you want to voluntarily suspend your benefits. At age 70 you resume collecting benefits. Your new benefit is worth $1,980 per month, which is 132% of your previous amount. This new amount is 99% of your original FRA benefit amount which was $2,000. By employing this strategy, you have created a larger benefit base for future COLA increases. Voluntary suspension at their FRA can be a great way to undo an ill-advised early claiming decision and boost guaranteed income which will last a lifetime.

Filing for Retroactive Retirement Benefits

If you are older than your FRA when you first claim Social Security benefits, you may be entitled up to six months of retroactive benefits which are paid as a lump sum. This retroactive period begins six months before filing the application to claim Social Security benefits. For example, an individual turns their FRA in September 2012. They decide to file their claim for Social Security benefits, one year later, in September 2013. They would be entitled to retroactive benefits beginning six months earlier from March 2013. If they also had a minor child, the child could also be eligible for retroactive benefits.

These retroactive benefits for months prior to reaching their FRA are not payable to a retired worker, spouse, widow or widower if this results in a permanent reduction of their monthly benefit. For example, if an individual's FRA is age 66 and they claim benefits at 66 and 3 months, they would not be entitled to six months retroactive benefits, since they only reached their FRA three months earlier. They could request a lump sum payment for 3 months of retroactive benefits.

If you have surpassed your FRA but not yet claimed retirement benefits AND you don't intend to wait until age 70 to collect your maximum benefits, this lump sum retroactive benefit can be an option if you need some cash. It may be a better alternative than dipping into your savings or investments to pay for a large vacation or home remodeling project.

File and Suspend Strategy

Singles think this is only a strategy for married couples. Normally, when implementing the file and suspend strategy, you are telling Social Security that you want to file for the purpose of triggering retirement benefits for a spouse and/or dependent children but delay collecting your own retirement benefits until later when they will be worth more as a result of accruing delayed retirement credits. This strategy can also work for singles.

Example 8

You've just reached your FRA but decide you really don't need the money yet. You want to delay collecting retirement benefits so you can earn your delayed retirement credits worth 8% each year until you reach age 70. This will maximize your own retirement benefit for later in life. Eighteen months later you receive a very bad medical diagnosis. With this diagnosis you know you're going to have large, unexpected medical expenses later. What can you do now relative to your Social Security situation?

You can implement a file and suspend strategy. By doing this you have the option, at any time, of requesting a lump sum payout of retirement benefits back to the date of your suspension. This could be the money needed for health care expenses. If you request this lump sum you forfeit the right to delayed retirement credits and the benefit you receive going forward is based on the age you were at when you suspended your benefits. If longevity is now no longer a concern for you, this lump sum payment could be the resources you need to pay those unexpected medical expenses.

Example 9

Let's look at a slightly different scenario in which a single individual could implement a file and suspend strategy. An individual reaches their FRA and decide to implement a file and suspend strategy and do nothing else. Being single why would they want to do this?

As we saw in the previous example, this strategy can create a hedge or quasi-insurance option for you. Three years have now passed and the individual changes his mind. He now wishes he had taken a lump sum of benefits earlier. At this point does he have to take a full lump sum payout for the entire three years or can he take a partial lump sum payout? The individual who initiated the suspension of benefits may request, at any time, to have those benefits reinstated effective for *any* month of the suspension period. Thus, he can request to have a partial period of the suspension period reinstated and receive a lump sum payment for that period. So this individual has a choice. As before, you will forfeit any delayed retirement credits earned during the same period.

Combination Strategy

As the name implies, this strategy combines two of the previously discussed options, which are implemented at different ages. Susan reaches her FRA of 66. Her PIA is $1,000 per month. She decides to file and suspend her benefits because she doesn't need the money. This will still enable her to collect her delayed retirement credits. At age 70 her monthly benefit will increase to $1,320 ($1,000 x 1.32) per month. Three years later, at age 69, she receives a life-threatening diagnosis. What are her options now?

She could wait one more year to collect her maximum monthly benefit. Or, she can contact the SSA now and request a reinstatement of her voluntarily suspended benefits, retroactive to her initial filing. This would entitle her to a lump-sum benefit payment of $36,000 ($1,000 per month x 12 months x 3 years), which she can use to help pay for medical expenses. However, by implementing this strategy and collecting a lump-sum benefit at age 69, she loses the 3 years of delayed retirement credits she has already earned and the opportunity for one more additional year to 70. Her future monthly will be her original PIA of $1,000 per month for the rest of her life.

If Susan had not employed the file and suspend strategy at 66 and was in need of money now, given her health condition at 69, her only option now would be to file for retroactive benefits. She would receive only 6 months of benefits as a lump-sum payment of $6,000, as if she had filed for benefits at age 68 1/2. These examples do not include any intervening COLAs which would have accrued.

"Get your (Social Security) tricks on Route 66. That's the magic number for maxing spousal benefits."

Mary Beth Franklin
Contributing Editor
InvestmentNews

CHAPTER ELEVEN

STRATEGIES FOR COUPLES

Many couples claiming their Social Security benefits think it is a simple decision to make. It can be if you just file at age 62 without giving any thought as to what the consequences may be long-term. If you approach it as a critical decision, which the two of you have to make together, in terms of how the outcomes will integrate within your overall retirement income strategy, one quickly discovers there are complex strategies which can be implemented to help add thousands of dollars of additional

A common mistake couples make is in looking at Social Security as their own separate individual earnings record and their own separate retirement benefit as opposed to integrating the two benefits together. Many individuals may try to determine at what age they would break-even. Should you wait to collect your monthly benefit until you reach your full retirement age, when you can collect 100% of your primary insurance amount or collect Social Security benefits early at age 62, when your benefit will be reduced by 25%? Maybe postponing until age 70 and collecting delayed retirement credits worth 8% each year after reaching your FRA. <u>Generally speaking</u>, the break-even point is about 15 years between taking reduced early benefits at age 62 and the higher PIA benefit at their FRA of 66. Another mistake made is looking at their own life expectancy and basing their filing decision on when to start collecting on just that. What they should really be considering is how long their spouse might live after the primary earner dies. This is critical and many times simply overlooked or ignored.

Here is a common thought process many couples use. Many times it is driven by the husband. The husband, who is the higher earner, believes he is going to die first. This could be because of circumstances in his family medical history or it could be his current health has been slowly deteriorating. His wife is relatively healthy and she thinks she'll live a long time. He claims his retirement benefits as early as possible to get whatever he can while he is still alive. Meanwhile, his wife plans to delay claiming her retirement benefits until her FRA.

Under most circumstances, this is probably the exact opposite of what you should do as a couple. If it turns out the husband is correct and dies first, by claiming benefits early, he has probably shortchanged his wife's survivor benefit with an opportunity cost, which could be worth thousands of dollars over the remainder of her lifetime. For couples, the goal should be to maximize the joint retirement benefits over both spouse's lives and ensure the maximum survivor benefit possible, a point many couples miss.

Women are more likely to live a longer life than men. If a couple lives to reach age 65, there is a 72% chance one of them will live to be age 85, a 45% chance one will live to reach age 90 and an 18% chance one will make it to age 95. If she did not have much of an earnings history for herself, she may be totally dependent on those survivor benefits she will receive based on her husband's earnings record when he dies. They need to make their decisions as a couple, as opposed to two separate "single" individuals'.

As you read further you will see it's tough to make generalizations about Social Security claiming strategies. Each spouse's age, their own retirement benefit amount, their existing financial circumstances and their health outlook all play key factors in determining how and when to claim retirement benefits. There are also tradeoffs to consider in collecting these benefits, whether it is at age 62, 66, 70 or any age in between. In the final analysis, some couples simply have no choice but to file for retirement benefits at age 62 because they need the additional income to meet their essential needs. If waiting is a possibility, don't claim benefits until you have assessed all your options and see how those various outcomes integrate within your overall retirement income strategy.

On June 26, 2013, the Supreme Court ruled Section 3 of the Defense of Marriage Act (DOMA) as unconstitutional. Social Security is now no longer prevented from recognizing same-sex marriages for purposes of determining entitlements to or eligibility for benefits. In December 2013, the SSA began processing claims for surviving members of same-sex marriages and paying benefits where they are due. However, the SSA can currently only pay benefits to same-sex couples who are legally married and reside in a state which recognizes their marriage.

Primary Insurance Amount

Your primary insurance amount (PIA) is the monthly benefit amount payable if you are a retired worker who begins receiving retirement benefits at their full retirement age or if you're disabled and have never received a retirement benefit reduced for age.

Full Retirement Age

Social Security retirement benefits are actuarially reduced if taken early and actuarially increased if taken later. Assuming your FRA is 66, starting at age 70, benefits are

76% larger than starting at age 62. Spousal benefits are 43% larger at your FRA than at age 62. Survivor benefits are 40% larger at your FRA than at age 60. Reaching your full retirement age (FRA) is a requirement in order to optimize some of the strategies which will be discussed. Individuals born before 1943 reach their FRA at age 65. Those born between 1943 and 1954 reach their FRA at age 66. Those born between 1955 and 1959 reach their FRA at different months during the year they turn age 66 (see chapter six), while individuals who were born after 1960 reach their FRA at age 67. Generally, one receives 100% of their PIA benefit if they wait until they reach their FRA before they begin to collect benefits. Filing any earlier than their FRA will permanently reduce the retirement benefit they are eligible to receive.

Delayed Retirement Benefits

Your benefit will be increase automatically from the time you reach your FRA until you reach age 70, if you delay claiming. The aggregate dollar amount you receive during this period will depend on your year of birth. For those born in 1943 through 1954, the SSA will add 8% per year to your PIA benefit for each year you delay claiming Social Security beyond your FRA. By waiting until age 70, you will receive four years of increases. At age 70, this increases your retirement benefit to 132% of whatever your PIA was at age 66. For example, if your PIA benefit at 66 is $2,000 per month, by delaying to collect retirement benefits until age 70, your PIA would now be worth $2,640 ($2,000 x 1.32) per month for the rest of your life. Once you reach age 70, delayed retirement credits end so there's no benefit to delay claiming your retirement benefits after you reach this age.

For individuals born in 1955 or later, their aggregate dollar increase in delaying past their FRA will be less due to the sliding scale in reaching their FRA. For example, someone born in 1960 reaches their FRA at age 67. They only have three years to earn the 8% in delayed retirement credits instead of four. By waiting until age 70, you will increase your retirement benefit to 124% of whatever your PIA was at their FRA. If their PIA at their FRA is the same $2,000 per month, by accruing their three years of delayed retirement credits, at age 70 their PIA would be worth $2,480 ($2,000 x 1.24) per month, a difference of $160 each month.

These examples do not factor in any cost-of-living adjustments (COLA) these individuals would be entitled to receive, which would further increase their PIAs at their FRA.

Spousal Benefits

Spousal benefits are worth 50% of the working spouse's FRA benefit **IF** the spouse waits until their own FRA to file and claim Social Security benefits. If the spouse decides to claim as early as age 62, the spouse would be eligible for 35% of the worker's PIA. The spousal benefit will always be between 35% and 50% of the covered worker's PIA, depending on the age at which the spouse applies for benefits. Between 62 and 66, proportional amounts apply. The percentage of benefits received will be reduced based on the number of months remaining until the spouse reaches their FRA. To view benefit reductions by FRA, click on your year of birth in the table at http://www.socialsecurity.gov/retire2/retirechart.htm.

If the working spouse claims a reduced early retirement benefit at say age 62, the other spouse, even prior to their own FRA, can claim spousal benefits, though these benefits will also be reduced. However, if the spouse waits until they reach their own FRA to claim spousal benefits, they will receive 50% of their spouse's FRA benefit. This is likely more than if they claim prior to reaching their own FRA.

If the spouse had enough earnings credits to qualify for her own retirement benefits, those benefits could be less than the 50% spousal benefit. In this case, the spouse is eligible for the higher benefit but it will be made up by a combination of the spouse's own benefit and a portion of the spousal benefit. The full amount of both benefits cannot be claimed. Also, both spouses cannot claim spousal benefits. One spouse must either file for Social Security benefits or file and suspend benefits in order to trigger spousal benefits for the other spouse. **Spousal benefits do not receive delayed retirement credits.** Spousal benefits do accrue COLAs. Delaying a claim for spousal benefits past the beneficiaries FRA has no additional benefit.

A spouse is eligible for Social Security benefits regardless of whether they have ever earned any income. However, in this case that spouse CANNOT claim spousal benefits until her husband files for his benefits.

Survivor Benefits

Once either spouse dies, spousal benefits are no longer an option. At this point, a survivor benefit could replace the spousal benefit or provide a new benefit to the surviving spouse. The surviving spouse can begin to claim benefits as early as age 60 but the benefit will be reduced based on the number of months remaining until the survivor reaches their FRA. If disabled, they can collect survivor benefits as early as age 50. If the surviving spouse waits until their own FRA to file and claim Social Security benefits, the survivor benefit is worth 100% of the deceased spouse's benefit they have collected or were eligible to receive at their FRA.

For example, the husband has reached his FRA of 66 and is eligible to collect $2,000 per month in retirement benefits. He has a non-working spouse. While he is 66 he dies in an automobile accident. The spouse would be eligible for a $2,000 per month survivor's benefit, providing she has at least reached her FRA. Extending the same example, the husband has turned age 67 and dies. He had opted to delay claiming retirement benefits. In this case, the spouse would be eligible for a $2,320 ($2,000 x 1.16) per month survivor's benefit because her husband is entitled to two years of delayed retirement credits, which are added to his PIA.

In the case where a surviving spouse is eligible for benefits and she claims before reaching her FRA, those survivor benefits will be reduced. If the survivor collects as early as age 60, benefits would be worth just 71.5% of their deceased spouse's PIA. If the surviving spouse is disabled, they would receive 71.5% of their deceased spouse's PIA any time from age 50 through 59. Survivor benefits are also available to a spouse of any age who is caring for the deceased worker's child who is under age 16. The survivor benefit for both the caregiving parent and child is worth 75% of the deceased worker's PIA.

If the deceased spouse was receiving reduced early retirement benefits, the survivor's benefit is based on a reduced amount but with a twist. If the surviving spouse is at their FRA or older when beginning to collect survivor benefits, the amount is limited to the larger of the reduced retirement benefit the deceased worker collected or 82.5% of the deceased worker's PIA. If the spouse was beyond their FRA and opted to collect delayed retirement credits and dies, the remaining spouse would be eligible to collect 100%, including any extra delayed retirement credits of what the deceased spouse already collected or was entitled to collect at the time they died.

Summary of Key Rules

When looking into the nuances of Social Security claiming strategies, shades of grey will be evident. Here is a summary of a few key rules when evaluating these strategies. If you fully understand these and first think about them as you read the following pages, it will help to eliminate some of the confusion you may feel.

- Spousal benefits are worth **50%** of the working spouse's FRA benefit **IF** the other spouse waits until their own FRA to file and claim for benefits.

- Spousal benefits are worth less than the 50% of the working spouse's PIA if the other spouse claims benefits **BEFORE** reaching their FRA.
- Spousal benefits are **NOT** entitled to the spouse's delayed retirement credits but **DO** receive COLAs.
- An individual can restrict their claim to **spousal benefits only** if they wait until their own FRA to claim the benefit.
- Survivor benefits are worth **100%** of the deceased worker's benefit.
- Survivor benefits are **NEVER** reduced as long as the survivor has reached their **OWN** FRA before collecting them.
- Survivor benefits **INCLUDE** any delayed retirement credits which the spouse has received **AND** any COLAs during the intervening periods.
- If the spouse passes between ages 66 and 70, the surviving spouse **ONLY** collects the delayed retirement credits up to death. The surviving spouse is not entitled to any delayed retirement credits which the deceased spouse did not receive.
- If financial circumstances allow you to delay collecting your retirement benefits until age 70, your annual benefit will be 76% greater than it would have been at age 62.

Claiming Strategies

There are four broad scenarios to consider when it comes to examining claiming strategies for couples and looking at spousal benefits. These scenarios are:

1. One spouse is the primary earner and the other spouse has not worked.
2. One spouse is the primary earner, while the other spouse has a nominal earnings record and there is a significant gap between their PIAs at their FRAs.

3. Both spouses have roughly the same earnings record and they both have similar PIAs at their FRAs.
4. There is a wide difference in ages between the two spouses.

The following examples are designed to educate the reader on the various scenarios which may arise when deciding on when to claim Social Security retirement benefits. These examples are not all inclusive of the different scenarios which may exist. The conclusions should not be construed as investment advice. You should consult with your investment or tax professional to see how any of these strategies may affect your own personal situation.

Over the next few pages a variety of strategies are presented, which couples can implement to maximize their combined Social Security benefits over their lifetimes. Each scenario is posed as a question, which then provides a solution to the question. A few "textbook" examples are given but as we all know, reality is usually never quite that simple. Some questions have very subtle differences. There may be alternative options available which did not get discussed in the example. A dose of "common sense" needs to be applied when looking at these examples and determining if they are close to your own situation.

We're going to ignore any earnings cap restrictions, federal taxation of benefits and intervening COLA increases which might affect retirement benefit outcomes. These are very important considerations, especially if you're working and collecting retirement benefits as you could lose all your benefits. Any COLA increases will be what they are and you have no control over them.

Retirement Benefit Do-Over Strategy

If you are already receiving Social Security retirement benefits, there is an obscure provision which allows you to repay the benefits you've collected and then reapply for benefits at a later age. This repayment to Social Security can be done interest and penalty-free. In December 2010, the SSA did change the rule somewhat. Most retirees who have been collecting benefits no longer have the option of repaying those collected benefits and then restarting their benefits at a higher amount later. Based on the new rule, you now have **once-in-a-lifetime opportunity to change your mind and repay your benefits but it must be within the first twelve months of claiming those benefits.** When you restart your benefits at a later date they will be based on your age at the time of the new filing, likely resulting in a higher benefit amount for you.

By repaying the benefits back to Social Security it will generate a Form SSA-1099 from Social Security. The form will show a negative number indicating you repaid benefits. If the deduction is $3,000 or less, it is subject to the 2%-of-adjusted-gross income limit which applies to certain miscellaneous deductions. This is claimed on Schedule A of your federal tax return. If the deduction is more than $3,000, you have a choice. You can choose between taking a tax deduction or a tax credit, whichever is more beneficial to you. See IRS Publication 915, *Social Security and Equivalent Railroad Retirement Benefits*, for further details concerning this process.

Example 10

You decided to file and begin claiming early retirement benefits because you didn't know how long you might live. You filed your claim when you reached age 62 and were entitled to collect a reduced early retirement benefit amount of $1,350 per month. Now, after 10-months of collecting benefits, you regret making this decision. Is there anything you can do?

The answer is yes. Implement the do-over strategy within the first 12 months of filing that benefit claim. You would need to repay Social Security those ten months of benefits you received which, in this case, is $13,500 ($1,350 x 10). There is one cautionary note in implementing this strategy. If your spouse or minor dependent children are receiving benefits on your earnings record during the period you collected benefits, you would have to repay those benefits also. If you wait longer than 12 months, you are stuck with your decision to claim early benefits. You will not be able to make any changes until you reach your FRA.

You will need to file SSA Form 521, *Request for Withdrawal of Application*, at your local Social Security office. Your benefits will stop in a relatively short period of time. The SSA will send you a letter explaining how much you need to repay, including any spousal or dependent benefits. If you were still working while you received benefits, you are also entitled to claim an itemized deduction or tax credit.

Voluntary Suspension of Benefits Strategy

Voluntary suspension of benefits is another option for those beneficiaries who decide to change their minds about the best age to claim Social Security benefits after the twelve month window has closed. Can someone who collects reduced early retirement benefits, at say age 62, suspend those benefits at a later date and still earn their delayed retirement credits?

The answer is yes. This strategy turns off benefits temporarily for the beneficiary once they reach their FRA. You don't have to repay any benefits to implement this strategy. You can voluntarily suspend your Social Security benefits once you reach your FRA and still be eligible to earn delayed retirement credits worth 8% each year until you reach age 70. However, if the spouse who initiated the voluntary suspension of benefits dies during this period, a surviving spouse CANNOT request retirement benefits for months prior to the death be reinstated and paid as an underpayment to the estate or widow(er). Only the individual who requested the voluntary suspension may request reinstatement.

Example 11

You will reach your FRA at 66. You made the decision to collect early retirement benefits beginning at age 62, the same age as your wife is. Since you claimed your retirement benefit early it was reduced by 25% to $1,500 per month. Had you waited until your FRA, your PIA would have been worth $2,000 per month. You collect those benefits from age 62 through 66, but during that time you wish you had waited for the bigger payout because you really didn't need the money anyway. What can you do?

Once you reach your FRA of 66, tell Social Security you want to voluntarily suspend your benefits. If you contact the SSA in January, for example, and request they suspend your retirement benefits you will still receive your January benefit in February. Your suspension would begin after that. Those benefits are suspended for four years. Once you reach age 70 you resume collecting your benefits.

By earning those four years of delayed retirement credits, worth 8% each year, your new benefit amount is now 132% of your previously claimed reduced early amount. In this case, your new benefit is worth $1,980 ($1,500 x 1.32) per month at age 70. This new amount is 99% of your original FRA benefit amount which was $2,000. By employing this strategy, you have created a larger benefit base for future COLA increases and a larger survivor benefit for your wife, if she outlives you. Survivor benefits are worth 100% of your retirement benefit, including any delayed retirement credits. You would also be entitled to any COLA increases during this intervening period.

Here is a scenario which often occurs between the husband and his wife. The husband says, look honey I can claim my benefit early and get this money now. Then I can suspend my benefit at my FRA and earn delayed retirement credits which will be better for you. This sounds reasonable to the wife. **There can be a serious drawback to using this strategy for married couples.** If the highest earning worker, the husband in this case, should die prematurely during the reduced collection period, before he has a chance to suspend benefits, he will inadvertently leave his surviving wife with a smaller survivor benefit. Over her lifetime this could ultimately be worth several thousand dollars in lost benefits to her at a time when she may need them the most.

Example 12

Let's extend the previous example and say the husband dies at age 63. He never made it to his FRA of 66 to voluntarily suspend benefits so he could earn his delayed retirement credits. Their plan failed. Let's say the wife lives until age 85. If their plan had worked and the husband made it to age 70, she would have been entitled to a survivor's benefit of $1,980 per month until she dies at age 85. With failure of the plan, she is now entitled to a survivor' benefit of $1,500 per month, $480 less. What do the cashflows look like?

With her husband passing early, she collects a survivor benefit for 22 years, which totals $396,000 ($1,500 x 12 months x 22 years). Had the husband made it to age 70 before passing, she would have collected a survivor benefit for only 15 years, which totals $356,400 ($1,980 x 12 months x 15 years), $39,600 less in total survivor benefits. Now your first thought might be, well that's not much of a difference and she collects more by me dying early. There is an eerie tradeoff which often gets overlooked, especially by the surviving spouse. The tradeoff which couples don't always take into account is, the wife loses that extra $480 each month in benefits. At age 65, that might not mean much to her. At age 75, that $480 could be a huge difference each month. From age 70, that extra $480 each month in benefits translates to an extra $86,400 in aggregate benefits over those 15 years until she passes at age 85.

This is why there are many shades of grey when dealing with Social Security claiming strategies. Delayed retirement credits affect only worker's and survivor benefits, not spousal benefits. If your wife is collecting spousal benefits based on your earnings record, her monthly benefit amount will not increase once you resume collecting your larger benefit at age 70.

File and Suspend Strategy

File and suspend is a strategy which can best work if one spouse has a substantially higher earnings record while the other spouse has little or no work history. It can also work if you have minor children under age 18 or under age 19 if still in high school. When implementing the file and suspend strategy, you are telling Social Security that you want to **file for the purpose of triggering benefits for a spouse and/or dependent children but delay collecting your own retirement benefits until later when they will be worth more.** Can both spouses file and suspend?

The answer is no. Only one member of the couple can apply for retirement benefits, then have those payments suspended so their current spouse can collect benefits. At least one spouse must wait until his or her normal FRA to implement this strategy. One spouse files with Social Security to receive their FRA benefits at age 66. That same spouse then requests that Social Security immediately suspend their benefits. By doing this they are entitled to receive delayed retirement credits until age 70. Their benefit would begin to accrue delayed retirement credits worth 8% per year until age 70. At that age they would be entitled to collect the maximum retirement benefit. Since the spouse didn't make an initial claim, the other spouse at their FRA, can file a restricted application to claim spousal benefits only based on the other spouse's earnings record. This spouse is still entitled to receive their own delayed retirement credits until age 70 based on their own earnings.

When might be the best time for a spouse to claim spousal benefits on her husband? In the scenario below, we're assuming the husband has a significantly higher retirement benefit than his wife does. Upon reaching his FRA, assuming age 66, he would file for Social Security benefits and then also suspend his benefits at age 66. By doing this it would allow his wife to collect spousal benefits on his earnings record. His own benefit would begin to accrue delayed retirement credits worth 8% per year until age 70. At that age he would be entitled to collect his maximum benefit. Here's how it works.

Example 13

We have a married couple who are in pretty good health.

- Husband's FRA: 66
- Wife's FRA: 66
- Husband's PIA: $2,500 per month
- Wife's PIA: $1,500 per month

This is $4,000 per month between the two of them if they claim benefits at their FRAs for the rest of their lives until one dies. Over the next four years, until age 70, they would collect a cumulative total of $192,000 in retirement benefits from Social Security, not including any intervening COLA increases they would receive by claiming at their FRAs.

Alternatively, the couple could implement the file and suspend strategy. The husband decides to file and suspend at his FRA of 66. By waiting until age 70, he receives his delayed retirement credits worth 8% per year which will increase his retirement benefit to $3,300 ($2,500 x 1.32) per month. Meanwhile, the wife at her FRA can collect a 50% spousal benefit based on her husband's earnings record, which in this case is $1,250 per month. She is then also eligible to earn her delayed retirement credits worth 8% each year. At age 70, her benefit would have increased to $1,980 per month, not including any intervening COLA increases. During this four year period she would have collected $60,000 in spousal retirement benefits.

Now with both individuals at age 70, the couple could file and claim retirement benefits and begin collecting nearly $5,300 per month in cumulative Social Security benefits, instead of the $4,000 per month if they had simple both filed at age 66. If they each make it to age 85, for example, they will have earned an extra $234,000 in retirement benefits by implementing this strategy. In addition, the larger benefit will serve as a bigger base for future COLA increases and lock in the largest survivor benefit for the wife **IF** the husband dies first.

Restricted Claim Strategy

The restricted claim strategy works best with dual-earning couples. For instance, the wife also has an earnings record. Although she can claim and collect retirement benefits as early as age 62, she may be better off waiting until she turns her FRA. Once her spouse files for retirement benefits, she can upon reaching her FRA, file a restricted claim for spousal benefits only. This allows her to collect 50% of her husband's full PIA, not including any delayed retirement benefits. By implementing this strategy she would allow her own benefits to accrue delayed retirement credits worth 8% per year until age 70. Upon reaching age 70, she would then switch to collect her maximum benefit.

Example 14

The wife is age 62 and her husband is also 62, but he has decided to claim reduced early retirement benefits. Can she file a restricted claim for spousal benefits now and then switch to her own retirement benefit at her FRA of 66?

The answer is no. She can only file to restrict her claim for spousal benefits only at her FRA of 66. She is only 62 now. However, since the husband has filed to receive reduced early retirement benefits at age 62, he could voluntarily suspend his benefits at his FRA of 66. He would then be entitled to earn his 8% each year in delayed retirement credits until age 70. When he reaches his FRA he can't file a restricted claim for spousal benefits only because he already made the decision to claim early benefits at age 62.

Example 15

This is a situational example of a husband who is 20 years older than his wife. He began collecting reduced early retirement benefits when he reached age 62. His wife is now 65. Can she file a restricted claim for spousal benefits only, in one year when she reaches her FRA of 66, even though her husband filed for retirement benefits at age 62?

The answer is yes, with a surprise. Since she will have reached her FRA, she can file a restricted claim for spousal benefits only and **collect 50% of whatever her husband's PIA was at his FRA**. In addition, her spousal benefit would be adjusted for 20 years of any intervening COLAs the husband had received. By implementing this strategy she receives a spousal benefit and can delay her own retirement benefit until age 70. This allows her to earn delayed retirement credits worth 8% each year, making her PIA worth 132% more when she reaches 70.

Example 16

A husband has reached his FRA at 66 and decides it makes sense to delay his benefits until he turns age 70. His wife, meanwhile, began collecting reduced early retirement benefits at age 62. Since his wife triggered a benefits claim, the husband is entitled to 50% of his wife's benefit while he waits until age 70 to collect his own. If he decides he wants to change his mind before he reaches age 70, he can do that and switch over and collect his own retirement benefit. Assume his wife's retirement benefit, at her FRA, would have been $1,750. She would actually be receiving less,

$1,312.50 ($1,750 x 0.75) per month, because she claimed early retirement benefits at age 62.

The husband, at his FRA, would receive 50% of his wife's PIA which is $875 ($1,750 / 2) per month for the next four years or $42,000 in total benefits. During the four years he delays, he is entitled to receive his 8% in delayed retirement credits each year. His benefit, at age 70, would now be 132% of whatever his PIA was at his FRA.

The spouse who files a restricted application must be at their FRA. If you apply for spousal benefits using this strategy prior to their FRA, the SSA considers this a deemed filing. Social Security considers you have filed for both your own retirement benefit and spousal benefits at the same time.

Example 17

A husband, who is 71, has still been working. He decides to retire at age 72. His wife is age 64 and is also still working. She plans to retire at age 65 from her job.

- Husband's FRA: 66
- Wife's FRA: 66
- Husband's PIA: $2,600
- Wife's PIA: $1,400

The husband started collecting his maximum retirement benefit when he reached age 70, which is $3,433 ($2,600 x 1.32) per month. Should his wife delay collecting her retirement benefits until she reaches her FRA of 66 when she could file a restricted claim?

It depends on the value the couple places on the tradeoff. The wife has one more year until she reaches her FRA. At that time she could file a restricted claim to collect a spousal benefit of $1,300 ($2,600 x .50) per month, 50% of her husband's PIA at his FRA. Spousal benefits do not qualify for delayed retirement credits but survivor benefits do. By doing this she can delay her own retirement benefits and collect the 8% each year in delayed retirement credits. At age 70 her retirement benefit would be worth $1,848 ($1,400 x 1.32) per month. On the other hand, because she is currently age 65, she could claim her own reduced early retirement benefits now. Since she is only one year away from reaching her FRA she will collect about 93% of her PIA, which in this case would be $1,302 ($1,400 x 0.93) per month. This is basically the same benefit as her spousal benefit, which she has to wait one more year to receive.

Here's the tradeoff the couple has to place a value on. If the wife claims retirement benefits early, she receives nearly $15,624 for the year BUT she forfeits the chance to collect a larger benefit five years from now ($1,848 per month at age 70) because she claimed benefits early. That opportunity cost amounts to an extra $448 per month when she reaches age 70. Does collecting an extra $15,624 now benefit the couple? Or should they wait one year to collect roughly the same amount plus a larger benefit later? That's the tradeoff the couple needs to consider.

The main goal for most couples should be to maximize survivor benefits. In this example the husband has already done this because he earned delayed retirement credits by waiting until he reached age 70 to claim his benefits. If the husband dies first, the wife's benefit would step up to $3,433 per month when the wife files for survivor benefits. Her own retirement benefit, if she either claimed early, claimed at her FRA or claimed spousal benefit would disappear at that point. If the wife should die first, the husband would not be entitled to a survivor benefit because his current benefit is larger than what his survivor benefit would be worth. The husband continues to receive his $3,433 per month while his deceased wife's benefit ceases. You can't collect both.

Combination Strategy

The file and suspend strategy is used many times in combination with the restricted claim strategy. This strategy can help married couples when both spouses are close in age and have similar earnings history's which allows them both to maximize their Social Security benefits. It also works best when the lower earner of the two spouses' retirement benefit is worth more than 50% of the higher earning spouse's benefit at their FRA.

Once you reach your FRA and your eligible for both a spousal benefit and a retirement benefit based on your own earnings record, a spouse has a choice. The first choice is the spouse can file a restricted claim for spousal benefits only and delay their own retirement benefits to a later date. Remember, only one of the spouses can choose to receive spousal benefits now and delay receiving their retirement benefits until later. In the second choice, the combo strategy is employed. The optimum situation arises when both spouses have reached their FRAs. One spouse files and suspends benefits, triggering spousal benefits for the other spouse, while delaying their own retirement benefits until they are worth more through accruing delayed retirement credits. The other spouse then files a restricted claim for spousal benefits only and collects 50% of the other spouses PIA while they also delay their own retirement benefit and also accrue delayed retirement credits. If both spouses wait until age 70 to collect they will both have achieved their maximum retirement benefit.

Example 18

The husband is 68 years old while his wife is age 70. Both have FRAs at 66. The husband also has the larger earnings record. The husband is currently not collecting any retirement benefits because he wants to delay claiming so he can earn his delayed retirement credits. The wife began collecting reduced early retirement benefits at age 62. Is the couple leaving retirement benefits on the table which they could be collecting?

The answer is yes. The key to this is the husband has already reached his FRA. He has two options he can choose from. First, he could implement a file and suspend strategy to trigger a higher spousal benefit for his wife. Since she claimed retirement benefits early, the spousal benefit would be less than 50% of his PIA at his FRA. The husband's retirement benefit would continue to earn delayed retirement credits worth 8% each year until 70. The second option is for the husband to file a restricted claim for spousal benefits only. Since he has already reached his FRA, he can collect 50% of his wife's PIA at her FRA, not 50% of a reduced benefit even though she began collecting her retirement benefits early at age 62.

Example 19

Let's examine the following situation.

- Husband's FRA: 66
- Wife's FRA: 66
- Husband's PIA: $2,000 per month
- Wife's PIA: $2,000 per month

When the husband turns age 66, he can file and suspend his retirement benefit. Since he has filed a claim, he triggers spousal benefits for his wife which are worth 50% of his PIA retirement benefit, which in this case would be $1,000 per month. Now, when his wife turns age 66, she can file a restricted claim for spousal benefits only. She would then collect her spousal benefit of $1,000 per month instead of collecting her own PIA benefit of $2,000 per month. Since both spouses have now delayed their retirement benefits they are each eligible to receive delayed retirement credits worth 8% each year until they reach age 70. When they reach age 70, their new retirement benefit would be worth 132% of their PIA benefit at their FRA. Since that amount was $2,000 each, they would now be entitled to a retirement benefit of $2,640 ($2,000 x 1.32) per month. Cumulatively, they would now be collecting $5,280 per month instead of $4,000 per month, a 32% higher cumulative monthly benefit. This translates into $63,360 every year in combined retirement benefits, instead of $48,000 when they reach age 70. What could you do with an extra $15,360 each and every year? This does not factor in any COLA increases.

Example 20

In this scenario, the wife has a lower earnings record and is three years older than her husband who has the higher earnings record.

- Husband's FRA: 66 and 6 months
- Wife's FRA: 66

What should she do when she reaches age 62?

If she collects early retirement benefits they will be reduced by 25%. If there is a wide gap between the two PIAs at their respective FRAs, collecting early shouldn't be of concern to her. Her focus should be on maximizing her survivor benefit. Even though her husband is three years younger than she is, statistically, she most likely will still outlive him.

Once he turns his FRA at 66 and 6 months, he has two options. He can file for his own retirement benefits and his wife will likely step up to a larger spousal benefit, though it would not be as large as if she had waited until her own FRA to claim those spousal benefits. The second option for him is to file a restricted claim for spousal benefits only and collect 50% of his wife's FRA, even though it is reduced because she collected early retirement benefits. He is allowed to do this because his wife has already claimed benefits. In this scenario the wife is still collecting her reduced retirement benefit, not spousal benefits. He can then earn his delayed retirement credits until age 70, when he can then switch to his maximum retirement benefit. This would now be 28% more than his FRA retirement benefit was because he only receives delayed retirement credits for 3 ½ years due to his FRA of 66 and 6 months. If he dies first his wife will be entitled to a survivor benefit worth 100% of what he received during his life or was entitled to at the time of his death. As long as she has reached her FRA of 66, her survivor benefit will not be reduced even though her retirement benefit was reduced because she file and collected retirement benefits early.

Example 21

Let's examine one more scenario having two different options to play on. The husband is currently age 64 while his wife is age 62. This is a situation where there is a significant difference in PIAs.

- Husband's FRA: 66
- Wife's FRA: 66
- Husband's PIA: $2,090 per month
- Wife's PIA: $822 per month

Here's something which should stand out immediately which we'll come back to later. If you take 50% of the husband's PIA, that is $1,045. This is more than the wife's PIA at her FRA. If the husband files and suspends his benefits at age 66 until age 70, can he file for spousal benefits when his wife reaches her FRA of 66?

The answer is no. He can either file and suspend OR file a restricted claim for spousal benefits only. He can't claim both strategies. However, when the wife reaches age 66, the husband can elect one strategy while the wife elects the other strategy. Here's how it would work.

Example 22

Extending on the previous example, at age 66, the husband elects to do nothing. He will now accrue delayed retirement credits of 8% each year until age 70. When his wife turns age 66, the husband will now be age 68, she claims her own PIA of $822 per month. Since she has now claimed retirement benefits, her husband files a **restricted claim for spousal benefits only**. He is entitled to collect 50% of his wife's PIA, which in this example would be $411 per month. They can now collect a combined retirement benefit of $1,233 ($822 + $411) per month for the next two years. When the husband turns age 70, he is eligible to switch and receive his own maximum retirement benefit of $2,759 ($2,090 x 1.32) per month, as a result of earning his delayed retirement credits of 8% each year for four years. Their combined retirement benefit would now be $3,581 ($2,759 + $822) per month.

Example 23

Alternatively, the husband elects to file and suspend benefits at age 66. He receives nothing for the next four years but he does earn his delayed retirement credits worth 8% each year. When his wife turns age 66, she files a restricted claim for spousal benefits only and collects 50% of her husband's PIA which is worth $1,045 per month. She is still eligible to earn delayed retirement credits on her PIA, which is $822 per month. When they each turn age 70, the husband collects his maximum retirement benefit of $2,759, the same as in the previous example. The wife now collects her maximum retirement benefit which is $1,090 ($822 x 1.32), which is more than the spousal benefit which is dropped. Their combined retirement benefit would now increase to $3,849 ($2,759 +$1,090) per month.

Example 24

In this situation we have the following couple. The husband is age 66 and the wife is 62.

- Husband's FRA: 66
- Wife's FRA: 66
- Husband's PIA: 2,200 per month
- Wife's PIA: $900 per month

Should the husband file and suspend to trigger spousal benefits for his wife?

Let's answer the question at the end this time. If the husband files and suspends, his wife is only 62 years old. She would be eligible for only about 35% of her husband's PIA, which in this case would be $770 ($2,200 x 0.35) per month. If she waits until her own FRA, this benefit would increase to $1,100 ($2,200 x .50) per month as she would now be entitled for 50% of his PIA. Since she is entitled to benefits on her own earnings record, she would receive her own retirement benefit first and would then be increased for any spousal benefit. The math works like this. She would receive 75% of her PIA since she is claiming at age 62. This would be $675 ($900 x 0.75). She would then receive an additional $95 in spousal benefits to bring her up to $770, which is the 35% of her husband's PIA. She would forfeit her ability to earn delayed retirement credits as she has now filed a claim for retirement benefits. The husband's benefit at age 70 would be $2,904 ($2,000 x 1.32) per month.

When working with claiming strategies there is usually a "however" in the mix. However, if the wife claims her early reduced benefit at 62, she would still receive $675 per month. The husband could then file a restricted claim for spousal benefits only on his wife's earnings record. Since he has already reached his FRA, he is entitled to receive 50% of his wife's FRA PIA, which is $450 ($900 x 0.50) per month. He can then defer collecting his own retirement benefits until age 70 and earn his delayed retirement credits. Which strategy is the better one?

Consider the immediate cashflows. In the file and suspend strategy, the husband collects nothing and the wife gets $770 per month. In the restricted claim strategy, the wife receives $675 per month while the husband collects $450 per month for a combined amount of $1,125 per month. The second strategy probably is most advantageous for the couple. The husband defers his own benefits in either one and earns the 8% in delayed retirement credits.

Spousal Strategies

Fewer women are expected to collect spousal benefits, as more women enter the workforce and earn as much, if not more, than their spouse or partner. The SSA projects the number of women collecting benefits based on their own work records will double to 36.4 million by the end of 2037. In 2012, there were 18.2 million women collecting benefits based on their own earnings record. Based on these projected numbers, the number of women collecting spousal benefits alone will decline slightly over the same period from 2.2 million to 2.1 million by 2037.

Individuals can restrict their claim to spousal benefits only, if they wait until their FRA to claim benefits. If there is a significant gap between PIAs the couple will receive at their FRAs, the spouse with the lowest earnings record should probably consider filing for reduced early benefits at age 62, particularly if they can use the extra money. This assumes the spouse is no longer working or if working, is not earning more than the earnings cap restriction would allow, since this would further reduce those already reduced benefits. Since spousal benefits do not qualify for delayed retirement credits, it usually doesn't make sense to delay collecting them, if eligible, beyond the FRA because they will not become any larger.

Example 25

This is a straight forward situation. Is it possible for a wife to take spousal benefits at age 62 and then switch to her own retirement benefits when she reaches her FRA of 66?

The answer is no. If she claims at age 62, she must accept the largest benefit which she is entitled to at the time. She also forfeits the right to engage in creative claiming strategies. If you claim early benefits at age 62, you don't get a second chance to claim more benefits later.

Example 26

In this example, we have a husband who is 66 and the wife is 64. Both are working and the husband's income is substantial more than his wife's income. Can the wife file for spousal benefits only?

The answer is no. She is two years away from reaching her FRA of 66. Since she has her own earnings record, if she wants to claim retirement benefits now, she would first have to file and collect reduced early retirement benefits. This could then possibly be increased by a spousal benefit. Since she might collect some spousal benefit, it would also be reduced because she is claiming before her FRA. It would be worth about 42% of her husband's PIA instead of the 50%, had she waited until her FRA. Depending on her earned income, she may be subject to the earnings cap restriction which would also reduce her benefit. Another reason to possible wait until her FRA is she would no longer be subject to the earnings cap restriction. She could then earn all she wants, although some earnings could be subject to federal income taxes.

To carry this example a bit further, if the husband waits until he is age 68, he could implement a file and suspend strategy. This would trigger spousal benefits only for his wife who will be at her FRA. She could file a restricted claim for spousal benefits only and defer her own retirement benefits until age 70. This assumes her own enhanced benefit at 70 would be worth more than 50% of her husband's PIA at FRA.

Claiming Retroactive Benefits

In this situation we have a couple who are both 67 years of age and have done nothing regarding their Social Security.

- Husband's FRA: 66
- Wife's FRA: 66
- Husband's PIA: $2,200

- Wife's PIA: $700

Their plan is to earn delayed retirement credits to maximize their retirement benefits. Both are in pretty good health. What options are available to the couple now?

The husband could file for retirement benefits retroactively going back six months. Once he files, he can voluntarily suspend his benefit during any period, beginning with the first month of entitlement. This now triggers a spousal benefit option for the wife. By doing this, the wife can retroactively file for spousal benefits only and receive six months of benefits. Since she has reached her FRA, she is entitled to 50% of her husband PIA, which in this case is a lump-sum benefit amount of $6,600 ($2,200 x 50% x 6). If she had filed retroactively on her own retirement benefit, her lump-sum benefit would have only been worth $4,200 ($700 x 6). This strategy preserves the husband's full benefit at age 70 of $2,904 ($2,200 x 132%) and maximizes the cumulative joint-life benefit.

Example 27

This next example involves declining health. The wife is 62 and in poor health. Her husband is age 72. Assume she could file for disability benefits at the same time she files for reduced early retirement benefits. Since she is already 62, she would receive her reduced early retirement benefit. If her disability claim is ultimately approved by the SSA, she would be paid an unreduced benefit retroactively, minus a five month waiting period. Whereas retirement benefits are reduced if they are claimed before the individual's FRA, disability benefits are based on average lifetime earnings at the time they are claimed. There is no reduction for age. If she is approved for disability benefits, once she has received benefits for 2 years, she is also eligible to qualify for Medicare even if she hasn't reached age 65 yet.

Example 28

Here we have the following situation. A man is age 64 and fully retired. His wife is age 59 and still working. Can the husband now file for spousal benefits only, which would be 50% of his wife's PIA then allow his own retirement benefit to grow with delayed retirement credits until age 70?

In this example the answer is no. Since he is only 64, if he claims before reaching his FRA of 66, he cannot segregate his benefit. He must collect the largest benefit which he is entitled to. In this example, it would be his retirement benefit. Since the wife is only age 59, she is not yet eligible to file for Social Security benefits. There are no spousal benefits available to the husband. If your spouse applies for early retirement benefits and you are receiving disability benefits, your spouse will automatically be deemed to be applying for a spousal supplement and the benefit reduction which goes with starting benefits early.

Example 29

In this situation the lower earning spouse is the oldest. The husband is 60 years old while his wife is age 62.

- Husband's FRA: 66
- Wife's FRA: 66
- Husband's PIA: $2,400 per month
- Wife's PIA: $1,700 per month

She decides to retire and collect reduced early retirement benefits. She will receive 75% of her PIA benefit which is $1,275 per month. Her husband makes the decision to wait until he reaches his FRA so he can collect 100% of his PIA benefit which is $2,400 per month. Can the wife collect a spousal benefit when he files his claim at age 66?

The answer is no. His wife cannot collect a spousal benefit because 50% of her husband's FRA benefit would be

$1,200, less than the amount she is already collecting which is $1,275 per month. She is entitled to the larger benefit.

Should her husband now pass away, after reaching his FRA of 66, she would be entitled to 100% of his $2,400 per month retirement benefit as a survivor benefit. Her lower benefit of $1,275 would disappear. She cannot collect on both. By employing this approach she can boost their household income by $15,300 ($1,275 x 12) each year. Even though her retirement benefit is permanently reduced, it will not affect her survivor benefit if he dies first, as long as he stays alive until his FRA before he claims benefits.

Example 30

Now let's twist the above situation around. Both the husband and wife are age 62 and have the same FRA of 66.

- Husband's FRA: 66
- Wife's FRA: 66
- Husband's PIA: $2,400 per month
- Wife's PIA: $1,000 per month

She decides to retire and collect a reduced early retirement benefit. She will see her benefit reduced by 25% to $750 per month. Her husband makes the decision to wait until he reaches his FRA to collect 100% of his PIA benefit which is $2,400 per month. What happens to the wife's benefit when he reaches his FRA?

She steps up to a larger monthly benefit but it won't be as large as if she waited until her own FRA to claim benefits. Had she waited until 66, her spousal benefit would have been $1,200 per month, 50% of her husband's PIA at his FRA. This difference between the spousal benefit of $1,200 and her FRA benefit of $1,000 at age 66 is $200. Since she claimed early benefits, her benefit amount was reduced to $750 per month. The SSA will now recalculate her benefit to add the spousal differential of $200 to her reduced benefit of $750 for a new monthly benefit of $950 per month. The formula is (A-B) + C, where A is ½ of the worker's PIA at their FRA, B is 100% of the spouse's PIA and C is the spouse's early retirement benefit. Starting early means C is less than B, the total is less than 50%.

Example 31

Let's expand the previous example again and say she was entitled to both her own retirement benefit and a spousal benefit. This is known as being dually entitled and the calculation is a little different. It describes a Social Security beneficiary whose retirement benefit, when based on their own earnings record, is lower than the spousal/survivor benefit they are entitled to receive. If the wife claims benefits at age 62, her $1,000 per month retirement benefit would be reduced by 25% to $750 per month. The $200 excess between her spousal benefit of $1,200 and her retirement benefit of $1,000 would be reduced by 48 months to $140. The two amount of $750 and $140 are added together to determine the new monthly benefit of $890.

Example 32

In this situation there is a four year difference in ages between the two spouses. The husband's current age is 66 while his wife is 62 years old.

- Husband's FRA: 66
- Wife's FRA: 66
- Husband's PIA: $2,000 per month
- Wife's PIA: $800 per month

What options are available to this married couple?

The husband could *file and suspend* to trigger spousal benefits only for his wife. But in this case, although she is 62 and is eligible to claim spousal benefits, she would be eligible for only 35% of her husband's PIA at his FRA. This is because she is filing before she has reached her own FRA.

She would be entitled to collect a $700 per month spousal benefit, not the 50% amount had she waited to her FRA.

Since she is also entitled to retirement benefits based on her own earnings record, Social Security will first pay her retirement benefit and then any difference remaining to bring her up to the appropriate spousal level amount. The math works like this. She would receive a reduced early retirement benefit worth 75% of her PIA. Since she is claiming at age 62, this is $600 per month. She would then receive an additional spousal benefit of $100 to get her back to the $700, which is equal to 35% of her husband's PIA at his FRA. If the wife collects early retirement benefits before her FRA, her retirement benefits are permanently reduced.

The alternative option would be for her to again file for reduced early retirement benefits at age 62. As before, she would collect $600 per month, which is 75% of her PIA at her FRA. At 66, her husband could then file a *restricted claim for spousal benefits only* on his wife's earnings record. Since he has reached his FRA, he is entitled to receive 50% of his wife's PIA, even though she filed to claim retirement benefits early. He receives $400 ($800 x 50%) per month. This would still enable the husband to accrue his delayed retirement credits until age 70, when they would be worth $2,640 per month.

This example assume the wife is not working while she is collecting benefits or if she is, she is not subject to any earnings cap restrictions. If she was, it would also affect her husband's spousal benefit.

Example 33

What if we add a twist is added to the previous example. The wife is collecting an reduced early retirement benefit of $700 per month. Remember, the wife has her own earnings record so she receives $600 from that and $100 from her spousal benefit (review the file and suspend portion of the previous example). Can she receive a spousal benefit when her husband begins to claim at age 70?

The answer is yes. The wife can receive a step-up in spousal benefits. Since the husband delayed receiving retirement benefits, he earned four years of delayed retirement credits, which will increase his retirement benefit to $2,640 ($2,000 x 1.32) per month.

Spousal benefits are worth 50% of the PIA at their FRA, a lesser benefit if collected early. Spousal benefits do not receive any benefit from delayed retirement credits but survivor benefits do. Once her husband claims at age 70 it triggers spousal benefits for the wife. Her retirement benefit would increase from $700 per month to $800 per month. The math works like this. First, you need to calculate the spousal differential. In this case, it is 50% of the husband's PIA, minus the wife's PIA ($1,000 - $800 = $200). Then add this spousal differential to the wife's reduced early retirement benefit amount of $600. Her step-up is the $600 + $200 = $800 per month. This becomes her new benefit amount once the husband begins collecting his retirement benefit. If the husband should pass away at age 74, the wife would be age 70. She would then be entitled to a survivor benefit of $2,640 per month. The husband would have maximized his survivor benefit for his wife.

Example 34

Is there a situation in which a spouse may never be eligible to collect a spousal benefit?

The answer to this question is yes. Let's examine the following situation where there is a four year difference in ages between the spouses and the wife has the lower earnings record. The husband is currently 60 years of age while his wife is currently age 64. They want to maximize their Social Security benefits over their lifetimes.

- Husband's FRA: 66
- Wife's FRA: 66
- Husband's PIA: $2,500 per month
- Wife's PIA: $1,500 per month

In two years, when she reaches her FRA, she would be eligible to collect her full PIA of $1,500 per month. She decides to postpone claiming benefits so she can earn her delayed retirement credits until age 70. When her husband reaches his FRA of 66, she will now be 70 years old. If he claims retirement benefits at his FRA, she could not step up to a bigger spousal benefit because her own benefit at age 70, including her delayed retirement credits would be worth more than the 50% spousal benefit on his PIA. At age 70 she can collect $1,980 ($1,500 x 1.32) per month, while 50% of her husband's FRA benefit is worth only $1,250 per month. She would never collect a spousal benefit.

If this situation had been reversed, she could have claimed a reduced early benefit on her own earnings record and then possibly stepped up to a larger spousal benefit once her husband claimed benefits. If he also waits until age 70 to collect benefits, he would have earned his maximum delayed retirement credits and assured his wife the largest survivor benefit possible of $3,300 ($2,500 x 1.32) per month when he dies, assuming of course she outlives him and she has reached her FRA.

Example 35

The previous examples assumed both spouses have had an earnings record. Let's look at an example where the wife has no earnings record and is several years older than her husband. These can be the most challenging scenarios because the Social Security rules make claiming strategies difficult to implement. For this example, the husband is age 55 and the wife is 61 years old. Even though the wife has no earnings record, she is still entitled to Social Security benefits as a spouse. This is where the simplicity ends. When can the wife collect retirement benefits?

Since the wife is not eligible for Social Security retirement benefits on her own, she must wait until her husband claims his retirement benefit in order for her to collect her spousal benefits. The earliest the husband can claim benefits would be at age 62, which would make his wife 68 years old. However, as we have learned, if the husband claims reduced early retirement benefits at age 62, his benefit would be reduced by 25%. The benefit his wife would receive at age 68 would also be reduced. If he is still working, he also could be subject to earnings cap restrictions. If the husband earns too much his benefits could be reduced or even totally eliminated, which would also impact his wife's spousal benefit. In addition, if the husband claims early, he is also reducing the survivor benefit his wife could be entitled to.

If the husband waits until his FRA, let's assume that is age 66, his wife will then be 72 years of age. At this point the husband could implement a file and suspend strategy, triggering full spousal benefits for his wife which would be 50% of his PIA. The wife could then file a restricted claim for spousal benefits only and begin collecting on her husband's earnings record. The husband would then begin to earn his delayed retirement credits and if he waits until age 70 to claim benefits, his PIA at his FRA would increase by 132% plus any intervening COLAs. This will NOT increase her spousal benefit amount but will entitle her to a larger survivor benefit if she outlives her husband. In this example, Social Security just doesn't generate any good claiming options for the wife.

Legal Separation

What are the rules for a married couple who have been legally separated for many years but not divorced? Since the rules as to what defines a spouse, according to the SSA are very clear, you are either married or you're not. There is nothing in between according to the Social Security rules.

Example 36

A couple are married but have been legally separated for a number of years. Both have reached their FRA. The husband has the higher earnings record while the wife does not yet have sufficient lifetime earnings credits to be eligible for retirement benefits on her own earnings record. Since they are estranged, can she collect spousal benefits before her husband files to claim retirement benefits?

The answer is no. The Social Security rules make no provisions for legal separation. So in this case, she is still married and is his spouse. All the rules regarding spousal benefits apply to her and she must wait until her husband files a claim for benefits before she would be entitled to spousal benefits. Since she is also not eligible for retirement benefits based on her own earnings record, even though she has reached her FRA of 66, she has zero cashflow coming in from Social Security. If their relationship was extremely bitter, the husband, who is also age 66, could just sit back and decide not to claim benefits until age 70. He would earn four years of delayed retirement credits. At age 70 he would be entitled to his maximum benefit which would be 132% of his PIA plus any COLA increases he would have been entitled to.

Spousal benefits do not accrue delayed retirement credits so she is also missing out on collecting some spousal benefits. By pursuing this strategy he would be denying his estranged spouse any Social Security benefits, assuming she had still not qualified for Social Security benefits during the intervening four year period. The decent thing for the husband to do would be to file and suspend benefits at his FRA at age 66. This would allow the wife to file for spousal benefits, entitling her to 50% of whatever his PIA is at his FRA. The husband would still be entitled to earning his delayed retirement credits.

Actually, if there was no hope at all for the marriage, the smart thing for her to do would have been to file for divorce at age 63. By the time she had reached either age 64 or 65, the divorce probably would have been final. Then one or two years later, at her FRA of 66, she would have had additional options under the divorce rules which we'll cover in the next chapter.

CHAPTER TWELVE

STRATEGIES FOR WIDOWS, WIDOWERS, DIVORCED AND DEPENDENTS

In this chapter we're going to cover those rules which do not apply to those who are either specifically single or married, the more non-traditional situations. There are philosophical and emotional issues involved when these events happen which may cloud judgment and decision making in the heat of the moment. These can be extremely important to those involved and should not be downplayed but we need to ignore them, for the moment, as we look at the issues surrounding claiming strategies involving these non-traditional circumstances. As we have seen, with all Social Security claiming strategies there are precise rules which must be followed. Patience can be a virtue in some of these situations. As you read this chapter, some of these rules will be repeated in the examples used. This will help to reinforce the concepts presented and further your understanding.

Marriage, Death, Divorce and Remarrying

In February 2014, a study was conducted by the Government Accounting Office (GAO). The GAO found over the last 50 years, from 1960 through 2010, the composition and work patterns of the American household have changed dramatically. The percentage of the population married has declined from 68% to 54%, while the percentage of divorced rose from 2% to 10%. Those widowed declined from 8% to 6%, while those never married increased from 22% to 31% over the period examined. At the same time, the proportion of single-parent households more than doubled. These trends were more pronounced for individuals with lower levels of income and education.

Taken from the same GAO report, from 1960 through 2011, the percentage of women age 62 and older receiving Social Security benefits based solely on their spouse or deceased spouse's earnings record, declined from 56% to 25%. Over the same period, the percentage of women receiving Social Security benefits based solely on their own earnings record increased from 39% to 48%.

Current statistics indicate that about 50% of all marriages end in divorce and multiple divorces are not uncommon. According to U.S. Census Bureau data, the number of Americans getting divorced rose for the third year in a row to about 2.4 million in 2012. This was after plunging during the 18-month recession, which ended in 2009. According to data from the federal government's National Center for Health Statistics, divorces were at a 40-year low in 2009. The divorce rate had more than doubled between 1940 and 1981, before falling by a third by 2009.

In a March 2013 working paper, published by Susan L. Brown, Ph.D. and I-Fen Lin, Ph.D., sociology professors at Bowling Green University, titled *"The Gray Divorce Revolution: Rising Divorce among Middle-aged and Older Adults, 1990-2010"*, the authors attempt to quantify the socio-demographic reasons for the rise in the divorce rate for couples over the age of 50, which were one in ten in 1990 and in 2010 were now one in four. Their study suggests several reasons for the increase. This includes:

- Baby-boomer expectations.
- Longevity is increasing.
- More women entering the workforce.
- Greater societal tolerance of divorce.
- Individuals with a previous divorce.

The baby boom generation was the first to bring self-fulfillment and personal happiness to the concept of marriage. After 20 or 30 years of marriage, if they're now dissatisfied with the way their marriage has evolved over time, they feel entitled to seek greener pastures elsewhere. With advances in medicine and health care, longevity has increased. Now in their 50s and 60s, with the prospects of living to 85 maybe even 95, many are thinking do I really want to spend another 30 or 40 years with this same person. As greater numbers of women have entered the workforce, the reliance on a single family "breadwinner" has diminished. Many women feel they have the economic resources to go it alone. Over the last 10-20 years, society has become increasingly more tolerate on many fronts. Divorce just doesn't carry the same stigma today that it once did. Lastly, if you've been through one divorce, the second one may not seem as scary. The authors cite the divorce rate for remarriages as 2.5 times the rate for first marriages. Many times there is an under appreciation of the stresses which can occur in blended families.

In a January 2014 paper titled, "*Recession and Divorce in the United States, 2008-2011*", published by Philip N. Cohen, Ph.D., sociology professor at the University of Maryland, his research indicates about 150,000 divorces were either postponed or avoided between 2009 and 2011 and linked these break-ups to the economic cycle at the time. Economic hardship adds stress to marriages that increases the risk of marital conflict and dissolution. Job loss and low earnings are perhaps the best studied aspects of economic hardship, with men's conditions usually found to be especially consequential. Home foreclosure, poverty, wage declines, job shift changes, fear of unemployment, or other economic threats (actual or perceived) may have similar stressing effects. On the other hand, there are two mechanisms by which economic hardship might reduce the occurrence of divorce, at least temporarily. First, the loss of a job or a decline in the value of a home may make divorce more costly relative to a spouse's or couple's available resources. Divorcing presents potential costs in housing, legal fees, childcare and losses from diminished economies of scale. Second, hard economic times within families may draw some couples closer together in resilience, so that even those considering divorce might set aside their conflicts and pull together, resulting in declining divorce rates.

In January 2014, Bloomberg ranked the U.S. states and the District of Columbia, based on the percentages of residents ages 15+ who were divorced. In Table 12.1, we examine the top five states which have the highest percentage of divorced and also the top five states with the most married individuals. The rankings were based on the 2012 U.S. Census American Community Survey.

Table 12.1 Top 5 States for the Most Divorced – 2012

Rank	State	Divorced	Married
1	Nevada	14.6%	45.6%
2	Maine	14.2%	50.8%
3	Oklahoma	13.5%	50.1%
4	Oregon	13.4%	49.0%
5 (tie)	Arkansas	13.3%	50.5%
5 (tie)	West Virginia	13.3%	49.9%

Source: Bloomberg

Table 12.2 Top 5 States for the Most Married - 2012

Rank	State	Married	Divorced
1	Utah	55.7%	9.5%
2	Idaho	55.0%	12.5%
3	Wyoming	52.9%	12.8%
4	Nebraska	52.8%	10.4%
5 (tie)	Montana	52.7%	12.3%
5 (tie)	Iowa	52.7%	11.4%

Source: Bloomberg

According to a U.S. Census Bureau paper titled, *"Number, Timing and Duration of Marriages and Divorces: 2009"*, first marriages, which end in divorce, last about 8 years, on average. What percentages of marriages make it to the 10th anniversary? Table 12.3 below displays this for men and women.

Table 12.3 Percent Reaching 10th Anniversary by Marriage Cohort and Sex; First Marriages 2009

Age Group	Men	Women
1960 - 1964	83.4%	82.8%
1965 - 1969	80.0	79.3
1970 - 1974	75.0	74.5
1975 - 1979	73.4	72.8
1980 - 1984	74.3	71.1
1985 - 1989	75.4	74.5
1990 - 1994	77.3	74.5
1995 - 1999	(X)	(X)

(X): Marriage cohort had not all had sufficient time to reach the stated anniversary at the time of the survey done in 2009.

Source: U.S. Census Bureau; Number, Timing and Duration of Marriages and Divorces: 2009

Since the early to mid-1980s, the percentage of marriages making it to the 10th anniversary has been increasing.

After these sobering statistics, a little humor is appropriate here. *With only taking Social Security into account, if you can't make the marriage work in the long run, at least try to stick it out until you cross the 10 year mark.* That's how long a marriage has to last in order for either spouse to collect Social Security benefits on the ex.

Let's first look at the rules in order to qualify for Social Security benefits as a spouse, ex-spouse or widow/widower. As you might expect, in dealing with the federal government there is a different answer for each category and exceptions to every rule.

Marriage

In order to qualify for and receive benefits as a spouse, you must have been married to the individual for at least one continuous year immediately before the day of the application for Social Security benefits. Even if you are not married, you may still be able to qualify for spousal benefits if you and the covered worker are the natural parents of the covered individual's child. Both the child and the parent, who is the primary caregiver, are entitled to dependent benefits equal to 50% of the covered worker's benefit. This benefit is subject to a family maximum amount, which ranges from 150% to 180% of the worker's benefit. The covered worker's benefit is not affected by the family maximum restrictions. A caregiving parent's dependent benefit ends when the child turns the age of 16.

Death and the Survivor Benefit

The shortest length-of-marriage requirement applies to survivor benefits. An individual can qualify for widow or widower's benefits if he or she were married to the deceased for at least 9 months, immediately prior to the day in which the individual died. They must also be married at the time of death. The nine month rule can be waived if:

- You are the mother or father of the decease's biological child.
- You legally adopted your decease's child while you were married to him or her and before the child attained age 18.
- The decease's death was the result of an accident or while serving in the military on active duty.

Surviving widowers have the same rights as surviving widows. The surviving spouse is entitled to benefits based on their deceased spouse's earnings record, as long as the covered worker had earned their 40 credits (10 years) to qualify for Social Security benefits. Survivor benefits are equal to 100% of what the deceased worker collected or was entitled to collect at their time of death. If the deceased worker was collecting reduced early retirement benefits, the surviving spouse could collect that amount or 82.5% of the deceased worker's PIA, whichever is larger. This applies even if he or she dies before reaching their FRA. Survivor benefits can be claimed as early as age 60, though at a reduced benefit amount.

Survivor's benefits and retirement benefits represent two different buckets of money. In many cases, a widow/widower can begin receiving one benefit at a reduced rate, then at their FRA or later, switch to the other benefit at an unreduced rate. An ex-wife may want to collect reduced survivor benefits initially, subject to any earnings cap restrictions then switch to her own benefits at age 70.

The window to reach full retirement age for spousal benefits and survivor benefits are slightly different. This can be an area of confusion for many individuals. Birth years for full survivor benefits are different than those for full retirement benefits. For anyone born from 1943 through 1954, the age for full retirement and spousal benefits is 66. For survivor benefits, it applies to birth years from 1945 through 1956 to receive full survivor benefits. For those born in 1960 or later, full retirement age is 67 but for survivor benefits it is 1962 or later. Collecting before your FRA will reduce the benefits you receive.

At the earliest claiming age of 60 (50 if disabled), a surviving spouse is entitled to 71.5% of their deceased spouse's full retirement benefit. This assumes the deceased spouse did not claim early benefits. At age 66 or later the surviving spouse would be entitled to 100% of her deceased spouse's PIA at their FRA. For survivors born from 1945 through 1956, who collect benefits as early as age 60, these benefits are reduced by .396% per month for every month they collect benefits before reaching their full survivor age.

Example 37

Let's begin with a straightforward example. A spouse has reached her FRA of 66 and begins collecting retirement benefits. She is entitled to receive $1,100 per month. Her younger husband then passes away at age 62. He was not collecting any Social Security benefits at his time of death. His PIA at his FRA is $2,200 per month. His reduced benefit at age 62 would have been $1,650 ($2,200 x 75%) per month. What benefit amount is she entitled to?

Though her husband has not yet reached his FRA, she is entitled to a step-up in her benefit amount to reflect her 100% survivor benefit. In this case that would be $2,200 per month since she waited until her own FRA to begin collecting retirement benefits. However, if she either had claimed her own retirement benefit early OR her husband began collecting early retirement benefits before he passed away, her survivor benefit would have been reduced.

Example 38

In this example, the husband is entitled to a PIA of $2,000 when he reaches his FRA. He decides to claim reduced early benefits at age 62. His benefit will be reduced by 25% so he will receive $1,500 ($2,000 x .75) per month. Three years later, he dies of a heart attack. His wife has reached her FRA. What survivor benefit is the spouse entitled to?

At first thought you might think it is what her husband was collecting, in this case, the $1,500 per month. Remember, the wife had already reach her FRA, so she is entitled to either $1,500 per month, which is what her late husband was collecting or 82.5% of his PIA. Whichever one results in the largest benefit that is what she will receive. In this example, the surviving spouse is entitled to $1,650 ($2,000 x .825) per month, since this amount is larger than the $1,500 he was collecting before he passed away.

Example 39

A couple is separated by seven years. He is 65 and his wife is 72. He is not collecting any benefits but his wife has been collecting her Social Security benefits since she turned age 62, at a reduced benefit rate. He is still working and his retirement benefit will be larger than hers. She passes away. Can he, as a widower now, file for survivor benefits and then switch to his benefit at age 70, which would maximize his own benefit amount?

The answer is yes. If he does this now, his benefit will be smaller than that which his late wife received because he is claiming survivor benefits before he reaches his FRA of 66. In this example, the husband would receive about 95% of his late wife's monthly benefit. He can continue collecting survivor benefits while he defers his own retirement benefits past his FRA. During this period his retirement benefits will accrue delayed retirement credits worth 8% per year, for each year he postpones claiming benefits between age 66 and 70. Survivor benefits do not accrue these delayed retirement credits. By implementing this strategy he will boost his retirement benefit to 132% of his PIA at 70 and also create a larger benefit base amount for any future annual cost-of-living adjustments received.

Since he was 65 when his wife passed away, another option for him would be to wait one year until he turns his FRA of 66. He would then be entitled to a survivor benefit of 100% of what the deceased worker was entitled to receive at their FRA. Since he has now reached his FRA, any earnings cap restrictions disappear. He could still defer his own retirement benefits until age 70 and earn four years of delayed retirement credits.

Example 40

A woman is currently age 64 and began collecting reduced early Social Security benefits when she turned age 62. As a result of claiming early, her benefit was permanently reduced by 25%. She is currently married to her husband who is 78 years old. Decades earlier she was previously married and that marriage lasted 12 years. Since her current husband is much older than she is, she wonders if the husband she is married to now should die, would she be able to collect benefits on her ex-spouse's earnings record once the ex turns age 62 in a couple of years? She believes her ex-spouses earnings record and PIA will be higher than her current husband's benefit is.

The answer is a *qualified* yes. She cannot collect benefits on her ex-spouse's earnings record while her current husband is still alive. If her current husband dies, the woman can collect 100% of his current PIA as a survivor benefit if she has reached her FRA, assuming it is age 66. If she hasn't reached her FRA, she would receive a smaller survivor benefit.

She has another option when her current husband passes. She could collect spousal benefits on her ex-spouse's earnings record, if that amount would result in a larger benefit and he is eligible to claim and has reached age 62. In this example, she would receive less than 50% of his PIA as a spousal benefit on her ex's earnings record because she began to collect her own retirement benefits early. She cannot claim both a survivor and a spousal benefit at the same time. If she should survive both her current and former ex-spouse, she would have her pick of which widow's benefit to collect. Lucky her!

Maximum survivor benefits are based on the ex-spouse's maximum benefit at the time of death. It will not grow if the surviving spouse delays collecting beyond their FRA but will be reduced if they collect early. Their own retirement benefit will increase by the 8% per year between their FRA and age 70 for delayed retirement credits.

Example 41

A husband reached his FRA, at which time he implements the file and suspend strategy, with the goal to create the maximum survivor benefit for his spouse. Two years later, at age 68, the unexpected happens. His wife, now pass her FRA, passes away. She also has her own earnings record but had not yet filed any type of claims with Social Security. Since the husband filed and suspended benefits, can he file for survivor benefits on his deceased wife?

The answer depends on what the PIA was for the wife. If the husband's PIA is less than his wife's PIA, the husband would be entitled to the difference between the two PIAs. His own benefit would continue to earn delayed retirement credits. If the deceased wife's PIA is smaller than the husband's, he would not be able to collect a survivor benefit.

Example 42

Let's extend the previous example further. Are there any other options available to the husband now that his wife has passed away?

The answer is yes. The husband had done the right thing with trying to maximize his survivor benefit for his wife by implementing the file and suspend strategy. This triggers spousal benefits for his wife, which she had not yet claimed, while letting his own retirement benefit earn delayed retirement credits. Now that his wife has passed, there is no need to maximize his survivor benefit.

The first option for the husband is just to do nothing and continue to earn his delayed retirement credits for another two years. At age 70, his retirement benefit will be 132% of his PIA and he will have maximized his lifetime guaranteed income from Social Security.

The second option for the husband is to begin collecting his own retirement benefits now. Since he delayed his own benefit for two years, his benefit will now be 116% of his PIA at his FRA.

There is a third option available to the husband. Since the husband filed and suspended his own retirement benefit two years earlier, he could request a lump sum payout back to the date of his suspension. This would be in lieu of his delayed retirement credits. He could collect two years' worth of retirement benefits at whatever his PIA is. Going forward, as if he claimed benefits at his FRA of 66, his monthly benefit would be his PIA.

Example 43

This next scenario will look at the complexities involved when one's health deteriorates and the steps which must be considered. In this situation the husband has recently turned age 62. The spouse will turn 62 next year. Both have FRAs of 66. The husband has the largest earnings record and his PIA at his FRA will be $2,150 per month. However, the husband was diagnosed with an inoperable cancerous brain tumor six months ago. His prognosis is not good. What options are available for this couple?

Having just turned 62, the husband believes his ability to make it to his FRA is low. Given this assessment, he should probably file to claim early retirement benefits even though they will be reduced by 25% and will also reduce the survivor benefits available for his wife. Also, his medical condition has left him unable to work. At this point, the husband should also file for Social Security disability benefits. There is a five month waiting period before disability benefits can commence after the date Social Security determines the disability began. If the husband is approved for disability benefits, the monthly check he receives from Social Security will be increased. If the SSA determines his disability began before he started receiving retirement benefits approved for disability benefits, this will increase survivor benefits for his spouse.

Where does this now leave the wife? Her own retirement benefits are substantially less than her husband's. When should she consider claiming her Social Security benefits? She will not turn age 62 until the next year, which at that point, she could then file for her own reduced early retirement benefits, though this will further reduce her potential survivor benefit when her husband passes away.

Survivor benefits are worth 100% of what the deceased worker collected or was entitled to collect at the time of death IF the surviving spouse waits until their own FRA to collect. There is a special minimum benefit rule for survivors when the worker had collected reduced retirement benefits. If the she has reached her FRA when she claims, she is entitled to the larger of what the deceased worker had collected or 82.5% of his PIA.

If the wife can delay collecting until she reaches her FRA, this will provide her with the most flexibility. Claiming reduced early benefits now will permanently reduce her own retirement benefits and if her husband should pass away within the next couple of years, her survivor benefit will be reduced because she claimed her own benefits before she reached her FRA. Alternatively, if her husband does pass way within the next couple of years and she had done nothing, she may then chose to claim her own retirement benefits early and then switch to her survivor benefit once she reached her FRA when they will be worth 100%.

Example 44

Let's add a twist to the previous example. Let's say the wife is older than her husband and the same medical scenario occurs later in their lives. The husband claimed retirement benefits at age 62. He has not reached his FRA but his wife has. If her husband should die before being approved for disability benefits, since she has already reached her FRA, her survivor benefits will be based on 82.5% of her deceased husband's PIA rather than the 75% benefit he received for claiming retirement benefits early.

Divorced

Claiming rules are a bit different for divorced spouses. This actual gives them an advantage which married couples do not have. They do not have to coordinate their claiming strategies or even communicate with each other. Divorced spouses can also collect benefits independently, as long as the **ex-spouse is eligible for benefits, even if he or she has not yet filed for benefits.** The divorced spouse must establish a relationship with Social Security first. The SSA is not going to provide any benefit estimate for an ex until it has verified the requester's relationship to the worker. The divorced spouse may have to submit both a marriage certificate and a divorce decree to prove they are a divorced spouse. In some cases, if the worker is already entitled to benefits and the ex-spouse was previously listed on their record, a marriage certificate or divorce decree may not be needed.

In order to qualify for and receive Social Security benefits, based on your ex's earnings record as a divorced spouse, you must have been married to your ex for at least 10 years and not be currently married. Divorced spouses not only have all the rights of currently married couples, they also have an additional benefit. You are able to begin collecting benefits on your ex's earnings record as early as 62, assuming your former spouse is also at least age 62 and eligible for Social Security benefits. This applies even if he or she has not yet applied for Social Security benefits. To exercise this option your divorce must have been finalized for at least two years. The rules indicate you are able to collect benefits on your ex-spouse as long as you're not entitled to higher benefits on your own earnings record. As a divorced spouse, your benefit is equal to 50% of your ex-spouse's FRA benefit amount or disability benefit if you start receiving benefits at your FRA. If you claim before your FRA, the benefit amount received will be reduced.

If she is entitled to her own benefits, Social Security will pay those first. If her spousal benefit, from her ex, is larger than her retirement benefit, the SSA will increase her benefit to bring it up to the larger amount.

Example 45

A couple has been married for 15 years. The husband is 67 years old and the wife is 65, when they decide to call it quits and file for divorce. The husband has been collecting retirement benefits and the wife, who owns her own business plans to keep running it. Her goal is to delay claiming retirement benefits until age 70, when she can claim her maximum retirement benefit. Can the wife claim spousal benefits at her FRA, even though the divorce will not have been finalized for two years yet? Note: we're going to ignore any possible earnings cap restrictions she might be subject to.

The answer is yes. There is an exception to the two year rule. The husband, soon to be ex, is already claiming retirement benefits. Once the wife reaches her FRA, she can claim spousal benefits, even if it's been less than two years. So in this example, once she reaches her FRA, assuming it is age 66, in one more year she is eligible to file a restricted claim for spousal benefits and collect 50% of her ex-husband's PIA. Since she is delaying her own retirement benefits she can earn delayed retirement credits until she turns 70, when they will be worth 132% of her PIA benefit.

Example 46

What about a situation where an individual has been married and divorced twice or more? Let's look at a trifecta situation. An individual was married in their first relationship for 12 years then got divorced. Eighteen months later they got remarried and that marriage lasted only five years. Two years after that they met the person of their dreams and got remarried for a third time. That marriage lasted 18 years before ending in divorce. All three ex's are still alive. Is the individual entitled to receive benefits from their ex's earnings records even though they were married and divorced three times?

The answer is yes with a qualifying but. You can use the earnings record of either the 1st or 3rd ex-spouse because those marriages lasted at least 10 years. If ex-spouse number two had the largest earnings record, sorry you're out of luck. You could choose to claim on either of the two other ex-spouses. Whichever earnings record would result in the highest benefit to you, as long as you are **still unmarried**, you could file a benefit claim on. Both ex-spouses would have had to reach age 62. Even if either ex-spouse remarries you can still claim benefits as long as you are currently unmarried.

As with married couples, a divorced spouse can collect reduced retirement benefits, such as spousal benefits, as early as age 62. Those benefits will be worth just 35% of the ex-spouse's benefit amount at that age. Any time you collect a benefit before you reach your FRA, you will receive the largest benefit to which you are entitled to. You cannot choose between collecting your own benefit or a spousal benefit, if you claim before your FRA.

If you wait until your FRA, assuming that is 66, to claim benefits you can restrict your claim to spousal benefits only and collect 50% of your ex's FRA benefit while deferring your own benefit until it is worth more at a later date. Each of the divorced spouses can simultaneously claim spousal benefits based on their ex's earnings record. If you employ this strategy, you can accrue delayed retirement credits worth 8% per year for every year you postpone claiming benefits up until age 70. At that age, you can then switch to your own retirement benefit, which would be worth 132% of your PIA at your FRA plus any intervening COLAs.

Example 47

Let's examine a scenario where the ex-husband decides to claim early retirement benefits. A couple were married for 17 years then got divorced. The husband, now 67, began collecting reduced early retirement benefits when he turned 62. The ex-wife is now 56 (her birth year is 1958). What options exist for the ex-wife now?

Unfortunately, there are none at the moment. The ex-wife must wait until she turns age 62, at which time she can claim reduced benefits on her ex's earnings record. When claiming benefits before her FRA, Social Security will pay the largest benefit to which she is entitled to, whether it is on her own work record or that of her ex-spouse. She cannot choose which benefit to receive. If she does decide to claim before her FRA, which in this case is 66 years and 8 months, her retirement benefit will be reduced by 28.33% at age 62. As an ex-spouse, if her benefit is larger than her own earnings record, her spousal benefit is worth 33.33% at age 62, compared with collecting at her own FRA benefit.

Even though her ex-spouse collected a reduced retirement benefit prior to reaching his FRA, spousal benefits are based on 50% of his PIA at his FRA if they are claimed at the FRA, less if collected earlier. If she claims before her FRA, she cannot choose which benefit to collect AND she will forfeit the chance to earn delayed retirement credits worth 8% for each year between her FRA and 70.

Example 48

In this situation we have a couple with similar earnings records in which the marriage lasted longer than 10 years before ending in divorce. Each ex-spouse is entitled to receive a retirement benefit of $2,000 per month at their FRAs, assuming that is age 66 for both. In this situation it might make sense for a spouse to restrict their claim to spousal benefits only and let their own retirement benefit accrue delayed retirement credits worth 8% each year until age 70. The spouse could collect $1,000 per month ($2,000 x 50%) for four years and at age 70 switch to their own retirement benefit which would now be worth $2,640 ($2,000 x 1.32) per month as a result of those delayed retirement credits.

Example 49

In this example let's look at the scenario where the ex-spouse has the larger PIA benefit, which will be $2,000 per month at age 66. The ex-wife has a much smaller PIA benefit worth only $500 per month when she reaches her FRA. This lower benefit could be based on intermittent work throughout her career or low-paying jobs. What should the ex-wife do in this situation?

In this situation the ex-wife might be better off filing an unrestricted claim based on her ex-spouse's earnings record. She would be able to receive 50% of his PIA benefit of $2,000, which would be $1,000 per month. This amount is worth more than her retirement benefit is worth. Even after four years of accruing delayed retirement credits her benefit would still be worth only $660 ($500 x 1.32) per month at age 70, if she restricted her claim to spousal benefits only and earned her delayed retirement credits on her earnings record.

In most cases, but not always, when there is a wide disparity in PIA benefits, the lower earning spouse may be better off claiming reduced early benefits at age 62, assuming she is no longer working or not earning more than the earnings cap restriction. This strategy would allow her to collect benefits as soon as possible if she needs the money. If she waits until her FRA, the strategy would allow her to claim the 50% spousal benefit of $1,000. However, since she would be claiming reduced early retirement benefits at age 62, that spousal benefit of $1,000 would be reduced by 30%, allowing her to receive $750 per month beginning at age 62.

She is still eligible for a much larger survivor benefit if her ex-spouse should die first. If she were at least at her FRA when this happens, she would be entitled to a survivor benefit worth 100% of what her ex-spouse received during his lifetime, including any delayed retirement credits. She could even receive this benefit if her ex-spouse had remarried. It will not affect the survivor benefits of his current wife.

As a divorced spouse if you remarry, you will completely nullify any spousal benefits based on the ex-spouse, no matter the age at which the person remarried. Generally, you cannot collect benefits on your former spouse's earnings record unless your later marriage ends, whether by death, divorce or annulment. Any number of ex-wife's can collect on the ex-husband's benefits, as long as they were married for 10 years or more. If an ex-wife is raising the ex-husband's child, as long as the child is under the age of 16, the child can also collect a small dependent benefit.

Example 50

We'll look at one more situational scenario involving divorce. A husband and wife have been divorce for a number of years. When the ex-wife reached her FRA of 66, she filed a restricted claim for spousal benefits only. This allows her to collect some income now while letting her own retirement benefit earn delayed retirement credits, which if she waits until age 70 to claim benefits, will be worth 132% of her PIA. The ex-wife subsequently heard about a strategy where an individual can file and suspend and preserve a lump sum payout option which could be used later. Can the ex-wife also do this?

The answer is yes but she probably would not want to. The ex-wife has already filed a restricted claim for spousal benefits only, allowing her to collect retirement benefits on her ex-husband's earnings record. If she files and suspends now, her spousal benefit would completely disappear and she would lose that monthly benefit. This presents an example of why it is a good idea to evaluate all your options before deciding on a claiming strategy. It could have unintended consequences.

Marriage, Divorce and Remarrying

A quick review at this juncture may be in order. An individual can receive retirement benefits as a divorced spouse on a former spouse's earnings record if:

- He or she was married to the former spouse for at least 10 years.
- Is at least 62 years old.
- Is currently unmarried.
- Is not entitled to a higher retirement benefit on his or her own earnings record.
- The divorce has been finalized for at least 2 years.

If the former spouse is eligible for a retirement benefit but has not yet applied for it, the unmarried divorced spouse can still receive a retirement benefit if he or she meets the eligibility requirements listed above. How do you think this applies to the next situation?

Example 51

This is an interesting scenario involving common-law marriage. A wife was legally married to her spouse for 20 years. The couple then divorces. The husband later remarries. Likewise, the ex-wife also remarries but this marriage is by common law. Nine years have now passed and they are still married. In this scenario, can the ex-wife (in her second marriage) who is now age 61, file for spousal benefits based on her marriage to her first husband when she turns 62?

The answer is it's going to depend. It's just not a clear cut answer as in the previous examples which have been illustrated. This has a legal twist to it. The Social Security Handbook defines a common law marriage as one in which neither a religious or civil ceremony was held. In certain states a common law marriage may be entered into if a man and a woman agree to be married for the rest of their lives. Most states will generally recognize a common law marriage which has been validly entered into in another state. Social Security will follow state laws when it comes to recognizing common law marriage. In the example used, which state the ex-wife lives in will probably be critical in determining an answer to the question, along with contacting the Social Security Administration or a local Social Security office in the state.

Example 52

The definition of what constitutes the family unit has been changing and evolving over recent years. The following scenario is occurring more frequently. It pulls many different elements into play when evaluating Social Security claiming options.

A couple had been married for 35 years. Divorce occurs and it has now been 12 years since the marriage ended. The ex-wife is now 63, still unmarried but has some health issues. The ex-husband is now 66 and earlier in his life remarried a much younger woman. He now also has a minor child from his second marriage. During his first marriage, the wife worked in her husband's business and in many years took no wages and hence paid no Social Security taxes. As many individuals who are self-employed do, there is a focus on taking the maximum allowable deductions. This in turn substantially reduces taxable income and the self-employment tax. These are the facts for the scenario above:

- Ex-Husband's FRA: 66
- Wife's FRA: 66
- Ex-husband's PIA: $1,950 per month
- Wife's PIA: $500 per month

The wife's circumstances change and now, at age of 63, she needs the money and decides to file for reduced early retirement benefits. Since she is still three years from reaching her FRA, her retirement benefits will only be reduced by about 20%. This will give her a retirement benefit of $400 per month.

As a divorced spouse she meets the requirements to be eligible for spousal benefits, even though her ex-husband has not yet claimed his benefits. He has reached his FRA of 66. The most a divorced spouse can receive is 50% of her ex-husband's retirement benefit at his FRA. However, because she started collecting her retirement benefit three years earlier, the amount of her spousal benefit is also reduced. The combination of her retirement benefit, increased by her spousal benefit will total about $750 per month.

Now let's look at the ex-husband's retirement situation. Since he has turned his FRA of 66, he could file and suspend his benefits. By implementing this strategy he accomplishes three things. First, he is now eligible to earn his delayed retirement credits worth 8% each year until age 70, if he waits that long. Four years' worth of delayed retirement credits will boost his retirement benefit by 32%. Second, he triggers spousal benefits for his new wife. Third, he triggers dependent benefits for his minor son. His current wife and minor son are each entitled to receive a benefit equal to 50% of his PIA at his FRA.

His son is eligible to collects dependent benefits until he turns age 18 or 19 if he is still in high school. Meanwhile his current wife can collect benefits as a caregiving spouse until her son turns age 16. However, she would be subject to earnings cap restrictions if she earns more than the prescribed limit and could forfeit some or all of her benefits. The husband's first wife, who now has health issues, receives only $750 per month in combined benefits. The current wife receives $975 per month (assuming no earnings cap restrictions) in spousal benefits by being the caregiving spouse and the minor son also receives $975 per month in dependent benefits for a combined benefit amount of $1,950 per month. Sometimes the way Social Security benefits are received doesn't always seem fair.

Marriage, Divorce and Death

Even if your former ex-spouse should become deceased, you may still be entitled to a survivor benefit worth 100% of what he or she was receiving or was entitled to at the time of death. This applies even if your former spouse had remarried and has a surviving spouse. You can continue to collect benefits as a surviving spouse or divorced spouse as long as you wait until age 60 or later to remarry.

If you are older than age 60 and remarried, you cannot collect benefits on your ex-husband's earnings record while your current husband is still alive. If your current husband dies, you can collect 100% of his survivor benefit if you have reached your FRA, less if you file a claim before your FRA. You also have the option to collect a spousal benefit on your ex-husband's earnings record, if that amount would result in a larger benefit to you. You can't claim both but you can switch benefits.

Example 53

A couple has been married for over 10 years. Circumstances arise and they decide to divorce. Later the husband becomes deceased. They are both about 56 years of age when he passes away. Can the surviving spouse collect survivor benefits?

Yes, but not yet. To collect survivor benefits as a divorced spouse, she must be unmarried and reached the age of 60. At that time, she could qualify for survivor benefits which are worth up to 100% of what her ex was entitled to collect at the time of his death, providing she has reached her FRA. If she claims before her FRA, her survivor benefit will be less. If she remarries after age 60 there is an exception. She can collect on her ex's survivor benefit or the spousal benefit of her new spouse, whichever results in the greater benefit, but not both. If we add a twist to the above scenario and say the husband had remarried before his death, his widow is entitled to the same survivor benefit too. They do not have to share the benefit amount.

Remarrying After Death of a Spouse

You can also collect benefits as a *surviving spouse* or *surviving divorced spouse* if you remarry. The key here is you must wait at least until you turn age 60 or age 50, if disabled, to walk down the aisle again. If you remarry before these ages you cannot receive Social Security benefits as a surviving spouse while you are married. If you wait to age 60 to remarry, you may also be entitled to spousal benefits based on your new spouse's earnings record after one year of marriage. If that benefit is more than your widow/widower's survivor's benefit you will receive a combination of benefits which equals the higher amount. You can collect one or the other, but not both.

Example 54

A woman was married to her first husband for 25 years. With both being of the same age, he passed away at age 58. The woman remarried just three weeks shy of turning age 60. Can she collect survivor benefits when she turns age 60?

The answer is no. Even though she was just three weeks from turning 60 before she remarried, the rules are very specific, she cannot collect survivor benefits. If she should outlive her second husband she would be able to choose the higher survivor benefit of the two. Points to consider are: if she waits until her full retirement age to collect survivor benefits, they are worth 100% of what the covered worker collected or was entitled to collect at the time of their death. She could then collect the higher of the two survivor benefits and delay her own retirement benefits until age 70, when she would have earned delayed retirement credits worth 8% per year for each year she postpones collecting them. Survivor benefits never grow any larger, delayed retirement benefits do.

Example 55

Let's look at a slightly different twist of the previous example. A couple had been married for over ten years. He passes away and she remarries before she reaches the age of 60. After just 3 years of marriage, she divorces her husband. Can she collect survivor benefits off of her deceased first spouse?

The answer is yes. At first thought you might think the answer should be no. She remarried before age 60 and her second marriage didn't last ten years. While this is correct, there is an exception to the rule. If you remarry before age 60, you are not entitled to survivor benefits on your deceased husband's earnings record UNLESS your subsequent marriage ends in death, divorce or annulment. So in this example, she would be re-entitled to survivor benefits on her deceased husband's earnings record since her subsequent marriage ended in divorce. Her survivor benefits could begin in the first month in which the subsequent marriage ended if all entitlement requirements are met.

Example 56

A woman is 64, but began collecting reduced early retirement benefits at age 62. Her retirement benefit amount is $8,000 each year. Her current husband is 75 years old, with prior health issues and collecting $16,000 each year in Social Security benefits. The woman was previously married to a younger man, many years ago. They were married for 15 years. Once her ex turns age 62 in four years, can she collect a spousal benefit on her ex-spouse? She believes he will have a greater earnings record than what her current husband has.

The answer is a "qualified" yes. She cannot collect benefits on her ex-husband's earnings record while her current husband is still alive. If her current husband dies, she can collect 100% of a survivor benefit if she has reached her FRA. In this case, that would be $16,000 per year in retirement benefits, which would be double her current benefit of $8,000 per year. If she claims before her FRA, her survivor benefit would be less. She would also have the option to collect a spousal benefit on her ex-husband's earnings record if that benefit amount would result in a larger benefit to her. At his FRA, her ex-spouse is entitled to the maximum retirement benefit which is $30,396. Her spousal benefit would be equal to 50% of what he was entitled to collect, which in this example would be $15,198 per year. However, since she claimed early retirement benefits at age 62, her benefits are permanently reduced. She would be entitled to a spousal benefit less than the $15,198 amount. You can't claim both but you can switch.

Dependent Children

According to the SSA, about 4.4 million children receive nearly $2.5 billion each month because one or both of their parents are disabled, retired or deceased. With more couples having children at older ages than in the past, remarriage of an older man to a younger women, then having children or just adopting additional children at an older age has become more common. It's much more likely a husband or wife could have a child under 18 when they begin collecting Social Security benefits, especially if they begin to collect early retirement benefits at age 62. Evolving family dynamics can now have a huge impact on retirement planning than just increasing life insurance coverage or updating IRA beneficiary forms. It can also influence when a parent should claim their Social Security retirement benefits.

A child can receive benefits if he or she is your biological (natural) child, adopted child, dependent stepchild and in some cases, a grandchild if the child's parents are dead or disabled and the child is your dependent. In some cases, your child could also be eligible for benefits on his or her grandparents' earnings. To receive dependent benefits a child must have:

- A parent who is disabled.
- A parent who is retired and is entitled to Social Security benefits.
- A parent who has passed away after having worked long enough in a job where he or she paid Social Security taxes.

The child must also be:

- Unmarried.
- Younger than age 18.
- Between ages 18 and 19 AND a full time student. No higher than 12th grade.
- Is age 18 or older and is disabled. The disability must have started before age 22.

Documentation, which may be needed, depending on the type of benefit involved can include:

- Child's birth certificate.
- Parent's Social Security number.
- Child's Social Security number.
- Proof of a parent's death.
- Medical evidence to prove a disability exists.

Benefit Amounts Payable

Within the family, a child can receive a dependent benefit based on 50% of the parent worker's PIA at their FRA. Even if the worker claims a reduced early retirement benefit or larger benefit by delaying their FRA, the child's benefit is based on 50% of the worker's full retirement benefit at their FRA. If the parent was eligible for Social Security but is deceased, the child can collect 75% of the parent's benefit.

There's limit to the amount of benefits which can be paid to a family. The family maximum benefit is determined as part of every Social Security benefit computation and can be from 150% to 180% of the parent's full retirement benefit amount. If the total amount payable to all family members exceeds this limit, benefits are reduced for each eligible person proportionately, until the total equals the maximum allowable limit. This computation does not include the worker's. Benefits are payable whether or not the parent is collecting, as long as they are old enough and are eligible for Social Security. To compute the reduced benefit amount, the SSA subtracts the worker's PIA from the applicable family maximum amount and divides the remaining balance among the other individuals entitled to benefits on the earnings record.

A word of caution is important here. If a worker claims reduced early retirement benefits and continues working, his benefits could be reduced or even wiped out completely if his earnings exceed annual limits. If the worker loses benefits due to the earnings cap restriction, other family members who get benefits based on that parent's earnings record could also lose benefits. As we saw earlier, once the parent turns their FRA, they could then voluntarily suspend their benefits. This enables the worker to earn delayed retirement credits worth 8% each year until age 70.

If you are taking care of a child under the age of 16, a spouse can claim a 50% spousal benefit, regardless of age, without being deemed to have claimed her own retirement benefits. If you are a widow/widower your benefit can be 75% at any age. If the child is not disabled, your benefits will end when the child turns 16. If your child is disabled, your benefits can continue if you exercise parental control and responsibility for a mentally disabled child or perform personal services for a child who is physically disabled. Benefits stop for the child when they reach age 18 unless the child is a student or is disabled. If a student, benefits continue until the child graduates from high school or until two months after reaching age 19, whichever comes first. If the child is disabled, benefits will continue at age 18. Disability benefits can continue if the disability began before age 22.

A situation which is less known to individuals involves parents, who are over age 62, and are dependent on their adult children for more than 50% of their support. If the adult child dies and would have been eligible for Social Security benefits, the elder parents can qualify for dependent benefits. Dependent parents of deceased adult children can collect up to 87.5% of the worker's benefit if one parent is claiming and up to 75% each if both parents are claiming benefits.

Example 57

This is a straightforward example. The husband is currently age 65. His wife is considerable younger at age 51 and doesn't work. They also have two children, ages 11 and 14. He wants to delay collecting his retirement benefit until age 70, so he is able to earn his delayed retirement credits and maximize his own retirement benefit. Is this the right thing to do as the example is stated?

It sounds like a good strategy but a better alternative would be this. He should obviously wait one year until he reaches his FRA of 66. At that time he should implement the file and suspend strategy to trigger spousal benefits, and in this example, dependent benefits for his minor children who will now be ages 12 and 15. But wait, his wife will only be 52 then. She could be entitled to receive spousal benefits because she is the primary caregiving parent of a minor child under age 16 (two in this example). Once the second child reaches 16, the wife's benefit would most likely stop. Each child could collect benefits until they reach age 18 or age 19 if still in high school. Since she is not working she doesn't have to worry about earnings cap restrictions. The husband is then able to earn his delayed retirement credits, 8% each year, until he reaches age 70.

All three family members could qualify for benefits on the husband's earnings record. They would qualify for 50% of the husband's PIA benefit at his FRA. However, they could be subject to the family maximum benefit limit, which was discussed earlier.

Earnings Cap Restrictions

Whether or not you should claim reduced early retirement benefits is not a simple decision to make. There are a lot of variables to consider. Keep in mind, anyone who collects Social Security benefits before they reach their full retirement age, currently age 66 for most individuals, is subject to earnings cap restrictions (see Chapter Eight) if they continue to work. This earnings cap penalizes individuals who collect any kind of Social Security benefits, whether retirement, spousal or survivor before their FRA. For 2014, they lose $1 in benefits for every $2 earned over $15,480 for the year. That means if you earn more than about $45,000, all your Social Security benefits would be wiped out. A more generous earnings cap applies in the calendar year when you reach your FRA, then disappear completely once you cross that threshold. At that point, you can continue to work while receiving Social Security benefits with no restrictions on their earnings. Benefits forfeited to the earnings cap do not disappear forever. They are merely deferred. The SSA will recalculate your benefits once you reach your full retirement age to account for those deferred benefits. In addition, any dependent benefits will be reduced also by any earnings cap restrictions.

You also could be subject to additional federal income taxes. The percentage of the Social Security benefit on which the income tax is applied is based on a sliding scale, depending on how much outside income the individual or couple has beyond their benefit(s). If the combined income for a single individual is between $25,000 and $34,000, up to 50% of the Social Security benefit is subject to tax. If the amount is more than $34,000, up to 85% of the benefit is taxable. For a married couple, filing jointly, if the combined income limit is between $32,000 and $44,000, up to 50% of the benefits are taxable. Above $44,000, up to 85% of the benefits are taxable.

"No longer will older Americans be denied the healing miracle of modern medicine. No longer will illness crush and destroy the savings that they have so carefully put away over a lifetime so that they might enjoy dignity in their later years. No longer will young families see their own incomes, and their own hopes, eaten away simply because they are carrying out their deep moral obligations to their parents, and to their uncles, and their aunts."

Lyndon B. Johnson
36th President of the United States
Remarks at the Signing of the Medicare Bill

37th Vice President of the United States
Senate Majority Leader
Senate Minority Leader
Senate Majority Whip
Democratic U.S. Senator – Texas

CHAPTER THIRTEEN

THE MEDICARE PROGRAM

Congress created Medicare under Title XVIII; Health Insurance for the Aged and Disabled as part of the Social Security Act and Medicaid under Title XIX in 1965 to provide health insurance to people age 65 and older or who were disabled regardless of income or medical history. The bill was signed into law by President Lyndon Johnson during the summer of that year. In 1972, Congress expanded Medicare eligibility to include younger people who have permanent disabilities and receive Social Security Disability Insurance (SSDI) payments, including those who have end-stage renal disease (ESRD). Congress further expanded Medicare eligibility in 2001, to cover younger people with amyotrophic lateral sclerosis (ALS, or Lou Gehrig's disease). Beginning in 2007, as required in the *Medicare Prescription Drug, Improvement and Modernization Act of 2003*, Part B premiums a beneficiary pays each month to cover medically-necessary services would become means-tested and based on annual income each year.

The Centers for Medicare and Medicaid Services (CMS), a federal agency within the U.S. Department of Health and Human Services (HHS) of the federal government, administers Medicare, Medicaid, the State Children's Health Insurance Program (SCHIP), the Clinical Laboratory Improvement Amendments (CLIA) and now the Health Insurance Marketplace. CMS creates and monitors detailed rules regarding how the Medicare insurance program should operate, so the program meets the best interest of its beneficiaries. Along with the Departments of Labor and Treasury, CMS also implements the insurance reform provisions of the *Health Insurance Portability and Accountability Act (HIPPA) of 1996.*

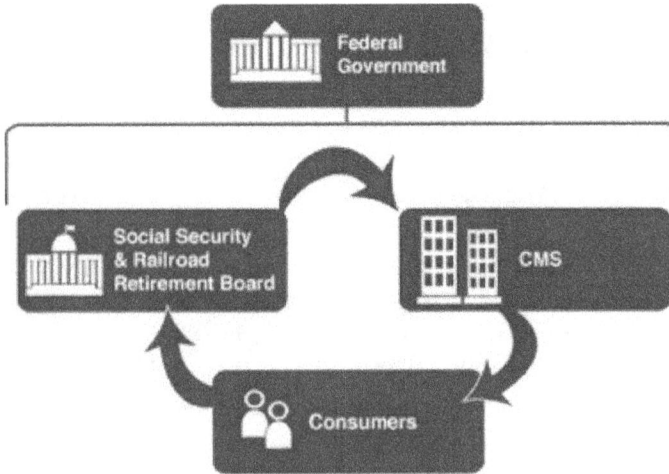

Courtesy: UnitedHealthcare® Medicare Solutions

The Social Security Administration (SSA) and the Railroad Retirement Board (RRB) are responsible for determining Medicare eligibility, enrolling consumers and processing premium payments for the Medicare program.

According to the *2013 Annual Report of the Boards of Trustees of the Federal Hospital Insurance and Federal Supplemental Medical Insurance Trust Funds,* in 2012,

Medicare covered 50.7 million people: 42.1 million aged 65 and older and 8.5 million who were disabled. About 27% of these beneficiaries have chosen to enroll in a Medicare Part C private health plan, which contracts with Medicare to provide Medicare Part A and Part B health services. Total expenditures in 2012 were $574.2 billion. Total income was $536.9 billion, which consisted of $523.5 billion in non-interest income and $13.4 billion in interest earnings. Assets held in special issue U.S. Treasury securities decreased by $37.3 billion to $287.6 billion.

THE AFFORDABLE CARE ACT

There is much confusion among many individuals who are on Medicare as to whether the Health Insurance Marketplace is something they either need to worry about or enroll in. The answer is very simple – **No**. If you are enrolled in original Medicare, a Medicare Advantage (Part C) plan, a Medicare Supplement plan or enrolled in a Medicare Prescription Drug (Part D) plan you do not have to be concerned with the Health Insurance Marketplace. You have creditable health care insurance coverage.

MEDICARE SUMMARY NOTICES

If you have original Medicare, every 3 months you receive a Medicare Summary Notice (MSN) in the mail, if you get Part A and Part B. This notice shows all the services and/or supplies that health care providers billed to Medicare during the 3 month period, what Medicare paid and what you may owe the healthcare provider.

You are also able to view your Medicare claims or file an appeal online. Claims are generally available for viewing within 24 hours after processing. You will need to first register at www.MyMedicare.gov. Complete your "Initial Enrollment Questionnaire" online. This will ensure your claims are correctly paid. Once this setup is completed, some of what you can do online is listed below.

- Manage personal information like medical conditions, allergies and implanted devices.
- Manage your personal drug list and pharmacy information.
- Track original Medicare claims and your Part B deductible status.
- View and order copies of your Medicare Summary Notices.
- Access to your personal health information by using Medicare's "Blue Button."
- Search for, add to and manage a list of your favorite providers and access quality information about them.

SUMMARIZING YOUR MEDICARE OPTIONS

This chapter is only going to provide a brief educational insight into the original Medicare program, which includes Part A and Part B. There are optional coverage choices, individuals can enroll in, which can cover care, procedures and prescription drugs which Medicare alone does not cover. There can be an additional cost to enroll in these plans and Medicare does NOT cover the cost you may incur by these plans.

In summary, Medicare health insurance options offered to consumers eligible to participate in Medicare can consist of a combination of one of the following:

- Original Medicare (Part A and Part B)
- Original Medicare + Part D
- Original Medicare + Medicare Supplement
- Original Medicare + Medicare Supplement + Part D
- Medicare Advantage Part C, which may or may not include prescription drug coverage.
- Original Medicare + Medicaid
- Employer-Sponsored Group Retiree Plans
- Employer Senior Supplement Group Retiree Plans

There can be penalties for not enrolling in Part A, Part B and Part D plans when you first become eligible unless you qualify for a special exemption.

EMPLOYER GROUP RETIREE PLANS

A group retiree is an individual who has retired from his/her previous employer or union and is looking for continued health care and/or prescription drug coverage through his/her previous employer or union. Health insurance companies have existing relationships with employer groups which allow them the opportunity to offer products and administer benefits for group retirees through contractual agreements and arrangements. With subsidized plans, the employer contributes to the premium but with endorsed plans, the employer does not pay any portion of the premiums.

Employer-provided health insurance for retirees has been declining for decades. According to Extend Health, a unit of the benefits consulting firm Towers Watson, 25% of employers who provide health insurance offer some type of financial assistance to retirees to help them with medical costs. This is down from more than 60% in the 1980s. Some companies are discontinuing their health plans for retirees and giving them a fixed amount of money to use towards their health expenses. 3M discontinued the company's traditional Medicare supplement plan in 2013 and is making contributions to retirees' health reimbursement accounts. With establishment of the Health Insurance Marketplace, early retirees now have guaranteed access to health insurance coverage, provided under the Affordable Care Act beginning in 2014. This may likely cause more large employers to strategically rethink their corporate health benefit strategy for retired former employees under age 65. Many companies may now consider dropping their coverage altogether for this former employee segment. For early retirees in that 55-64 age bracket, some individuals may find their premiums could decrease through the use of the Health Insurance Marketplace for individuals.

Employees from the public sector are also not immune from these changes either. More municipalities, which used to cover retiree health care expenses at 100%, are now requiring formers workers to pay a monthly premium. While the premiums are usually modest, benefit coverage is also less than what it was. This trend will likely accelerate in the future with retired public employees having to contribute a larger percentage towards their health benefits through increasing premiums.

Senior supplement group retiree plans are only available through employer groups. These plans help pay for some or all of the costs not covered by original Medicare. They have similar coverage as the federal Medicare supplement plans. Joining a Medicare Advantage plan may limit or end the individual's employer or union coverage for both the individual and/or family members covered by his/her group coverage plan for medical and/or prescription drugs. It's important for the individual to understand how their employer or union coverage will work with original Medicare before a decision is made about whether to enroll in a Medicare Advantage plan.

Speak with your former employer or union benefits administrator or the office that answers your health coverage questions before you make any changes to your existing health insurance coverage.

WHO ARE MEDICARE BENEFICIARIES

The following two tables present an overview of selected demographic and coverage data as it applies to Medicare beneficiaries. The tables contrast the years 2010 with 2012.

Table 12.1 Demographics Fact Sheet

November 2010	November 2012
50% of all individuals on Medicare have incomes below $22,000.	No change.
50% of all Medicare beneficiaries have less than $53,000 in savings.	50% of all Medicare beneficiaries have less than $77,000 in savings.
45% have 3 or more chronic conditions.	40% of 3 or more chronic conditions.
>25% or more have a cognitive/mental impairment.	No change.
17% are under 65 and disabled.	No change.
12% are age 85+.	13% are age 85+.

Source: Kaiser Family Foundation; Medicare at a Glance, Jan. 2012

Table 12.2 Coverage Fact Sheet

November 2010	November 2012
25% were enrolled in Medicare Advantage.	23% were enrolled in Medicare Advantage.
20% had a Medicare Supplement plan.	21% had a Medicare Supplement plan.
>30% have employer-sponsored plans provide supplemental.	25% have employer-sponsored plans provide supplemental.
21% of Medicare beneficiaries qualify for Medicaid.	20% of Medicare beneficiaries qualify for Medicaid.
11% of Medicare beneficiaries had no supplemental coverage.	12% of Medicare beneficiaries had no supplemental coverage.

Source: Kaiser Family Foundation; Medicare at a Glance, Jan. 2014

MEDICARE ENROLLMENT

Enrollment for Part A and/or Part B can occur in one of four circumstances below:

1. Under 65 and Already Enrolled in Social Security or the Railroad Retirement Board.
2. Turning Age 65 - Initial Enrollment Period (IEP).
3. General Enrollment Period (GEP).
4. Special Enrollment Period (SEP).

You can sign up for Medicare when you first become eligible, during what is called the Initial Enrollment Period (IEP). This is a 7-month period that begins 3 months before the month you turn 65, the month you turn 65 and 3 months after the month you turn 65. If you do not enroll in Medicare during your IEP you may have to pay a penalty unless you're eligible for an SEP. This penalty may apply to both Part A and Part B of original Medicare.

MEDICARE PART A: HOSPITALIZATION INSURANCE

Individuals, who are eligible for Medicare coverage, have their Medicare Part A premiums entirely waived if the following conditions apply:

- Are 65 years or older and a U.S. citizen or have been a permanent legal resident for 5 continuous years and they or their spouse has paid Medicare taxes for at least 10 years.
- Are under 65, disabled, and have been receiving either Social Security Disability Insurance (SSDI) benefits or Railroad Retirement Board disability benefits. They must receive one of these benefits for at least **24 months** from date of entitlement (first disability payment) before becoming eligible to enroll in Medicare.

- Are receiving continuing dialysis for End Stage Renal Disease (ENRD) or need a kidney transplant.
- Are eligible for SSDI and have amyotrophic lateral sclerosis (ALS, or Lou Gehrig's disease).

Premium Costs for Medicare Part A

Those who do not meet these criteria and are 65 and older must pay a monthly premium to remain enrolled in Medicare Part A, if they or their spouse have not paid Medicare taxes over the course of 10 years (40 quarters) while working. According to the CMS, 99% of Medicare beneficiaries do not pay premiums for Part A.

If you aren't eligible for premium-free Part A, you may be able to buy Part A if you meet one of the following conditions:

- You're 65 or older, and you have (or are enrolling in) Part B and meet the citizenship and residency requirements.
- You're under 65, disabled and your premium-free Part A coverage ended because you returned to work. If you're under 65 and disabled, you can continue to get premium-free Part A for up to 8 1/2 years after you return to work.

The monthly premium for 2014 is $234.00 for individuals having 30-39 quarters of Medicare-covered employment. For those who are not eligible for premium-free Part A hospital insurance and have less than 30 quarters of Medicare-covered employment, the monthly premium is increased to $426 per month.

Medicare Part A Coverage

Medicare Part A covers five areas of health care.

- Inpatient Care in Hospitals

- Inpatient Care in a Skilled Nursing Facility
- Nursing Home Care Services
- Hospice Care Services
- Inpatient Care in a Religious Nonmedical Health Care Institution

Hospitalization Coverage

Medicare Part A provides coverage for hospital care. This includes:

- Inpatient hospital care
- Skilled nursing facility care
- Long-term care hospitals

Inpatient Hospital Care

Hospitalization covers inpatient care in hospitals such as critical access hospitals and inpatient rehabilitation facilities. These costs can include:

- Semi-private room.
- Meals.
- General nursing.
- Medications as part of your inpatient treatment.
- Hospital services and supplies.
- All but the first three pints of blood. However, if the hospital gets blood from a blood bank at no charge, you shouldn't have to pay for it or replace it.

Medicare does not cover and **excludes:**

- Private duty nursing.
- Private room unless medically necessary.
- Television and telephone in your room (if there's a separate charge for these items.
- Personal care items, such as slippers or razors.

Inpatient mental health care coverage is limited 190 days per lifetime.

Skilled Nursing Facility Care

Part A covers skilled nursing care in a skilled nursing care facility (SNF) under certain conditions for a limited time. These Medicare covered services include but are not limited to:

- Semi-private room.
- Meals.
- Skilled nursing care.
- Physical and occupational therapy (Part B).
- Speech language pathology services (Part B).
- Medical social services.
- Medications.
- Medical supplies and equipment used in the facility.
- Ambulance transportation to the nearest supplier of needed services which are not available at the SNF.
- Dietary counseling. A registered dietician or nutritional professional who meets certain requirements can provide these services which can include nutritional assessment, one-on-one counseling and therapy services.

Long-Term Care Hospitals

Long-term care hospitals (LTCH) specialize in treating patients who have more than one serious condition and may improve with time and care, then return to home. **This is not to be confused with long-term care facilities.** You will not have to pay a second deductible for your care in a LTCH if:

- You are transferred to a LTCH directly from an acute care hospital.

- You are admitted to a LTCH within 60 days of being discharged from an inpatient hospital stay.

There are deductibles and coinsurance amounts you're responsible for. These deductibles and coinsurance amounts are increasing for 2014. For each benefit period, Medicare pays all covered costs except the Medicare Part A deductible, which for 2014, is $1,216 during the first 60 days and coinsurance amounts for hospital stays that last beyond 60 days but no more than 150 days. For each benefit period you pay:

- A total deductible of $1,216 for a hospital stay lasting from 1-60 days.
- $304 coinsurance per day for days 61-90 of a hospital stay.
- Days 91 and beyond, $608 coinsurance per each "lifetime reserve day" after day 90 for each benefit period in 2014.
- Beyond lifetime reserve days you are responsible for all hospital costs.

Lifetime reserve days are additional days Medicare will pay for when you're in the hospital for more than 90 days. You have a total of 60 reserve days which can be used during your lifetime. For each lifetime reserve day, Medicare pays all covered costs except for a daily coinsurance.

Staying overnight in a hospital doesn't always mean you're an inpatient. **For Medicare purposes you're considered an inpatient the day a physician formally admits you to a hospital with a physician order.** Many Medicare beneficiaries', who thought they were admitted to a hospital, instead had observation status only. This is a Medicare classification which can cost individuals thousands of extra dollars if they need post-hospital nursing care. Most states don't require hospitals to notify patients of their admission status. Medicare covers the first 100 days of care in a skilled nursing facility but only for patients who were first formally admitted to a hospital for three consecutive days.

Federal data shows the number of Medicare patients classified as under observation has jumped sharply in recent years to 1.4 million in 2011 from 920,000 in 2006. This trend is not limited to patients who spend less than 48 hours in the hospital. The number of observation stays, lasting more than 48 hours, totaled 112,000 in 2011 compared with just 27,600 in 2006.

If you're going to be in a hospital overnight always ask the physician if you're going to be an inpatient, outpatient or have observation status. Otherwise, you may be the recipient of an extremely large and unwanted hospital bill, in which you now may need to file an appeal with Medicare. The Center for Medicare Advocacy has a self-help packet which explains the observation status issue in detail and also provides detailed guidance for filing appeals with Medicare at www.medicareadvocacy.org/self-help-packet-for-medicare-observation-status/.

Skilled Nursing Care

For qualified skilled nursing care to be covered by Medicare, it must be obtained in a Medicare-certified facility. There needs to be a minimum 3-day medically necessary prior inpatient hospitalization stay for a related illness or injury. Transfer to a Medicare-certified facility within 30 days from hospital discharge must occur. The services in the nursing home must be for a condition that was treated during hospitalization (conditions test apply). Your physician must certify that you need daily skilled care like intravenous injections or physical therapy.

Medicare coverage will pay, in full, the first 20 days. For skilled nursing facility, the coinsurance amount in 2014 is $152.00 per day for days 21 through 100, for each benefit period. In 2013, this was $148 per day. There is no coverage after 100 days. **The deductible for Part A is not an**

annual deductible but per episode of care deductible.
Part A doesn't cover copays, long-term care or custodial care
such as a nursing facility.

Home Health Care

A physician or certain health care providers, who work with
a physician, must see you face-to-face before the physician
can certify you need home health services. To qualify, the
beneficiaries' physician must have determined medical care
is needed in the home and the physician has prepared a
written plan of care. Needed care must include:

- Intermittent (not full time) skilled nursing care.
- Physical therapy.
- Speech therapy.
- Continued occupational services.

The beneficiary must be home-bound, which means leaving
home is a major effort. Absences from home must be
infrequent and of short duration to receive medical care. If
a Home Health Care Agency is used it must be Medicare
approved. Medicare Part A will cover 100% of **medically
necessary**, Medicare approved home health care visits.
Any Durable Medical Equipment (DME), such as
wheelchairs, hospital beds, oxygen and walkers, which may
be needed, Medicare will pay 80% of approved charges,
leaving you responsible to pay the remaining 20%. Medicare
does NOT cover or pay for:

- 24 hour-a-day care at home.
- Meals delivered to your home.
- Homemaker services such as cooking, cleaning or
  shopping.
- Personal care.

Hospice Care

If you qualify for hospice care, you'll have a specially trained team and support staff helping you and your family in coping with your illness. The beneficiary must have their physician certify they're terminally ill and have 6 months or less to live. If you're already getting hospice care, a hospice physician or nurse practitioner will need to see you about 6 months after you entered hospice to recertify you're still terminally ill. Hospice care is usually provided for in your home and includes the following services when your physician includes them in the plan of care for palliative care for your terminal illness. You pay nothing for hospice care but there is a copayment for drugs and a coinsurance charge for inpatient respite care. Hospice coverage includes:

- Physician services.
- Nursing care.
- Medical equipment.
- Medical supplies.
- Medications for symptom control of pain.
- Hospice aid and homemaker services.
- Physical and occupational therapy.
- Speech language pathology services.
- Social work services.
- Dietary counseling.
- Grief and loss counseling for you and your family.
- Short-term inpatient care.
- Short-term respite care.
- Any other Medicare covered services needed to manage your pain and other symptoms related to your terminal illness, as recommended by your hospice team.

Hospice doesn't pay for your stay in a facility (room and board) unless the hospice medical team determines you need short-term inpatient stays for pain and symptom management, which can't be addressed at home. Drugs for symptom control and pain relief are subject to a copay of up to $5.00 per prescription.

Medicare also covers inpatient respite care, which is care you get in a Medicare-approved facility so your usual caregiver can rest. You can stay up to 5 days each time you get respite care. Inpatient respite care is subject to a 5% coinsurance payment. You can continue to get hospice care as long as the hospice medical director or hospice physician recertifies you're terminally ill.

When you make the decision to choose hospice care, you have decided you no longer want care to cure your illness and/or you physician has determined efforts to cure your illness are not working. Medicare will not cover any of these once you choose hospice care:

- Treatments intended to cure your illness.
- Prescription drugs to cure your illness.
- Care from any hospice provider that was not set up by the hospice medical team.
- Room and board.
- Care in an emergency room, inpatient facility care or ambulance transportation unless it's either arranged by you hospice team or is unrelated to your terminal illness.

Some additional resources which may help include:

- National Hospice and Palliative Care Organization (NHPCO)
- Hospice Association of America (HAA)
- Hospice Foundation of America (HFA)

Religious Nonmedical Health Care Institution

In these facilities, religious beliefs prohibit conventional and unconventional medical care. If you qualify for hospital or skilled nursing facility care, Medicare will only cover the inpatient, non-religious, non-medical items and services, such as room and board or items and services which don't require a physician's order or prescription.

MEDICARE SAVINGS PROGRAMS

The federal government offers Medicare Savings Programs for low-income individuals, which the states' administer through Medicaid. They pay some or all of beneficiaries' premiums and coinsurance. The programs are called Qualified Medicare Beneficiary (QMB), Specified Low-income Medicare Beneficiary (SLMB), Qualifying Individual (QI) and Qualified Disabled Working Individuals (QDWI). If an individual can answer yes to the following 3 questions, call your State Medicaid Program to see if you qualify for a Medicare Savings Program in your state:

1. Do you have or are you eligible for Medicare Part A?
2. Is your income for 2014 at or below the income limits listed below?
3. Do you have limited resources below the limits listed below?

Resource limits for the QMB, SLMB, and QI Medicare Savings Programs are $7,080 for a single individual and $10,620 for a married couple. Resource limits for the QDWI program are $4,000 for a single individual and $6,000 for a married couple. Countable resources include:

- Money in a checking or savings account.
- Stocks.
- Bonds.

Countable resources **don't** include:

- Your home.
- One car.

- Burial plot.
- Up to $1,500 for burial expenses if you have put that money aside.
- Furniture.
- Other household and personal items.

The household income values listed below are for the 48 contiguous states and the District of Columbia. Alaska and Hawaii (not shown) have their own values.

- QMB: $11,736 ($978 monthly) for a single individual and $15,756 ($1,313 monthly) for a married couple. Program helps pay Part A and Part B premiums plus deductibles, copays and coinsurance is guaranteed if you meet the qualifications.
- SLMB: $14,028 ($1,169 monthly) for a single individual and $18,852 ($1,571 monthly) for a married couple. Program helps pay Part B premium and has no fixed budget. Everyone who qualifies gets the benefit.
- QI: $15,756 ($1,313 monthly) for a single individual and $21,180 ($1,765 monthly) for a married couple. Program helps pay Part B premium but program has a fixed budget. When the money is exhausted no one else can qualify that year.
- QDWI: $46,980 ($3,915 monthly) for a single individual and $63,060 ($5,255 monthly) for a married couple. Program helps pay for Part A premiums only.

Information is available at 1-800-MEDICARE (1-800-633-4227), Social Security at 1-800-772-1213. For individuals who have hearing difficulties and/or are speech impaired, information is available at TTY/TDD 1-877-486-2048. Ask for information about Medicare Savings Programs.

MEDICARE PART B: MEDICAL INSURANCE

Original Medicare Part B is a voluntary program, which covers the medical insurance component of your health care. Only Part B charges a monthly premium, assuming you have the premium-free Part A. Part B helps cover medically-necessary services like physician's services, outpatient care, durable medical equipment, home health services, and other medical services. Part B also covers some preventive services. Part B coverage includes:

- Medically-necessary services: services or supplies that are needed to diagnose or treat your medical condition and which meet accepted standards of medical practice.
- Preventive services: health care to prevent illness (like the flu) or detect it at an early stage, when treatment is most likely to work best.

If you obtain these preventive services from a health care provider who accepts assignment you usually pay nothing. Medicare may cover some services and tests more often than the timeframes listed by Medicare if needed to diagnose a condition. Part B premiums increased in 2012 for the first time since 2009. Such increases used to be routine before that. There is a law that prevents premiums from rising if Social Security's cost-of-living adjustment isn't enough to cover the increase. During the low inflation environment, which has prevailed following the Great Financial Crisis, there were no increases in Medicare premiums because there were no increases in Social Security payments.

PREMIUM COSTS

The standard Part B premium for 2014 is $104.90. The last five years have been among the slowest periods of average Part B premium growth in the programs' history. According to Jonathan Blum, CMS principal deputy administrator, he noted that for the third year in a row Medicare premium costs are meeting or beating expectations. Medicare premiums for 2014 are lower than the $109.10 they were projected to be for 2014.

If you are considered a high earner, you will pay the standard premium plus a fixed dollar amount based on your modified adjusted gross income (MAGI), as reported, **on your federal tax return from 2 years ago**. It is a two year period because that is the most recent tax return information provided to Social Security by the IRS. For 2014, your premium would be based on your 2012 federal tax return, which was filed in 2013, to determine if you are considered a high earner.

There are five Medicare income brackets. Currently less than 5% of beneficiaries are affected by these income-related premiums. High income beneficiaries are defined as singles earning more than $85,000 and couples, filing jointly, exceeding $170,000. If you're a high income beneficiary and you are single and filed an individual tax return, or married and filed a joint tax return, your premium is based on your modified adjusted gross income (MAGI). MAGI is the total of your adjusted gross income (gross income minus adjustments to income) plus tax-exempt interest income. If this exceeds $85,000 for single individuals or $170,000 for those married, the following premiums will apply for 2014, based on your 2012 Federal Income Tax Return. These income levels are the same as they were in 2013.

- Individuals with a MAGI above $85,000 up to $107,000 and married couples with a MAGI above $170,000 up to $214,000. Standard premium + $42.00. **Total Premium $146.90**.
- Individuals with a MAGI above $107,000 up to $160,000 and married couples with a MAGI above $214,000 up to $320,000. Standard premium + $104.90. **Total Premium $209.80**.

- Individuals with a MAGI above $160,000 up to $214,000 and married couples with a MAGI above $320,000 up to $428,000. Standard premium + $167.80. **Total Premium $272.70**.
- Individuals with a MAGI above $214,000 and married couples with a MAGI above $428,000. Standard premium + $230.80. **Total Premium $335.70**.

If you are married and lived with your spouse at some time during the taxable year, but filed a separate tax return, the following premiums will apply:

- Individuals with a MAGI of $85,000 or less. **Standard premium $104.90**.
- Individuals with a MAGI above $85,000 up to $129,000. Standard premium + $167.80. **Total Premium $272.70**.
- Individuals with a MAGI above $129,000. Standard premium + $230.80. **Total Premium $335.70**.

There are investment products which are not counted as income by Medicare. These include;

- Distributions from health savings accounts (HSA).
- Distributions from ROTH IRAs.
- Distributions from ROTH 401(k)s.
- Proceeds from a reverse mortgage.
- Income and loans from cash-value life insurance.
- Certain distributions from annuities in non-qualified plans.

If you're receiving Social Security, RRB, or Civil Service benefits, your Part B premium is deducted from your benefit payment. If you don't get these benefit payments and choose to sign up for Part B, you will receive a bill for the premium due. If you choose to buy Part A because you don't qualify for premium-free, you will always receive a bill for your Part A premium.

MEDICAL SERVICES AND ASSIGNMENT

One of the things you learn as a Medicare recipient is whether or not your health care providers accept assignment. Assignment is an agreement by your physician, other health care provider or supplier who will be paid directly by Medicare. These physicians and health care providers agree to accept the payment amount Medicare approves, for the service or product provided, and agrees not to bill you for any more than the Medicare deductible and/or co-insurance. **You are likely to pay more for physicians or providers who don't accept assignment.** Before you go on Medicare it is a good idea to contact your current physicians and other health care providers you use, to determine if they accept assignment.

If the Part B deductible applies, you must pay all costs until you meet the yearly Part B deductible, before Medicare begins to pay its share. The deductible for Part B in 2014 is $147.00. This is the same as it was for 2013. After your deductible is met, you typically pay 20% of the Medicare-approved amount of the service if the physician or other health care provider accepts assignment. **There is no yearly limit or cap for what you pay out-of-pocket.**

COVERED SERVICES

Medicare may cover some services and tests more often than the timeframes listed if needed to diagnose a condition. You pay nothing for most preventive services if you get the services from a physician or other health care provider who accepts assignment. For some preventive services, you may have to pay a deductible, co-insurance, or both. Listed below are some of the medical services which Medicare covers.

- Abdominal Aortic Aneurysm Screening
- Alcohol Misuse Counseling
- Ambulance Services
- Ambulatory Surgical Centers
- Blood
- Bone Mass Measurement (Bone Density)
- Breast Cancer Screening (Mammograms)
- Cardiac Rehabilitation
- Cardiovascular Screenings
- Cervical and Vaginal Cancer Screening
- Chemotherapy
- Chiropractic Services (limited)
- Clinical Research Studies
- Colorectal Cancer Screenings
- Defibrillator (Implantable Automatic)
- Depression Screening
- Diabetes Screenings
- Diabetes Self-Management Training
- Diabetes Supplies
- Durable Medical Equipment (like walkers)
- EKG (Electrocardiogram) Screening
- Emergency Department Services
- Eyeglasses (limited)
- Flu Shots
- Foot Exams and Treatment
- Glaucoma Tests
- Hearing and Balance Exams
- Hepatitis B Shots
- HIV Screening
- Home Health Services
- Kidney Dialysis Services and Supplies
- Kidney Disease Education Services
- Laboratory Services
- Medical Nutrition Therapy Services
- Mental Health Care (outpatient)
- Obesity Screening and Counseling
- Occupational Therapy

- Outpatient Hospital Services
- Outpatient Medical and Surgical Services and Supplies
- Physical Therapy
- Pneumococcal Shot
- Prescription Drugs (limited)
- Prostate Cancer Screenings
- Prosthetic/Orthotic Items
- Pulmonary Rehabilitation
- Rural Health Clinic Services
- Second Surgical Opinions
- Speech-Language Pathology Services
- Surgical Dressing Services
- Tobacco Use Cessation Counseling
- Tests (other than lab tests)
- Transplants and Immunosuppressive Drugs
- Urgently-Needed Care
- "Welcome to Medicare" Preventive Visit Yearly "Wellness" Visit

Note * Items – In all areas of the country you must get your covered equipment, supplies, replacement or repair services from a Medicare-approved supplier for Medicare to pay. Some area of the country may have a DME Competitive Bidding Program. In order to get certain items you must use specific suppliers called "contract suppliers" or Medicare will not pay for the item and you will likely pay full price for the item yourself.

WHAT MEDICARE DOES NOT COVER

Many consumers are unaware Medicare doesn't cover all health care services and costs. On average, Medicare covers 48% of health care costs for enrollees. This leaves 52% of the health care costs being the responsibility of the enrollee. These out of pocket expenses can include the following.

- Long-term or custodial care
- Routine dental care
- Dentures
- Cosmetic surgery
- Acupuncture
- Care while travelling outside of the U.S., except under certain circumstances
- Hearing aids
- Exams for fitting hearing aids
- Vision exams and prescription eyewear
- Deductibles
- Coinsurance
- Copayments
- Supplemental insurance plans
- Routine physicals, with the exception of the one-time "Welcome to Medicare" physical exam within the first 12 months of enrolling in Medicare Part B
- Custodial care is non-skilled personal care. It is designed to help individuals with six activities of daily living like bathing, dressing, eating, toileting, continence and transferring (getting in and out of bed or a chair).

This chapter will not cover options consumers have beyond original Medicare, such as Medicare Advantage and Medicare Supplement/Medigap plans. For readers who are interested, there is a companion book titled, *"Navigating the Maze of Medicare"*, covering both these plans as well as prescription drug plans, long-term care and Medicaid.

PRESCRIPTION DRUG COVERAGE

Medicare doesn't cover most prescription drugs. If you're currently not taking many prescriptions, this may not be an issue at the moment. If you are taking an extensive list of prescription drugs, as you turn 65 you may want to consider optional health care coverage which can include those prescriptions. Most Medicare Advantage Part C plans will include prescription drug coverage. Your other choice will be a standalone Medicare Prescription Drug Part D plan to work in conjunction with original Medicare.

SOME FUTURE PRESPECTIVE ON MEDICARE

The Health Insurance Marketplace has nothing to do with Medicare so if you're currently enroll in original Medicare, have a Medicare Advantage plan or Medicare Supplement/Medigap plan or have health coverage through a retiree employer-sponsored health plan there is nothing for you to worry about. You have creditable health coverage and will not face a penalty.

The ACA significantly expanded several preventive health measures for Medicare recipients. It also reduces or eliminates out-of-pocket costs for a variety of life-saving screenings. Beneficiaries once had to pay coinsurance amounts of 20% for many preventive services. Beneficiaries used to receive a one-time only "Welcome to Medicare" visit with their primary care physician (PCP) at no cost. Now beneficiaries can receive an annual wellness visit with their PCP at no out-of-pocket expense. This is not a full physical but involves a comprehensive health risk assessment. Medicare now also covers screenings for cancer, depression, obesity, diabetes and other chronic illnesses. It also extends to alcohol counseling, smoking cessation and nutritional consultations. For more information about preventive service, Medicare has a *"Guide to Medicare's Preventive Services"* which is available at www.medicare.gov/Pubs/pdf/10110.pdf.

The ACA also mandates greater prescription drug coverage on Medicare Part D Prescription Drug plans. Prior to the ACA enactment, beneficiaries had to pay 100% of drug costs if they reached the coverage gap or donut hole as it is also called. Since 2011, beneficiaries have been paying a reduced amount each year. For 2014, beneficiaries will pay 47.5% for brand-name prescriptions and 72% for generic prescriptions. The ACA gradually closes this coverage gap each year until 2020, when these amounts will be reduced to and stay at 25% for both. Beginning in 2014, employer-sponsored plans have to provide certain preventive health screening procedure at no cost to employees.

The initial rollout of the Health Insurance Marketplace was a dysfunctional mess. However, the federal government is getting the systems and software fixed. The Obama administration simply has too much riding on this legislation to allow it to implode. We're still just in the early innings of the ballgame, though it remains to be seen whether this will be a success in the long run. The line from the Kevin Costner movie, *Field of Dreams,* comes to mind. *"If you build it they will come."* Sufficient enrollment numbers (especially of healthy younger adults), affordable premiums and a quality network of health care providers are essential in the long run to make the program viable.

Obamacare cuts government funding to Medicare by $716 billion between 2013 and 2022, in order to pay for part of the law's $1.9 trillion in new health care spending for younger individuals over the same time frame. Much of this comes from new measures to reduce fraudulent spending. Entitlement programs will come under greater scrutiny in years to come. While health care technology innovation is very rich in this country it comes with a price; a price which entitlement programs may just not want to cover regardless of patient benefits and outcomes. There is only so much money to go around. In the economic environment we're in, Medicare and Medicaid are meant to be backstop programs. They're not intended to get you anything and everything. If the federal government perseveres and accomplishes its goal and health care reforms become a success, a future presidential administration might use the Health Insurance Marketplace as an effective replacement for the single-payer health care entitlement programs of Medicare and Medicaid. They would both be simply absorbed within the Health Insurance Marketplace.

FURTHER QUESTIONS

Have additional questions about Medicare, Social Security, Railroad Retirement, Medicaid, Veterans Affairs or Long Term Care? Additional resources are listed below.

1. Visit www.medicare.gov:

- For Medigap policies in your area visit www.medicare.gov/medigap.
- For updated phone numbers visit www.medicare.gov/contacts.

2. Call 1-800-MEDICARE (1-800-633-4227):

- For general or claims-specific information customer service representatives are available 24 hours a day, 7 days a week. TTY users should call 1-877-486-2048. You can get information 24 hours a day, including weekends. If you need help in a language other than English or Spanish let the customer service representative know the language.

3. Social Security (1-800-772-1213)

- Get a replacement Medicare card.
- Change your name or address.
- Eligibility, entitlement and enrollment information for Part A and/or Part B.
- Apply for Extra Help with prescription costs.
- TTY users should call 1-800-325-0778.

4. Coordination of Benefits Contractor

- Find out if Medicare or your other insurance pays first and to report changes in your insurance information.

- Call 1-800-999-1118.
- TTY users should call 1-800-318-8782.

5. Department of Defense

- Information about the TRICARE for Life (TFL) and the TRICARE Pharmacy program.
- TFL call 1-866-773-0404.
- TTY users should call 1-866-773-0405.
- Pharmacy call 1-877-363-1303
- TTY users should call 1-877-540-6261.
- Visit www.tricare.mil/mybenefit.

6. Department of Health and Human Services – Office for Civil Rights

- Think you were discriminated against or if your health information privacy rights were violated.
- Call 1-800-368-1019.
- TTY users should call 1-800-537-7697.
- Visit www.hhs.gov/ocr.

7. Department of Veterans Affairs

- You're a veteran or have served in the U.S. military.
- Call 1-800-829-4833.
- TTY users should call 1-800-829-4833.
- Visit www.va.gov.

8. Office of Personnel Management

- Information about the Federal Employee Health Benefits Program for current and retired Federal employees.
- Call 1-888-767-6738.
- TTY users should call 1-800-878-5707.

- Visit www.opm.gov/insure.

9. Railroad Retirement Board (RRB)

- Receiving benefits from the RRB.
- Call 1–877–772–5772.
- Visit www.rrb.gov.

10. Below are some additional telephone numbers that may be useful.

- Senior Medicare Patrol: 1–877–808–2468 to find out location of nearest office.
- Medicare Fraud Hotline: 1–800–447–8477 if you suspect fraud.
- Do Not Call Registry: 1–888–382–1222.

11. Resources for Long-Term Care

- The *National Clearinghouse for Long-Term Care Information* website, www.longtermcare.gov. The *U.S. Department of Health and Human Services* developed this website to provide information and resources to help you and your family plan for future long-term care (LTC) needs.
- To find out about in-law apartments visit the *National Resource Center on Supportive Housing and Home Modification* website, www.gero.usc.edu/nrcshhm.
- Visit the *U.S. Department of Housing and Urban Development-Persons with Disabilities* section 811, www.hud.gov, to find subsidized housing for persons with disabilities.
- The local community Area Agency on Aging can be found by visiting the *Eldercare Locator* website, http://www.eldercare.gov, or calling 1–800–677–1116 to obtain information about available services in

your area. You may also find more information about board and care facilities in your area from the *Administration on Aging (AoA)* website, www.aoa.gov.

- You may also find more information about assisted living facilities in your area from the *Administration on Aging (AoA)* website. You can also contact the *Assisted Living Federation of America (ALFA)*, www.alfa.org and the *National Center for Assisted Living (NCAL)*, www.ahcancal.org.

- You can find out if a CCRC is accredited and get advice on selecting this type of long-term care community from the *Commission on Accreditation of Rehabilitation Facilities*, www.carf.org/home. You can also get more information about continuing care retirement communities from the *Administration on Aging (AoA)* and the *American Association of Homes and Services for the Aging (AAHSA)*, www.healthfinder.gov.

- To find out information on accreditation of nursing homes in your area, look at the *Joint Commission on the Accreditation of Healthcare Organizations' (JCAHO)* website, www.jointcommission.org.

12. State Health Insurance Assistance Program

SHIPs are state programs which get their money from the Federal government to give local health insurance counseling to people with Medicare. Services include:

- Getting free personalized Medicare counseling on decisions about coverage.
- Help with claims, billing or appeals.

Information is available on programs for individuals with limited income and resources.

"American workers and families face a retirement crisis in which a majority of households are at risk for downward mobility in retirement and a significant share face not being able to meet basic expenses in old age."

Nari Rhee, Ph.D.
Manager of Research
National Institute on Retirement Insecurity
From the report, "Race and Retirement Insecurity in the United States"

CHAPTER FOURTEEN

THE FUTURE FOR SOCIAL SECURITY

"Illusions commend themselves to us because they save us pain and allow us to enjoy pleasure instead. We must therefore accept it without complaint when they sometimes collide with a bit of reality against which they are dashed to pieces." – Sigmund Freud

The amount of misunderstanding and misinformation regarding the workings of the Social Security system is just staggering. Much of this arises from *which* numbers are communicated to the public. Social Security is not the cause of our current federal deficits.

There are two trust funds which the Social Security Administration controls: Old-Age and Survivors Insurance (OASI) Fund and the Disability Insurance (DI) Fund. Very seldom are the two trust funds discussed separately in the media. Social Security taxes are paid into the Social Security Trust Fund, which is maintained by the U.S. Treasury. The trust funds are a separate, off-budget, self-financed program with their own dedicated funding source. They are treated separately, in certain ways from other federal spending and other trust funds of the Federal Government. Whereas the federal government can run huge annual deficits and borrow the needed money to fund ongoing operations, the trust funds CANNOT borrow money. Social Security would have pay out less in order to balance their books. Benefits would need to be cut or taxes would have to be raised.

In 1981, Social Security was facing a short-term financing crisis. Congress and President Reagan appointed the National Commission on Social Security Reform to study and make recommendations to avert the crisis. The Commission was informally known as the Greenspan Commission after its Chairman, Alan Greenspan. At the time Greenspan was Chairman of Townsend-Greenspan & Co., Inc., an economic consulting firm in New York City. Estimates indicated the OASI Trust Fund would run out of money as early as August 1983. Congress and the President also realized the enormous strain the impact of the baby boom generation, retiring in the early part of the 21st century, would place on the future Social Security system.

The Commission's report, issued in January 1983, became the basis for the Social Security Amendments of 1983. With large bipartisan support, landmark legislation was passed by Congress to shore up the program. Taxes were raised, which subjected a percentage of OASDI benefits to federal income tax. This boosted inflows and set the stage for dramatic growth in the trust funds. This revenue, which the U.S. Treasury collects, is allocated back to the OASI and DI trust funds. In other words, these tax revenue dollars are put back into the Social Security trust funds which support its programs. The tax money you pay into Social Security is used to pay benefits to:

- Individuals who have already retired.
- Individuals who are disabled.
- Survivors of workers who have died.
- Dependents of beneficiaries.

Current year expenses are paid from current Social Security tax revenues. When revenues exceed expenditures, as they did between 1983 and 2009, the excess is invested in special series, non-marketable U.S. Government bonds. The Social Security Trust Fund indirectly finances the federal government's general purpose deficit spending. These surpluses, which began in 1983, were expected to continue for several more years. The Great Financial Recession induced declines in payroll taxes and an uptick in benefit claims, especially within the DI program.

Trustees of the Social Security Trust Funds

Each year, the Board of Trustees' of the Federal Old-Age and Survivors Insurance and Federal Disability Insurance Trust Funds, report to the Speaker of the House and President of the Senate on the current and projected financial status for both the Social Security and Medicare programs. Social Security and Medicare together accounted for 41% of Federal expenditures in fiscal year 2013. The recent report submitted is for July 2014, reporting on the fiscal year 2013 and is the 74th such report by the Trustees'.

2014 Trustees' Report – The Current Status

In their report, *"The 2014 Annual Report of the Board of Trustees' of the Federal Old-Age and Survivors Insurance and Federal Disability Insurance Trust Funds"*, an estimated 163 million individuals had earnings covered by Social Security and paid payroll taxes. At the end of 2013, the OASDI program was providing benefit payments to about 58 million individuals. This included 41 million retired workers and their dependents, 6 million survivors of deceased workers and 11 million disabled workers and dependents of disabled workers.

The Trustees conclude neither Medicare nor Social Security can sustain their projected long-run programs in full under currently scheduled financing. Legislative changes are necessary to avoid disruptive consequences for beneficiaries and taxpayers. Both programs will experience cost growth, substantially in excess of GDP growth through the mid-2030s. This is due to the rapidly aging population caused by the baby-boom generation entering retirement and lower-birth-rate generations entering employment. For Medicare, the issue is growth in expenditures per beneficiary exceeding growth in per capita GDP.

Total expenditures for Social Security have exceeded *non-interest income* for the combined trust funds since 2010. Revenues come from the following sources:

- Net payroll tax contributions.
- General Fund (GF) reimbursements.
- Taxation of benefits.
- Net interest.

While expenditures go to the following:

- Scheduled benefits.
- Administrative costs.
- Railroad Board (RRB) interchange.

Table 14.1, on the next page, presents the combined operations of both the OASI and DI Trust Funds for fiscal years 2010 and 2013. For 2010, looking at non-interest income only, revenues totaled nearly $664 billion. Expenses totaled nearly $713 billion, leaving a deficit of $49 billion for both funds combined. However, when interest income of nearly $118 billion is added back, the deficit disappears and the net operations are in the black by $68 billion for 2010.

The 2013 deficit of tax income relative to cost was $76 billion. Again, looking at non-interest income only for 2013, revenues totaled $752.2 billion. Expenses totaled $822.9 billion, leaving a deficit of nearly $71 billion for both trust funds combined. When interest income of nearly $103 billion is added back, the deficit disappears again, with net operations in the black by just over $32 billion for 2013.

Table 14.1 Combined Operations: OASI and DI Trust Funds (Dollar amount in billions)

Income					
Calendar Year	Net payroll tax contributions	General Fund reimbursement	Taxation of benefits	Net interest	Total
2010	$637.3	$2.4	$23.9	$117.5	$781.1
2013	$726.2	$4.9	$21.1	$102.8	$855.0

Cost				
Calendar Year	Schedule benefits	Administrative costs	RRB interchange	Total
2010	$701.6	$6.5	$4.4	$712.5
2013	$812.3	$6.2	$4.5	$822.9

Source: Trustees' of the Social Security and Medicare Trust Funds Report 2014

Table 14.2 below, displays an income statement for just the operations for the Social Security program for the same comparable years.

Table 14.2 Operations of the OASI Trust Fund (Dollar amount in billions)

Income					
Calendar Year	Net payroll tax contributions	General Fund reimbursement	Taxation of benefits	Net interest	Total
2010	$544.8	$2.0	$22.1	$108.2	$677.1
2013	$620.8	$4.2	$20.7	$98.1	$743.8

Cost				
Calendar Year	Schedule benefits	Administrative costs	RRB interchange	Total
2010	$577.4	$3.5	$3.9	$584.9
2013	$672.1	$3.4	$3.9	$679.5

Source: Trustees' of the Social Security and Medicare Trust Funds Report 2014

For 2013, if you again look at non-interest income only, revenues totaled nearly $646 billion. Expenses totaled nearly $680 billion, leaving a deficit of $34 billion for the OASI fund. When interest income of $98 billion is added back the deficit disappears again, with net operations in the black by just over $64 billion for 2013.

While yearly benefit payments exceeded yearly income from payroll taxes by just over $51 million in 2013, trust fund balance, for just the operations of the OASI Trust Fund, still grew by just over $64 billion once income from interest, tax receipts and other sources were included.

The DI Trust Fund presents an entirely different problem. Table 14.3 below, displays an income statement for just operations for the Disability Insurance program.

Table 14.3 Operations of the DI Trust Fund
(Dollar amounts in billions)

Income					
Calendar Year	Net payroll tax contributions	General Fund reimbursement	Taxation of benefits	Net interest	Total
2010	$92.5	$0.4	$1.9	$9.3	$104.1
2013	$105.4	$0.7	$0.4	$4.7	$111.2

Cost				
Calendar Year	Schedule benefits	Administrative costs	RRB interchange	Total
2010	$124.2	$3.0	$0.5	$127.7
2013	$140.1	$2.8	$0.6	$143.4

Source: Trustees' of the Social Security and Medicare Trust Funds Report 2014

While the OASI Trust Fund generated an increase in asset reserves, the DI Trust Fund generated a deficit, just over $32 billion for 2013. Since 2010, income has risen by nearly 7%. However, during this same period costs rose just over 12%. 2013 is the fifth consecutive year for such deficits.

The Treasury Department invests trust fund reserves in interest-bearing securities of the U.S. Government. For 2013, the combined trust fund reserves earned interest at an effective rate of 3.8%, down from 4.1% in 2012. The trust fund investments provide a reserve to pay benefits whenever total program costs exceed income. At the end of 2013, the combined reserves of the OASI and DI Trust Funds were 320% of estimated expenditures for 2014. For comparison, the combined reserves at the end of 2011 were 341% of expenditures for 2012. Table 14.4 below, displays the change in asset reserve balance for both the OASI and DI Trust Funds for 2013.

Table 14.4 OASDI Combined Asset Reserves

Asset Reserves (in billions)			
	OASI	DI	OASDI
Asset reserves at the end of 2012	$2,609.7	$122.7	$2,732.3
Net increase in asset reserves in 2013	64.3	-32.2	32.1
Asset reserves at the end of 2013	$2,674.0	$90.4	$2,764.4

Source: *Trustees' of the Social Security and Medicare Trust Funds Report 2014*

Long-Term Projections

Non-interest income fell below program costs in 2010 for the first time since 1983. According to the Trustees' estimates, Social Security's costs will exceed non-interest income throughout the 75-year projection period. The Trust Fund Ratio peaked in 2008, declined through 2012 and is expected to decline steadily in future years.

Table 14.5, on the next page, displays three key dates for events, which have been projected by the Board of Trustees' since 2009. According to the 2014 report, the combined trust fund reserves are still growing and will continue to do so through 2019. Beginning with 2020, the cost of the program is projected to exceed income. The U.S.

Treasury will then need to redeem trust fund asset reserves to the extent that cost exceeds tax revenue and interest earnings until depletion of total trust fund reserves in 2033. These projections combine both the OASI and DI Trust Funds and are unchanged in the 2014 report.

Table 14.5 Key Dates for Social Security Trust Fund

Event	2009	2010	2011	2012	2013
First year outflow exceeds income, excluding interest.	2016	2015	2010	2010	2010
First year outflow exceeds income, including interest.	2024	2025	2023	2012	2021
Year trust fund assets are exhausted.	2037	2037	2036	2033	2033

Source: 2009-2013 Social Security Trustees Reports

The year 2033 is widely reported by the media as the year Social Security will be broke. However, even after the year 2033, payroll tax income alone would be sufficient to pay about 77% of scheduled benefits through 2087.

Social Security's Disability Insurance (DI) program satisfies neither, the Trustees' long-range test of close actuarial balance or their short-range test of financial adequacy. It faces the most immediate financing shortfall of any of the separate trust funds. DI Trust Fund reserves, expressed as a percent of annual cost (the trust fund ratio), declined to 85% at the beginning of 2013. Table 14.6, on the next page, is the same table which has been projected by the Board of Trustees' since 2009. This table displays the two trust funds separately in terms of the years assets are projected to be exhausted.

Table 14.6 Key Dates for the OASI and DI Trust Funds

Event	2009	2010	2011	2012	2013
Year OASI Trust Fund assets are exhausted.	2039	2040	2038	2035	2035
Year DI Trust Fund assets are exhausted.	2020	2018	2018	2016	2016

Source: 2009-2013 Social Security Trustees Reports

The Trustees project trust fund depletion in 2016. DI costs have exceeded non-interest income since 2005 and the trust fund ratio has declined since peaking in 2003.

In a July 2014 presentation, before the Senate Finance Committee, the SSA's chief actuary warned by 2016 continuing tax income in the DI Trust Fund will be sufficient to cover only 80% of scheduled DI benefits. Either scheduled revenues need to be increased by 25% or costs need to be reduced by 20% or some combination of these.

In another study, the Congressional Budget Office (CBO) released their report, *"The 2013 Long-Term Projection for Social Security: Additional Information"* in December 2013. The numbers for 2013 were derived from information which had been reported in Department of the Treasury's Final Monthly Treasury Statement of Receipts and Outlays of the United States Government for Fiscal Year 2013 Through September 30, 2013.

In their report, the CBO calculated that in fiscal 2013, Social Security spending totaled $808 billion. This represents almost 25% of all federal spending for the year. OASI payments accounted for about 83% of those outlays while DI payments made up about 17%. The revenues added to the Social Security system totaled $745 billion. Revenues from taxes, along with intra-governmental interest payments are credited to Social Security's two trust funds, the OASI and DI. The program's benefits and administrative costs are paid from those funds. Although legally separate, the funds often are described collectively as the OASDI Trust Funds.

Figure 14.1 Revenue/Outlay Projections for Social Security as a Percentage of GDP

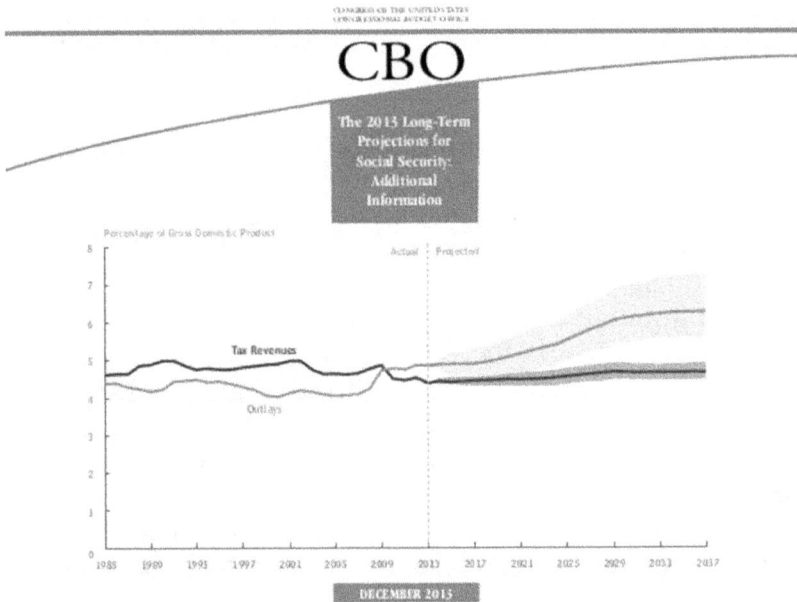

Source: CBO Report; The 2013 Long-Term Projection for Social Security

In 2010, for the first time since the enactment of the Social Security Amendments of 1983, annual outlays for the program exceeded annual tax revenues. That is, outlays exceeded total revenues, *excluding* interest credited to the trust funds. In 2012, outlays exceeded noninterest income by about 7%. The CBO projects that the gap will average about 12% of tax revenues over the next decade. As more individuals of the baby boom generation retire, outlays will increase, relative to the size of the economy. Tax revenues will remain at an almost constant share of the economy. As

320

a result, the gap will grow larger in the 2020s and will exceed 30% of revenues by 2030.

Also in the report, the CBO projects that under current law, the DI Trust Fund will be exhausted in fiscal year 2017 and the OASI Trust Fund will be exhausted in 2033. If a trust fund's balance fell to zero and current revenues were insufficient to cover the benefits specified in law, the Social Security Administration would no longer have legal authority to pay full benefits when they were due. In that case, retirement benefits would be cut by 25% as revenue from the dedicated payroll tax would be sufficient to only finance about 75% of scheduled benefit payments.

In 1994, with the DI Trust Fund just 8 months away from reserve depletion, Congress passed legislation which redirected revenues from the OASI Trust Fund to prevent the imminent exhaustion of the DI Trust Fund. In part, because of that experience, it is a common analytical convention to consider the OASI and DI Trust Funds as combined. The CBO projects, if some future legislation shifted resources from the OASI Trust Fund to the DI Trust Fund, the combined OASDI trust funds would be exhausted in 2031. Reallocation is a simple process which Congress has done, in a bipartisan manner, 11 times since 1957.

Shortfalls for Social Security, which the CBO is currently projecting, are larger than those the agency projected a year ago. The 75-year imbalance has increased from 1.95% to 3.36% of taxable payroll. This higher projection results from a number of factors, including increases in projections of life expectancy and of the disability incidence rate, both of which raise projected outlays for benefits and decreases in the projection of income taxes on benefits. For 2013, rather than using the Social Security trustees' projections of life expectancy (as was done previously), the CBO used its own, which incorporate faster growth of that measure than the Social Security Trustees' anticipate. In addition, the CBO increased its projection of the share of workers who will receive Social Security disability benefits, resulting in higher projected spending for Social Security. Of the 1.4 percentage-point increase in the 75-year imbalance, a higher projection of life expectancy accounts for 0.6 percentage points, a higher projection of the disability incidence rate accounts for 0.1 percentage points, reductions in income tax rates enacted in January 2013 (which reduce the revenues for Social Security from income taxes on benefits) account for 0.4 percentage points and other factors (including a projection period that extends a year later and updated data) account for 0.4 percentage points.

Social Security remains just one the many challenges facing policy makers. In the their July 2014 report, *The 2014 Long-Term Budget Outlook*, the CBO projects that if current laws remain generally unchanged, the total amount of federal debt held by the public at 74% of GDP would exceed 100% of GDP by 2039, 25 years from now.

Figure 14.2 Components of Total Federal Spending

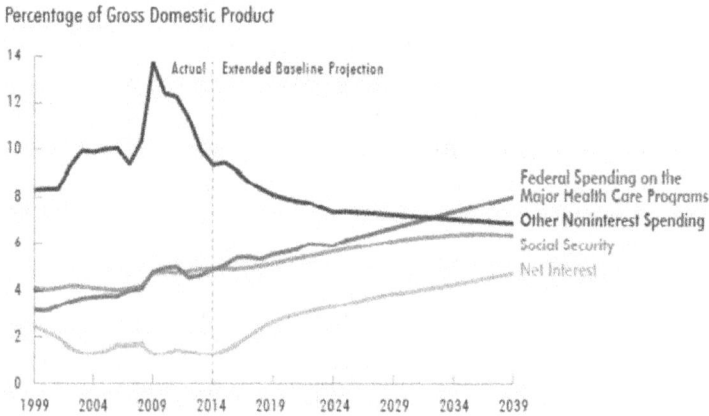

Source: CBO Report; The 2014 Long-Term Budget Outlook

Federal spending would increase to 26% of GDP by 2039, under the assumptions of the extended baseline compared with 21% in 2013 and an average of 20.5% over the past 40 years. as displayed in Figure 14.2 on the previous page.

Federal spending for just Social Security, Medicare, Medicaid, the Children's Health Insurance Program and the subsidies for health insurance purchased through the Health Insurance exchanges would rise sharply to a total of 14% of GDP by 2039, twice the 7% average seen over the past 40 years. As the CBO projects, the current spending path is unsustainable.

Solutions to the Financing Dilemma

The last major overhauls of the Social Security system occurred in 1977 and 1983. Each took about 17 years to fully implement all the changes. Congress and some future presidential administration will clearly have to come to some bipartisan agreement to correct the deficiencies which exist within the current Social Security system. When all the issues are debated and analyzed, there are only three broad options available. The first is to raise revenues which go into Social Security. The second is to cut outlays or benefits to the beneficiaries of the Social Security programs. The third would be to fundamentally change the entire Social Security program. Within those first two options, there are a number of different choices and combinations which can clearly correct the glide path Social Security is on. The current path is not sustainable in the long run.

Increase Revenues

Social Security derives its income from three sources: payroll contributions, interest payments on the $2.8 trillion invested in U.S. Treasury bonds and taxation of benefits. Given Social Security is so heavily payroll tax dependent, one option for raising revenues is by increasing those payroll taxes. Payroll taxes could be increased from their current 12.4% (both employer and employee contribution) levels. However, this type of tax increase would disproportionately affect those who earn low wages relative to those who are considered high income earners. A twist on this option would be to just increase the employer contribution component only, making corporate America more responsible for funding Social Security.

A second option is to either raise or eliminate the wage cap ceiling on which Social Security taxes are paid on. For 2014, that cap is $117,000. About 6% of wage earnings earn above this limit. The FICA tax is the lowest hanging fruit but could also have the greatest impact. This option would impact only the highest income earners who are also likely to collect the largest benefits. According to Strengthen Social Security, a coalition of over 300 state and national organizations, between 60% and 90% of the total Social Security deficit could be eliminated by modifying or eliminating this cap. The Center for Economic and Policy Research, a progressive think tank, estimates eliminating the cap on payroll taxes would affect only the wealthiest 5.2% of wage earners.

A third option would be to increase the rate on which Social Security benefits can be taxed. Current taxable limits range from 50% to 85% of benefits, depending on combined income.

Decrease Outlays/Benefits

When Social Security was created in 1935, the full retirement age was set at 65. At the time, average life expectancy was 61.7 years. Today, nearly eighty years later, the full retirement age for most is now age 66, only one year longer. Yet, according to data compiled by the SSA, a man reaching age 65 today can expect to live, on average, until age 84. A woman turning age 65 today can expect to live, on average, until age 86. This is over twenty years longer in life expectancy than in 1935 and these are just averages. About one out of every four 65-year-olds alive today will live past age 90 and one out of ten will make it past age 95.

To reduce outlays, one option would be to allow the full retirement age to creep up to age 70 over a period of years for those born in 1960 or later. Those born after 1960, currently reach their full retirement age at 67. In October 2013, Alicia Munnell, Ph.D., director of the Center for Retirement Research at Boston College, published a paper titled, *"Social Security's Real Retirement Age is 70"* . The paper makes the argument to eliminate the full retirement age. By implementing this change, it would clearly signal that claiming at age 70 provides the appropriate benefit and would encourage individuals to work longer. The shift to age 70 might be appropriate given the increase in life expectancies, health and education for the majority of workers. However, it will also result in low replacement rates for the many workers who retire early. This would also be equivalent to about a 20% reduction in retirement benefits.

A second option is to change the way cost-of-living adjustments (COLAs) are calculated. The CPI-W is currently used, which is the Consumer Price Index for Urban Wage Earners and Clerical Workers, for COLA calculations. Some congressional representatives advocate using the chained CPI in the calculation. Many economists argue this is a better representation of inflation. Unlike the CPI-W, which economists say tends to overstate inflation, the chained CPI accounts not only for price increases but also for the substitutions consumers make based on those increases. For example, if beef prices are increasing, the chained CPI assumes that to some extent consumers will switch to chicken to stave off the price increases. This switch would ultimately lead to a lower calculated inflation rate, a lower annual COLA and reduced benefit increases for Social Security beneficiaries. One could argue neither of these options accurately reflects the needs and spending patterns of retirees, the long-term disabled and other Social Security recipients. While food and other types of consumer goods are roughly in line with the CPI numbers, health care and long-term care expenses have risen far faster and consume a larger percentage of the household budget for many retirees.

A third option is to reduce the connection between the CPI and COLA. Today they are tied, so increases in Social Security benefits are directly proportional to the inflation rate. In the future, the COLA could only be a fraction of the CPI, thereby further reducing the COLA Social Security beneficiaries would receive. Understanding what the potential effect of using the chained CPI approach in COLAs is something that near-retirees (late 50s to early 60s) and especially pre-retirees (40s to mid-50s) really need to grasp. The gradual effect of any CPI change will probably generate far less outcry from both politicians and the public then a retirement age increase or additional taxes on benefits, both of which would be felt immediately in the short run.

How much could payments change? Estimates show that under the chained CPI, your COLA would be about 0.3% below the CPI. That works out to $3 less on every $1,000. While this doesn't sound like much, the issue is that this amount keeps compounding over time. The COLA for 2013 was 1.7 percent. If your monthly Social Security benefit was $1,250 for 2012, it would have increased to $1,271.25 for 2013. With the chained CPI, you would be getting $1,267.50 or $3.75 less a month and $45 less a year. Again, this might not seem like a big reduction but if the COLA is the same next year, the difference increases to $7.61 a month and $91.32 for the year. As you project 30 years into the future, this gap accelerates and begins to become a serious amount of money. If you're 62 and take early retirement this year, by age 92, when health care costs can skyrocket, you'll be losing a full month of income every year. While a change to a chained CPI would not affect those already late into retirement, it could significantly affect the degree to which those who will become retirees are able to depend on Social Security.

From a Think Tank Perspective

There are some in academia who advocate the current Social Security program should be completely eliminated with some type of private accounts established in its place. These accounts would be tied to capital market returns to generate retirement income. Larry Kotlikoff, a professor of economics at Boston University, is one who advocates this approach. Kotlikoff also believes the Social Security program is in far worse shape than it was in 1983, when the Greenspan Commission proposals were implemented.

Then there are groups who believe certain provisions in the program should be changed. The Heritage Foundation, a research and educational think tank institution, advocates spousal benefits have become outdated because many women have worked long enough to receive their own benefit off their earnings record. Senator Marco Rubio has advocated a Federal Thrift Plan be offered to all Americans to help supplement Social Security and improve retirement readiness as part of a 5-point plan aim at stabilizing the Social Security's long-term finances.

Social Security Works, a coalition which advocates strengthening the Social Security system to protect and improve the economic security of disadvantaged and at-risk populations. They receive their funding from public donations and through a grant from Atlantic Philanthropies. The group opposes fixing the problem by cutting Social Security benefits. The groups' position is that dramatic growth of income inequality, where wages at the top have grown so much faster than average wages has caused Social Security to lose income. The group asserts Congress could nearly eliminate the entire shortfall by raising the Social Security payroll tax cap so the 6% of workers who make more than 117,000 a year contribute on all of their wages just like everyone else. The group's research indicates two-thirds of senior households rely on Social Security for a majority of their income while more than a third relies on it for 90% of their income or more.

In the fall of 2013, a survey was released which was conducted at the University of Chicago by the Associated Press and the NORC Center for Public Research. Funding for the survey was provided for by the Alfred P. Sloan Foundation. The survey included 1,024 participants who were age 50 or older. The research found seniors generally have a hands-off attitude towards Social Security. It is viewed as a hard earned entitlement they have contributed to and have been promised to receive. Some of the findings from the research include:

- 62% said they are opposed to any change in the way Social Security benefits are calculated.
- 58% opposed any efforts to gradually increase the full retirement age from what is now in place while 29% would support it.
- 41% support reducing Social Security benefits for seniors with higher incomes while 44% were opposed to the idea.
- There is wide support to raise the cap on earnings which are subject to the Social Security tax.

In a July 2014 report, from the nonprofit National Center for Policy Analysis (NCPA), the federal government has two options to keep Social Security functioning.

1. To retain the current benefits structure, increase Social Security payroll taxes by 3.3%. The study calls this the "baseline" program.
2. Impose a "reform" program. This would entail keeping tax rates where they are but raising the retirement age for workers eligible for benefits starting in 2023. In addition, the benefit formula for high earners would be less generous.

With the baseline program, an average earner born in 1985 would pay 13.5% of their lifetime income in taxes and in turn receive benefits equal to 9.6% of income, resulting in a lifetime net tax of 3.8%. With the reform program, the same worker would pay a lower tax rate of 10.2% and would receive benefits of 8.2%. This results in a lower lifetime net tax of 2%. In addition, the reform program would retain the current program's progressivity for very low wage earners. Low wage workers would pay 10.2% and receive benefits of 14.5%, a net lifetime benefit of 4.3% of earnings. In the baseline program, these low wage workers would pay 13.5% and receive benefits of 15.8%, a net lifetime benefit of 2.3% of earnings. The NCPA favors the adoption of the reform program.

With mid-term elections approaching in 2014, the earliest something may be done regarding Social Security, from a Congressional perspective, is probably the spring of 2015. So for now, 2033 or maybe 2031, seem to be key years on the Social Security and Disability Income timeline. If nothing is accomplished to correct the funding issues, the consequences could be an immediate 25% reduction in benefits at that point. An individual might have to save over an additional $10,000 per year, starting now, to compensate for the cumulative loss of those benefits. That could create social unrest in this country and would not be something any President or congressional leaders would want to happen on their watch.

Obama Budget for 2015

On March 4, 2014, President Obama released his 2015 budget proposal. In the $3.9 trillion proposed budget, some 214 pages in length, buried on page 150, is a sentence spelling out the plan to prevent duplicative or excessive benefit payments through both the Social Security's retirement program and disability insurance. Exact wording of the sentence states, "In addition, the budget proposes to eliminate aggressive Social Security-claiming strategies, which allow upper-income beneficiaries to manipulate the timing of collection of Social Security benefits in order to maximize delayed retirement credits."

This language is vague enough that there is no specific procedure by which the SSA would eliminate these claiming strategies. Yet the language seems to be unusually strong for a government document.

This inclusion *could* have arisen from research which the SSA funded back in 2008-2009, to look at a range of issues including the cost of using various claiming strategies and what the costs could potentially be to the Social Security program. In a working paper titled, *"Unusual Social Security Claiming Strategies: Costs and Distributional Effects"* authors Alicia Munnell, Ph.D., Alex Golub-Sass and Nadia Karamcheva, Ph.D. conducted a study examining unconventional claiming strategies which have the potential to pay higher lifetime retirement benefits to some individuals, thus also increasing costs within the Social Security system. The first was what the authors called the "Free Loan" strategy. It is called the Do-Over strategy throughout this book. This strategy allowed an individual to claim benefits at a given age and later repay the full nominal amount of those benefits received back to Social Security without any time restrictions, penalties or accrued interest imposed. The individual could then file again later to obtain an increased benefit from the delayed filing. The authors calculated the annual cost could range from $5.5 billion to $11.0 billion, with gains likely to be concentrated among households in the upper portion of the wealth distribution. In December 2010, the SSA announced a modification of this option using a rule change which didn't require congressional approval. As a result, beneficiaries only have only a 12-month window now in which to do this.

The second strategy the authors looked at was the "Claim and Suspend" strategy. This is called file and suspend by most today. They estimate only 27% of couples benefit from this strategy. The potential cost of allowing couples this option was estimated to have an annual cost of about $0.5 billion. This estimate assumes couples follow an optimal claiming strategy, which the evidence suggests many do not.

The third strategy was the "Claim Now, Claim More Later" strategy. This is called filing a restricted claim for spousal benefits only and is available to married couples only. Under the conventional strategy, couples claim benefits at optimal ages which maximize their expected lifetime benefits. In reality, couples tend to claim early. When the authors used actual claiming behavior as the base case, rather than optimal behavior using conventional strategies, potential costs were estimated to be about $23.3 billion. Based on real-life reported behavior, using the expanded options, the authors estimate this strategy has an annual cost of between $9.7 billion and $11.8 billion. The main beneficiaries of this strategy are two-earner couples, with a significant portion of the benefits going to those in the upper portion of wealth distribution.

In an August 2013 article, which appeared in the Journal of Financial Planning titled, *"Understanding Unusually Social Security Claiming Strategies"*, the article focuses on just the File and Suspend strategy along with the Restricted Claim for Spousal Benefits strategy from the paper the same authors, Munnell, Golub-Sass and Karamcheva had done earlier.

In a piece written by Darla Mercado for InvestmentNews, she cites a couple of sources who differ on exactly what the administration might be conveying in its 2015 proposed budget. One camp indicates this could be defined as a rule change which the administration could implement. The other camp thinks this proposal may be targeting spousal claiming strategies. If this is the case, any change to the formula for spousal benefits would require Congressional approval.

The Obama administration has used rule changes before with Social Security. In December 2010, the SSA announced a rule change which limited the time period for beneficiaries to implement the do-over strategy to within 12 months. In that change also was that an individual could

331

only exercise the strategy once in their lifetime. The rule change went into effect immediately after it was announced by the SSA. Could the study by Munnell, Golub-Sass and Karamcheva in 2009 have influenced the administration to target that specific strategy? It's quite possible. Based on the targeted savings from that earlier study presented, the filing a restricted claim for spousal benefits might be next target. The last major overhaul of Social Security took place in 1983, when a reform commission was chaired by Alan Greenspan. Some of those changes didn't take effect for more than 10 years.

Many times, proposed changes are "run up the flagpole" ahead of time, to gauge both Congressional and public opinion. When I view proposals put forth by a presidential administration or by Congressional committees affecting American taxpayers, the question I ask myself is this; is this proposal designed to fix a problem within the program to make it stronger or is this proposal designed to simply cut benefits to a specific segment of Americans and redistribute the wealth? The cost savings to the SSA by eliminating these claiming strategies seems modest when compared to the "big picture" of the issues surrounding Social Security. In this case, it's simply to cut retirement benefits to a small group of Social Security beneficiaries. These actions are nothing more than band aid solutions. How long will the can continue to be kicked down the road. Maybe the time has come for a Presidential and Congressional bipartisan appointment of the Greenspan Commission on Social Security Reform - Part II.

"In politics, nothing happens by accident. If it happens, it was planned that way." – Franklin D. Roosevelt

About the Author

Stephen J. Stellhorn is the founder of MSM Capital Management, LLC (MSM). MSM is a Florida licensed insurance agency which provides Medicare health plans, long-term care, life, individual health and final expense insurance along with annuities to consumers. He also writes a blog and posts videos on his author website (stephenstellhorn.com), covering retirement concerns individuals and couples may face as they plan for and live through the various phases of retirement.

Stellhorn has a financial services career which spans over twenty-five years in banking, investments and insurance. He has held positions in retail and institutional bond sales, fixed income portfolio management, U.S. Government bond trading, bank balance sheet management, brokerage branch sales management and insurance and financial planning. Prior to beginning his business career, Stellhorn was a paramedic while pursuing his business degree.

He holds the Retirement Management Analyst (RMA℠) designation through the Retirement Income Industry Association® (RIIA®), of which he is an individual member. He has passed the FINRA securities exams for the Series 7, 8, 24, 4, 27, 55, 63 and 65, and also the MSRB securities exams for the Series 52 and 53. Stellhorn has also passed the State of Florida Life, Health & Variable Annuity 2-15 insurance exam. He is a Florida licensed insurance agent.

Stellhorn completed the Retirement Management Analyst Program at Boston University's Center for

Professional Education. He also completed and received a Certificate in Financial Planning from Kaplan University. He is a graduate of The Florida State University, earning dual Bachelor of Science degrees in International Business and Biological Science. He is a member of the fraternity of Phi Gamma Delta.

Past firms he has been associated with include Waddell & Reed Financial Advisors, AXA Advisors, LLC, Charles Schwab & Co., ABN AMRO North America, European American Bank (EAB), NCNB, Pan American Bank, Mabon Nugent & Co. and Southeast Bank.

He resides in Tampa, Florida with his lovely wife Linda, three boomeranging college students and his beloved Shih Tzu, Jagger.

Appendix A

History of Increases in Social Security Benefits and Automatic Cost-of-Living Adjustments

Automatic benefit increases, also known as cost-of-living adjustments (COLAs) have been in effect since 1975. The 1975-82 COLAs were effective with Social Security benefits payable for June (received by beneficiaries in July) in each of those years. After 1982, COLAs have been effective with benefits payable for December (received by beneficiaries in January). COLAs received from 1973 through 2013 are shown below.

(1) The COLA for December 1999 was originally determined as 2.4% based on CPIs published by the Bureau of Labor Statistics. Pursuant to Public Law 106-554, this COLA is effectively now 2.5%.

October 1950	77.0%	1971	
October 1952	12.5%	October 1972	20.0%
October 1954	13.0%	April/July 1974	11.0%
February 1959	7.0%	July 1975	8.0%
February 1965	7.0%	July 1976	6.4%
		July 1977	5.9%
March 1968	13.0%	July 1978	6.5%
February 1970	15.0%	July 1979	9.9%
		July 1980	14.3%
February	10.0%	July 1981	11.2%

July 1982	7.4%	January 2003	2.1%
January 1983	3.5%	January 2004	2.7%
January 1984	3.5%	January 2005	4.1%
January 1985	3.1%	January 2006	3.3%
January 1986	1.3%	January 2007	2.3%
January 1987	4.2%	January 2008	5.8%
January 1988	4.0%	January 2009	0.0%
January 1989	4.7%	January 2010	0.0%
January 1990	5.4%	January 2011	3.6%
January 1991	3.7%	January 2012	1.7%
January 1992	3.0%	January 2013	1.7%
January 1993	2.6%	January 2014	1.5%
January 1994	2.8%	January 2015	
January 1995	2.6%	January 2016	
January 1996	2.9%	January 2017	
January 1997	2.1%		
January 1998	1.3%		
January 1999	2.5%[1]		
January 2000	3.5%		
January 2001	2.6%		
January 2002	1.4%		

Source: Social Security Administration

Appendix B

Average Wage Indexing Series

When the SSA computes a person's retirement benefit, they use the national average wage indexing series to index that person's earnings for benefit computation purposes. Such indexation ensures a worker's future benefits reflect the general rise in the standard of living which occurred during his or her working lifetime.

Year	AWI	Annual Change
1951	2,799.16	—
1952	2,973.32	6.22%
1953	3,139.44	5.59%
1954	3,155.64	0.52%
1955	3,301.44	4.62%
1956	3,532.36	6.99%
1957	3,641.72	3.10%
1958	3,673.80	0.88%
1959	3,855.80	4.95%
1960	4,007.12	3.92%
1961	4,086.76	1.99%
1962	4,291.40	5.01%
1963	4,396.64	2.45%
1964	4,576.32	4.09%
1965	4,658.72	1.80%

Year	AWI	Annual Change
1966	4,938.36	6.00%
1967	5,213.44	5.57%
1968	5,571.76	6.87%
1969	5,893.76	5.78%
1970	6,186.24	4.96%
1971	6,497.08	5.02%
1972	7,133.80	9.80%
1973	7,580.16	6.26%
1974	8,030.76	5.94%
1975	8,630.92	7.47%
1976	9,226.48	6.90%
1977	9,779.44	5.99%
1978	10,556.03	7.94%
1979	11,479.46	8.75%
1980	12,513.46	9.01%
1981	13,773.10	10.07%
1982	14,531.34	5.51%
1983	15,239.24	4.87%
1984	16,135.07	5.88%
1985	16,822.51	4.26%
1986	17,321.82	2.97%
1987	18,426.51	6.38%
1988	19,334.04	4.93%
1989	20,099.55	3.96%
1990	21,027.98	4.62%
1991	21,811.60	3.73%
1992	22,935.42	5.15%
1993	23,132.67	0.86%
1994	23,753.53	2.68%
1995	24,705.66	4.01%
1995	24,705.66	4.01%

Year	AWI	Annual Change
1996	25,913.90	4.89%
1997	27,426.00	5.84%
1998	28,861.44	5.23%
1999	30,469.84	5.57%
2000	32,154.82	5.53%
2001	32,921.92	2.39%
2002	33,252.09	1.00%
2003	34,064.95	2.44%
2004	35,648.55	4.65%
2005	36,952.94	3.66%
2006	38,651.41	4.60%
2007	40,405.48	4.54%
2008	41,334.97	2.30%
2009	40,711.61	-1.51%
2010	41,673.83	2.36%
2011	42,979.61	3.13%
2012	44,321.67	3.12%
2013		
2014		
2015		
2016		
2017		
2018		
2019		
2020		
2021		
2022		
2023		
2024		
2025		
2025		

Year	AWI	Annual Change
2026		
2027		
2028		
2029		
2030		
2031		
2032		
2033		

Source: Social Security Administration

Appendix C

Contribution and Benefit Bases

Social Security's Old-Age, Survivors, and Disability Insurance (OASDI) program limits the amount of earnings subject to taxation for a given year. The same annual limit also applies when those earnings are used in benefit computations. This limit can change each year with changes in the national average wage index and is called the annual limit contribution and benefit base.

Year	Amount	Year	Amount
1937-50	$3,000	1981	$29,700
1951-54	3,600	1982	32,400
1955-58	4,200	1983	35,700
1959-65	4,800	1984	37,800
1966-67	6,600	1985	39,600
1968-71	7,800	1986	42,000
1972	9,000	1987	43,800
1973	10,800	1988	45,000
1974	13,200	1989	48,000
1975	14,100	1990	51,300
1976	15,300	1991	53,400
1977	16,500	1992	55,500
1978	17,700	1993	57,600
1979	22,900	1994	60,600
1980	25,900	1995	61,200

Year	Amount
1996	$62,700
1997	65,400
1998	68,400
1999	72,600
2000	76,200
2001	80,400
2002	84,900
2003	87,000
2004	87,900
2005	90,000
2006	94,200
2007	97,500
2008	102,000
2009	106,800
2010	106,800
2011	106,800
2012	110,100
2013	113,700
2014	117,000
2015	
2016	
2017	
2018	
2019	
2020	

Source: Social Security Administration

Appendix D

Period Life Table 2010

A period life table is based on the mortality experience of a population during a relatively short period of time. This is the 2010 period life table for the Social Security area population. The Social Security area population is comprised of (1) residents of the 50 States and the District of Columbia (adjusted for net census undercount); (2) civilian residents of Puerto Rico, the Virgin Islands, Guam, American Samoa and the Northern Mariana Islands; (3) Federal civilian employees and persons in the U.S. Armed Forces abroad and their dependents; (4) non-citizens living abroad who are insured for Social Security benefits; and (5) all other U.S. citizens abroad.

For this table, the period life expectancy at a given age is the average remaining number of years expected prior to death for a person at that exact age, born on January 1, using the mortality rates for 2010 over the course of his or her remaining life.

	Male			Female		
Exact age	Death probability [a]	Number of lives [b]	Life expectancy	Death probability [a]	Number of lives [b]	Life expectancy
0	0.006680	100,000	76.10	0.005562	100,000	80.94
1	0.000436	99,332	75.62	0.000396	99,444	80.39
2	0.000304	99,289	74.65	0.000214	99,404	79.43
3	0.000232	99,259	73.67	0.000162	99,383	78.44

	Male			Female		
Exact age	Death probability [a]	Number of lives [b]	Life expectancy	Death probability [a]	Number of lives [b]	Life expectancy
4	0.000172	99,235	72.69	0.000132	99,367	77.46
5	0.000155	99,218	71.70	0.000117	99,354	76.47
6	0.000143	99,203	70.71	0.000106	99,342	75.47
7	0.000131	99,189	69.72	0.000099	99,332	74.48
8	0.000115	99,176	68.73	0.000093	99,322	73.49
9	0.000096	99,164	67.74	0.000090	99,313	72.50
10	0.000082	99,155	66.74	0.000090	99,304	71.50
11	0.000086	99,147	65.75	0.000096	99,295	70.51
12	0.000125	99,138	64.76	0.000111	99,285	69.52
13	0.000205	99,126	63.76	0.000137	99,274	68.52
14	0.000319	99,106	62.78	0.000170	99,261	67.53
15	0.000441	99,074	61.80	0.000207	99,244	66.54
16	0.000562	99,030	60.82	0.000245	99,223	65.56
17	0.000690	98,975	59.86	0.000282	99,199	64.57
18	0.000820	98,906	58.90	0.000318	99,171	63.59
19	0.000949	98,825	57.95	0.000352	99,139	62.61
20	0.001085	98,731	57.00	0.000388	99,105	61.63
21	0.001213	98,624	56.06	0.000423	99,066	60.66
22	0.001304	98,505	55.13	0.000454	99,024	59.68
23	0.001345	98,376	54.20	0.000476	98,979	58.71
24	0.001350	98,244	53.27	0.000494	98,932	57.74
25	0.001342	98,111	52.34	0.000511	98,883	56.77
26	0.001340	97,980	51.41	0.000531	98,833	55.79
27	0.001342	97,848	50.48	0.000553	98,780	54.82
28	0.001356	97,717	49.55	0.000579	98,726	53.85
29	0.001380	97,584	48.62	0.000608	98,668	52.88

	Male			Female		
Exact age	Death probability [a]	Number of lives [b]	Life expectancy	Death probability [a]	Number of lives [b]	Life expectancy
30	0.001408	97,450	47.68	0.000641	98,608	51.92
31	0.001435	97,313	46.75	0.000677	98,545	50.95
32	0.001466	97,173	45.82	0.000719	98,479	49.98
33	0.001499	97,031	44.88	0.000765	98,408	49.02
34	0.001539	96,885	43.95	0.000818	98,332	48.06
35	0.001592	96,736	43.02	0.000879	98,252	47.10
36	0.001660	96,582	42.08	0.000948	98,166	46.14
37	0.001741	96,422	41.15	0.001022	98,073	45.18
38	0.001837	96,254	40.22	0.001100	97,972	44.23
39	0.001953	96,077	39.30	0.001185	97,865	43.27
40	0.002084	95,889	38.37	0.001279	97,749	42.32
41	0.002241	95,689	37.45	0.001387	97,624	41.38
42	0.002439	95,475	36.53	0.001518	97,488	40.43
43	0.002686	95,242	35.62	0.001676	97,340	39.50
44	0.002975	94,986	34.72	0.001858	97,177	38.56
45	0.003297	94,704	33.82	0.002055	96,997	37.63
46	0.003639	94,392	32.93	0.002262	96,797	36.71
47	0.003997	94,048	32.05	0.002480	96,578	35.79
48	0.004366	93,672	31.17	0.002709	96,339	34.88
49	0.004750	93,263	30.31	0.002947	96,078	33.97
50	0.005156	92,820	29.45	0.003209	95,795	33.07
51	0.005596	92,342	28.60	0.003484	95,487	32.18
52	0.006078	91,825	27.76	0.003751	95,155	31.29
53	0.006605	91,267	26.93	0.004000	94,798	30.40
54	0.007174	90,664	26.10	0.004246	94,418	29.52
55	0.007805	90,013	25.29	0.004520	94,017	28.65

	Male			Female		
Exact age	Death probability [a]	Number of lives [b]	Life expectancy	Death probability [a]	Number of lives [b]	Life expectancy
56	0.008464	89,311	24.48	0.004836	93,593	27.77
57	0.009095	88,555	23.69	0.005185	93,140	26.91
58	0.009676	87,750	22.90	0.005570	92,657	26.04
59	0.010245	86,901	22.12	0.006001	92,141	25.19
60	0.010865	86,010	21.34	0.006489	91,588	24.34
61	0.011592	85,076	20.57	0.007046	90,994	23.49
62	0.012444	84,090	19.81	0.007686	90,352	22.65
63	0.013451	83,043	19.05	0.008419	89,658	21.83
64	0.014608	81,926	18.30	0.009249	88,903	21.01
65	0.015927	80,729	17.57	0.010201	88,081	20.20
66	0.017370	79,444	16.84	0.011255	87,182	19.40
67	0.018895	78,064	16.13	0.012372	86,201	18.62
68	0.020484	76,589	15.43	0.013538	85,135	17.84
69	0.022191	75,020	14.75	0.014793	83,982	17.08
70	0.024139	73,355	14.07	0.016233	82,740	16.33
71	0.026364	71,584	13.40	0.017882	81,397	15.59
72	0.028808	69,697	12.75	0.019693	79,941	14.87
73	0.031480	67,689	12.12	0.021671	78,367	14.16
74	0.034442	65,558	11.49	0.023866	76,669	13.46
75	0.037855	63,300	10.89	0.026437	74,839	12.77
76	0.041725	60,904	10.30	0.029368	72,860	12.11
77	0.045932	58,363	9.72	0.032519	70,721	11.46
78	0.050469	55,682	9.17	0.035870	68,421	10.83
79	0.055465	52,872	8.63	0.039555	65,967	10.21
80	0.061179	49,939	8.10	0.043828	63,357	9.61
81	0.067698	46,884	7.60	0.048808	60,580	9.03

| | | Male | | | Female | |
Exact age	Death probability [a]	Number of lives [b]	Life expectancy	Death probability [a]	Number of lives [b]	Life expectancy
82	0.074923	43,710	7.11	0.054434	57,624	8.47
83	0.082891	40,435	6.65	0.060762	54,487	7.93
84	0.091725	37,084	6.21	0.067889	51,176	7.41
85	0.101575	33,682	5.78	0.075926	47,702	6.91
86	0.112568	30,261	5.38	0.084968	44,080	6.44
87	0.124795	26,854	5.00	0.095093	40,335	5.99
88	0.138305	23,503	4.64	0.106352	36,499	5.56
89	0.153107	20,253	4.30	0.118777	32,617	5.17
90	0.169195	17,152	3.99	0.132384	28,743	4.80
91	0.186543	14,250	3.70	0.147181	24,938	4.45
92	0.205115	11,592	3.44	0.163161	21,268	4.13
93	0.224867	9,214	3.20	0.180314	17,798	3.84
94	0.245744	7,142	2.98	0.198615	14,588	3.58
95	0.266454	5,387	2.79	0.217125	11,691	3.34
96	0.286625	3,952	2.62	0.235558	9,153	3.13
97	0.305869	2,819	2.47	0.253602	6,997	2.94
98	0.323783	1,957	2.34	0.270923	5,222	2.76
99	0.339972	1,323	2.22	0.287178	3,807	2.60
100	0.356971	873	2.10	0.304409	2,714	2.45
101	0.374819	562	1.99	0.322673	1,888	2.31
102	0.393560	351	1.88	0.342033	1,279	2.17
103	0.413238	213	1.78	0.362555	841	2.03
104	0.433900	125	1.68	0.384309	536	1.91
105	0.455595	71	1.59	0.407367	330	1.79
106	0.478375	39	1.50	0.431809	196	1.67
107	0.502293	20	1.41	0.457718	111	1.56

	Male			Female		
Exact age	Death probability [a]	Number of lives [b]	Life expectancy	Death probability [a]	Number of lives [b]	Life expectancy
108	0.527408	10	1.32	0.485181	60	1.45
109	0.553778	5	1.24	0.514292	31	1.35
110	0.581467	2	1.17	0.545149	15	1.26
111	0.610541	1	1.09	0.577858	7	1.17
112	0.641068	0	1.02	0.612530	3	1.08
113	0.673121	0	0.95	0.649282	1	1.00
114	0.706777	0	0.89	0.688238	0	0.92
115	0.742116	0	0.83	0.729533	0	0.84
116	0.779222	0	0.77	0.773305	0	0.77
117	0.818183	0	0.71	0.818183	0	0.71
118	0.859092	0	0.66	0.859092	0	0.66
119	0.902047	0	0.60	0.902047	0	0.60

[a] Probability of dying within one year.
[b] Number of survivors out of 100,000 born alive.
Note: The period life expectancy at a given age for 2010 represents the average number of years of life remaining if a group of persons at that age were to experience the mortality rates for 2010 over the course of their remaining life.

Source: Social Security Administration

Index

www.ingramcontent.com/pod-product-compliance
Lightning Source LLC
Chambersburg PA
CBHW050502210326
41521CB00011B/2287